Hilmer & Sattler und Albrecht

Bauten und Projekte
Buildings and Projects

Hilmer & Sattler und Albrecht

Bauten und Projekte
Buildings and Projects

Einführung/Introduction
Klaus Jan Philipp

Edition Axel Menges

© 2004 Edition Axel Menges, Stuttgart/
London
ISBN 3-932565-39-8

Druck/Printing: Druckhaus Münster GmbH,
Kornwestheim
Bindearbeiten/Binding: Buchwerk GmbH,
Darmstadt

Englische Übersetzung/English translation:
Christina Rathgeber, Berlin

Layout-Konzept/Layout concept: Peter Lange-
mann, München/Munich
Redaktion und Layout/Editorial work and
layout: Alexander Waimer, Berlin

Inhalt

Contents

Vorwort

Der im März 2000 erschienene erste Band mit dem Titel *Hilmer & Sattler* findet mit diesem Buch seine chronologische Fortsetzung. Der erste Band beinhaltet die Projekte des Büros bis einschließlich 1997. Der zwei Jahre zuvor abgeschlossene Masterplan des Potsdamer und Leipziger Platzes und der 1997 vollendete Bau der Gemäldegalerie in Berlin bilden sicherlich die Kulminationspunkte unserer Arbeit.

Diese beiden großen Projekte waren in langjährigen Diskussionen, in differenzierter Abwägung entstanden, wurden mit Tusche auf Papier gezeichnet, kaum anders, als dies Architekten in früheren Jahrhunderten getan haben.

Das Jahr 1997 stellte für das Büro in vielerlei Hinsicht eine Zäsur in unserer Arbeit dar:

Durch die allgemeine Einführung der EDV im Planungsprozeß erhöhte sich in dieser Zeit der zeitliche Druck nicht nur auf den Teil der Architektenarbeit, welcher die exakte Darstellung der Ideen beinhaltet, sondern auch auf die Geschwindigkeit von Entwurf und Planung allgemein. So betrug z. B. die Zeitvorgabe bei der Planung der Gemäldegalerie zwischen Wettbewerb und Baubeginn mehr als vier Jahre, zehn Jahre später stand bei dem vergleichbaren Projekt des Beisheim-Towers nur etwas mehr als ein Jahr zur Verfügung. Obwohl dies auf den ersten Blick keinen Eingriff in den kreativen Prozeß der Architektur bedeutet, sondern nur in den Prozeß der technischen Zeichnung, ist hier doch ein leiser Wandel zu spüren: Konnten vorher noch Sonderzulassungen für neue Fassadenmaterialien erwirkt werden, wird gestalterische Vielfalt jetzt eher durch Kombination und Abwandlung von bereits bestehenden Konstruktionen erreicht.

Zum zweiten konnte in den sechs Jahren zwischen dem Redaktionsschluß im Herbst 1997 und dem im Herbst 2003 eine Vielzahl von Bauten realisiert werden. Durch die oben erwähnte neue Technologie war dies ohne eine allzu große Ausweitung des Büros möglich.

Als dritte Neuerung firmiert das Büro seit 1997 unter dem Namen »Hilmer & Sattler und Albrecht«, was den gleichberechtigten Status unseres Juniorpartners Thomas Albrecht besser ausdrückt, auch wenn die differenzierte Verwendung der beiden »und« der gewachsenen Konstellation Rechnung trägt.

Das vorliegende Buch wurde redaktionell von unserem langjährigen Mitarbeiter Alexander Waimer betreut, der auch das Layout besorgte. Ihm sei an dieser Stelle herzlich gedankt.

München, im Januar 2004

Heinz Hilmer
Christoph Sattler
Thomas Albrecht

Foreword

The book is a chronological continuation of the first volume of *Hilmer & Sattler* that appeared in March 2000. The first volume dealt with the firm's projects up to and including 1997. The culmination of these years can definitely be seen in the master plan for Potsdamer Platz and Leipziger Platz, completed two years earlier, and in the construction of the Gemäldegalerie (picture gallery) in Berlin, completed in 1997.

Both of these large projects resulted from years of discussion and the consideration of various alternatives. They were drawn in ink on paper, little different from the way that architects worked in previous centuries.

In a number of ways the year 1997 marked a major break for our firm.

The general introduction of electronic data processing into the planning process during this period meant that time pressure was increased not only on the part of the architectural work, which consists of the exact presentation of the ideas, but also on the overall speed of the design and planning. For example, for the Gemäldegalerie, the time-span between the competition and the start of construction was more than four years, ten years later, there was a span of little more than one year for a comparable project, the Beisheim tower. Although at first glance this does not intrude on the creative process of architecture, but rather on the process of technical drawing, a change has quietly taken place. Whereas previously special permission for new façade materials could be obtained, it is now the case that diversity of form is achieved more likely through the combination and adaptation of already existing constructions.

Secondly, in the six years between the time of going to press in the autumn of 1997 and of 2003 a number of buildings were constructed. This was made possible by the technology mentioned above and not by an undue expansion of the firm.

The third new aspect is that since 1997 the firm has the name, »Hilmer & Sattler und Albrecht«. This better expresses the equal status of our junior partner, Thomas Albrecht, even if the different use of »and« is also a recognition that this partnership has evolved.

This book, including its layout, was put together by Alexander Waimer, who has worked for the firm for many years. We would like to take this opportunity to thank him for his effort.

Munich, January 2004

Heinz Hilmer
Christoph Sattler
Thomas Albrecht

Klaus Jan Philipp

Kontinuität in sich wandelnder Zeit. Die Architektur von Hilmer & Sattler und Albrecht

Will man das Œuvre von Hilmer & Sattler und Albrecht der vergangenen sieben Jahre gegenüber ihrem Werk seit der Gründung des gemeinsamen Büros 1974 mit einem einzigen Wort charakterisieren, so heißt dieses Wort »Kontinuität«.[1] Denn außer dem Eintritt von Thomas Albrecht, der dem Büro seit 1986 angehört und seit 1994 Partner ist, hat sich nicht viel verändert. Noch immer arbeiten Hilmer und Sattler dialogisch und symbiotisch zusammen, und Albrecht ist als Dritter in diese Symbiose eingebunden, aus dem Dialog wurde ein Trialog.[2] Die grundsätzliche Auffassung des Büros ist dieselbe geblieben: Noch immer ist ein »Haus ein Haus« und nichts anderes, noch immer steht das Bekenntnis zur kompakten, räumlich komplexen europäischen Stadt unverrückbar, und noch immer liegt die Kohärenz ihrer architektonischen Sprache in der sinnreichen Bezugnahme auf historisch erprobte städtebauliche und architektonische Typologien. Wer ganz genau hinschaut und unbedingt Veränderungen oder kleine Abfärbungen des aktuellen Zeitgeists erkennen will, der muß sich schon sehr anstrengen. Vielleicht sind die Bauten in München ein bißchen moderner als die in Berlin, welche sich immer ganz eindeutig auf historische Vorbilder beziehen. Vielleicht widmet das Büro heute den Details mehr Aufmerksamkeit, vielleicht ist auch Ausblenden der Eigenleistung und das völlige Zurücktreten hinter das historische Bauwerk wie im Fall der Renovierung der Neuen Wache oder des Alten Museums von Karl Friedrich Schinkel eine neue Tendenz. Sonst aber sind die Architekten ihrem architektonischen Credo treu geblieben. Die symbiotische Entwurfsmethode, die *per se* individualistische Ausuferungen und spektakuläre Einzelleistungen ausschließt, führt weiterhin zu einer »Normalität«, die im besten Sinne das Hauptkennzeichen ihrer Architektur geblieben ist.

Sie sind konservativ, indem sie sagen, daß nicht jeden Tag eine neue Architektur erfunden werden müsse. Sie sind konservativ, indem sie nicht daran glauben, daß eine gläserne Architektur demokratisch sei und eine steinerne oder geschlossene nicht demokratisch. Ihre Architektur will nicht auffallen, paßt sich an und fügt sich Situationen, die andere vielleicht zu einer lauten Geste genutzt hätten. Bescheidenheit wird als eine Zier verstanden, und sie kommen weit mit ihr. Denn konservativ eingestellt ist auch die Klientel – die meisten Wohnbauten sind für die oberen Zehntausend, nicht für die Yuppies, sondern für die, denen man ihren Reichtum nicht ansehen soll, die eigentlich nicht auffallen wollen und sich nur innerhalb ihrer »Klasse« durch bestimmte Zeichen erhöhen, die anderen verborgen bleiben. Feine Unterschiede sind es denn auch, die die Bauten von Hilmer & Sattler und Albrecht gegenüber ihrer Umgebung auszeichnen. Die kleine Überraschung, der dezente Reichtum, die verborgene edle Einfassung, der versteckte Luxus, es sind diese feinen Besonderheiten, die die Bauten der drei Architekten aus der Masse hervorheben.

1–3. Christoph Sattler, Thomas Albrecht, Heinz Hilmer (von links nach rechts) im Berliner Büro, August 2003. (Photo: Frigga Uhlisch.)

1–3. Christoph Sattler, Thomas Albrecht, Heinz Hilmer (from left to right) in the Berlin office, August 2003. (Photo: Frigga Uhlisch.)

Eine Zukunft

für unsere Vergangenheit?

Architektur des neuen Millenniums

Die Architektur zu Beginn des neuen Millenniums hätte unspektakulärer nicht ausfallen können: »Business as usual«. Da sich auch ein *fin de siècle* nicht wie zu Ende des 19. Jahrhunderts wiederholt hat, war trotz der hochgesteckten Erwartungen an das neue Millennium kein neuer Aufbruch zu erwarten. Die vom Bund Deutscher Architekten gestartete Initiative »Baukultur« vermochte bislang nicht den Erfolg zu wiederholen, den 1975 das europäische Jahr der Denkmalpflege besonders in Deutschland ausgelöst hatte, und dem das Büro Hilmer & Sattler so viel verdankte. Die Idee einer *Zukunft für unsere Vergangenheit* – so der Titel einer äußerst erfolgreichen Wanderausstellung 1975/76 – ergriff damals alle Schichten der Bevölkerung und ist in den vergangenen zwanzig Jahren fest in unserem Denken verwurzelt. Ein Zurück in die zügellose Zerstörung historischer urbaner Umwelt, wie es bis in die siebziger Jahre hinein gang und gäbe war, erscheint heute undenkbar. Im gleichen Zuge ist aber das Unbehagen an moderner Architektur in einem Maße gewachsen, daß modernes Bauen mit Anonymität und Kälte gleichgesetzt wird. Außergewöhnliche Highlights läßt man sich zwar gerne gefallen und pilgert nach Bilbao oder zu anderen spektakulären Bau-Ereignissen. Ein Umdenken hingegen, ein tieferes Verständnis für die Rolle guter oder zumindest anspruchsvoller Architektur hat auf breiter Basis bislang noch nicht stattgefunden.

Alles bleibt also zunächst beim alten. Nur die Fronten scheinen sich ein wenig zu verhärten. Zumindest gilt dies mit Blick auf eine sich *in nuce* befindliche Architekturdebatte, die, wenn sie weitergeführt würde, vielleicht wirklich etwas bewegen könnte. Auf der einen Seite steht die Gruppe der Modernen, die sich die Rettung der »Baukultur« auf die Fahnen geschrieben hat und auf neue Materialien, Techniken und Konstruktionen mit Blick auf Nachhaltigkeit und Ökologie besonderen Wert legt. Auf der anderen Seite stehen die Traditionalisten, die ebenso auf der Suche nach der verlorenen »Baukultur« sind, diese jedoch mit anderen Mitteln zurückerlangen wollen.

Zu Beginn des Jahres 2003 tagten kurz hintereinander zwei Konferenzen, die sich um eine neue »Baukultur« in Deutschland bemühten: Zunächst sei die Veranstaltung des Bundesministeriums für Verkehr und Bauen in Bonn genannt, die die ersten Ergebnisse der Initiative »Baukultur« zusammenfaßte und diskutierte. Programmatisch fand diese Veranstaltung im Plenarsaal des ehemaligen Deutschen

4. *Eine Zukunft für unsere Vergangenheit? Denkmalschutz und Denkmalpflege in der Bundesrepublik Deutschland, Europäisches Denkmalschutzjahr 1975,* Katalog zur Wanderausstellung 1975/76, München 1975, Umschlagrücken.

4. *Eine Zukunft für unsere Vergangenheit? Denkmalschutz und Denkmalpflege in der Bundesrepublik Deutschland, Europäisches Denkmalschutzjahr 1975,* catalogue for the travelling exhibition 1975/76, Munich, 1975, reverse cover.

Klaus Jan Philipp

Continuity in changing times. The architecture of Hilmer & Sattler und Albrecht

If one were to characterize the work of Hilmer & Sattler und Albrecht in the past seven years in comparison to the work carried out since the founding of the firm in 1974, then one would have to choose the word »continuity«.[1] Aside from the partnership with Thomas Albrecht, who has worked for the firm since 1986 and has been a partner since 1994, not much has changed. Hilmer and Sattler still work in symbiosis and in dialogue with each other. Albrecht is the third man in this symbiosis, the dialogue has become a trialogue.[2] The firm's basic understanding of architecture has remained the same. It is still the case that a »building is a building« and nothing else. There is still a steadfast commitment to the compact, spatially complex European city and the coherence of their architectural language lies in the meaningful reference to historically tested urban design and architectonic typologies. If somebody decidedly wants to find small changes resulting from contemporary influences, then one must look very closely and make a great effort. Perhaps the buildings in Munich are somewhat more modern than those in Berlin, which always make clear references to historic precursors. Perhaps the firm today devotes more attention to details. Perhaps a new tendency can be seen in the evanescence of their own work and the complete withdrawal behind the historic building, as in the case of the renovation of the Neue Wache (New Guard House) or the Altes Museum (Old Museum) by Karl Friedrich Schinkel. The architects have otherwise remained true to their architectonic credo. The symbiotic design method, that by definition excludes individualistic escalations and spectacular solo performances, continues to lead to a »normality« that in the best sense of this word, is the distinguishing feature of their architecture.

They are conservative in saying that a new architecture does not have to be invented daily. They are conservative in not believing that glass architecture is democratic and that a stone or self-contained architecture is undemocratic. Their architecture does not want to attract attention, it adapts to situations that others might have used to make an attention-grabbing gesture. Modesty is understood as a virtue and it stands them in good stead. Their clients are also conservative, most of the residential buildings are for the upper ten thousand, not for yuppies but rather for those who do not want their wealth to be seen. These people do not want to attract attention and are only visible within their »class« through certain signs, not apparent to others. Fine distinctions are also that which distinguish the buildings of Hilmer & Sattler und Albrecht from their surroundings. The small surprise, the discreet riches, the concealed border of a high quality, the luxury that is never ostentatious – it is these sort of exceptional qualities that set the buildings of the three architects apart.

Bundestags statt, also jenem Raum, der als Inbegriff demokratischen Bauens gilt. Behnischs offene, durchglaste, unhierarchisch spielerische Architektur schien der angemessene Rahmen für die Diskussion einer kommenden Baukunst, die nicht nur modern und vielleicht reflexiv ist, sondern die auch geeignet scheint, »Baukultur« zu begründen. Christoph Ingenhoven erklärte dazu lautstark das »Ende der Toleranz« gegenüber den Neohistoristen unter den Architekten.[3] Wenige Wochen zuvor hatten sich in Berlin Architekten in der von Josef Paul Kleihues gegründeten Internationalen Bauakademie anläßlich des 222. Geburtstages ihres Helden Karl Friedrich Schinkel zu einem Symposium getroffen. Schinkel wurde hier zum »Schutzpatron« einer Veranstaltung, die ebenfalls einer neuen »Baukultur« aufhelfen will. Nur diesmal mit scharfen Stimmen gegen die Moderne und Postmoderne, gegen Konstruktivismus und Dekonstruktivismus.[4]

Wird hier an zwei streng gehüteten Fronten – denn man lud sich gegenseitig nicht ein – die Debatte aus den frühen neunziger Jahren nun in zwei Fraktionen institutionalisiert weitergeführt, oder bricht hier ein Konflikt der Architektur des 21. Jahrhunderts auf? Denn nie zuvor scheint es auf der einen Seite avantgardistischer zugegangen zu sein und auf der anderen Seite konservativer als heute. Oder spiegelt sich hier nur die ganz normale Wirklichkeit des Bauens in der Bundesrepublik Deutschland, und lösen sich nicht Phasen des Bewahrens und wenig Spektakulären mit Phasen des Experimentellen und Atemberaubenden ab? Vielleicht aber stehen wir vor einer ähnlichen Situation wie zu Beginn des 19. Jahrhunderts, als man sich im Besitz der ganzen Geschichte der Architektur glaubte und über diese Geschichte frei verfügen konnte. Ullrich Schwarz hat kürzlich Wege der Moderne beschrieben und zu einer erneuten Revision der Moderne aufgerufen, die drei Gewißheiten voraussetzt und in gewisser Weise an die Diskussion vor 200 Jahren erinnert:

»Die heutige Architektur folgt keinem dominanten Stil mehr, sie verfügt über alle Stile.

Die heutige Architektur ist skeptisch gegenüber allen großen Programmen. Sie sucht nicht um jeden Preis das Neue, aber sie wird auch nicht nostalgisch. Eine neue Qualität des Zeitgenössischen entsteht.

Die heutige Moderne ist aufgeklärt – auch über sich selbst; sie ist entzaubert – auch vom eigenen Zauber. Dennoch wird sie nicht zynisch, opportunistisch oder entmutigt. Sie entfaltet konstruktiv ihr kreatives Potential in einer herausfordernd offenen Situation. Sie erkundet Möglichkeiten in einem Raum der Unbestimmtheit. Sie weiß, daß es keine ganz einfachen Lösungen mehr geben kann und keine Dogmatik des einen einzigen Weges.«[5]

Auch wenn Schwarz bei diesem Text gewiß nicht zuvorderst – vielleicht auch gar nicht – an die Architektur von Hilmer & Sattler und Albrecht gedacht hat, so ist auch sie doch darin aufgehoben. Denn wenn eine neue Qualität des Zeitgenössischen im Entstehen begriffen ist, dann gehört auch die solide, unspekulative Architektur des in München und Berlin ansässigen Büros dazu. Einem auf Wiedererkennbarkeit angelegten, gleichsam als Markenzeichen fungierenden Stil folgen die Architekten in München und Berlin auch nicht, sondern vielmehr gezielt gewählten Typologien. Sie suchen nicht das Neue, sind aber auch nicht nostalgisch aus einem romantischen Bedürfnis nach einer heilen Welt. Und Hilmer & Sattler und Albrecht sind aufgeklärt, denn sie wissen sehr genau ihre Position innerhalb der

Architecture of the new millennium

The architecture at the start of the new millennium could not have been more unspectacular. »Business as usual«. As there was no repetition of the *fin de siècle* that had marked the end of the 19th century, despite great expectations, the new millennium did not mark a break with the past. To this point the »building culture« (Baukultur) initiative started by the Bund Deutscher Architekten (Association of German Architects) has been unable to repeat the success that the European Year for the Preservation of Historical Monuments enjoyed in 1975, particularly in Germany, and to which the firm Hilmer & Sattler owes so much. The idea of a future for our past (*Eine Zukunft für unsere Vergangenheit*) – the title of an extremely successful touring exhibition in 1975/76 – caught the imagination of the population at all levels and in the past twenty years has become a concept deeply rooted in our minds. A return to the unrestrained destruction of the historical, urban environment, as was all too common well into the 1970s, is today unthinkable. At the same time, however, the unease with modern architecture has grown to such an extent, that it is now equated with anonymity and coldness. Occasionally, exceptions are made and pilgrimages are undertaken to Bilbao or to other spectacular pieces of architecture. A real change of view, a deeper understanding of the role played by good or at least ambitious architecture has, however, not taken place on a broad basis.

Everything is still the way it was. Perhaps the lines have been drawn a bit more clearly. This is at least the impression one gets when one looks *in nuce* at a current architectural debate. If this debate is continued, it might even change something. On the one side is the group determined to rescue modernity. Dedicated to saving »building culture«, they put special value on new material, technologies and constructions that are enduring and meet certain ecological standards. On the other side are the traditionalists who are also looking for the lost »building culture« but want to retrieve this through other means.

At the beginning of 2003 two conferences took place in quick succession devoted to a new »building culture« in Germany. One of these conferences, held in Bonn under the auspices of the Federal Ministry for Traffic and Construction, summarized and discussed the first findings of the Baukultur initiative. Fittingly, this conference was held in the assembly room of the former German parliament, a room that can be considered the quintessence of democratic architecture. Behnisch's open, glazed light-handed construction, lacking any display of hierarchy, seemed to be the appropriate setting for the discussion of an architecture in the future that would not only be modern and perhaps reflective but that could also serve as the foundation for a »building culture«. Christoph Ingenhoven loudly proclaimed the »end of the toleration« of the neo-historicists amongst the architects.[3] A few weeks earlier, architects had met for a symposium in Berlin's Internationale Bauakademie, founded by Josef Paul Kleihues. Their immediate reason for meeting was the 222nd birthday of their hero, Karl Friedrich Schinkel. Schinkel was the patron saint of a conference that also wanted to support a new »building culture«. In this case, however, voices were raised against modernity and Post-Modernism, against constructivism and deconstruction.[4]

Were these two strictly segregated camps – no invitations were extended from one side to the other – merely a continuation of the debate of the early 1990s in

5. Hilmer & Sattler und Albrecht, Bauinschrift am Verlags- und Redaktionsgebäude der *Frankfurter Allgemeinen Zeitung*, Berlin-Mitte, 1999. (Photo: Stefan Müller.)

5. Hilmer & Sattler und Albrecht, inscription on the publishing and editorial offices of the *Frankfurter Allgemeine Zeitung*, Berlin-Mitte, 1999. (Photo: Stefan Müller.)

modernen und der historischen Architektur zu bestimmen. Da sie über ein sehr breites Wissen der gesamten Architekturgeschichte verfügen und sich vor allem in den verschiedenen Bautypen und städtebaulichen Typologien selbstverständlich bewegen, sind sie gleichsam ihre eigenen Interpreten und Historiker. Sie haben das versteckte Zitat, die beziehungsreiche Anspielung der postmodernen Architektur entzaubert, indem sie ihre Anregungen bekennen und benennen und ihre Zitate selbst ganz deutlich aussprechen. Gegen die vielzitierte Schnellebigkeit und den dauernden Wandel, gegen das nun schon seit 40 Jahren von den Modernen beschworene, herbeigesehnte oder gefürchtete Nomadentum der modernen Gesellschaft, setzen Hilmer & Sattler und Albrecht ganz auf Stetigkeit.

So haben die Architekten die Bauinschrift wiederentdeckt: An der Neorenaissance-Fassade des Verlags- und Redaktionshauses der *Frankfurter Allgemeinen Zeitung* in Berlin-Mitte fanden sie den für eine Inschrift vorgesehenen Türsturz leer vor, was ihnen Gelegenheit gab, hier den Namen »Frankfurter Allgemeine« in der für die Zeitung typischen Fraktur einmeißeln zu lassen. Im obersten Stockwerk des Beisheim-Gebäudes ragt nicht nur eine im Licht gleißende Metallspitze in den Himmel, sondern hier sind auch an der Front zum Platz die Initialen des Beisheim-Centers »BC« in den Stein eingraviert, während an beiden Seiten des Kopfbaus der ausgeschriebene Name eingelassen ist. Ebenso ziert die Inschrift »Stadtbibliothek« die neue Bibliothek in Pforzheim. Wer seine Bauten so kennzeichnet, der rechnet nicht mit einem schnellen Besitzerwechsel oder einer baldigen Umnutzung, sondern es wird deutlich ausgesprochen: Hier wurde für die »Ewigkeit« gebaut.

Hilmer & Sattler und Albrecht gehören jedoch nicht in einen Topf mit den dumpfen Revisionisten und Historisten. Dazu bewegt sich ihre Architektur auf einem viel zu hohen Niveau. Und sie machen moderne Architektur. Sie bauen mit modernen Materialien, ökonomisch und ökologisch auf dem Stand der Zeit. Der technischen Verläßlichkeit ihrer Bauten kann jeder Bauherr vertrauen. Ihre Bauten oszillieren zwischen Gegenwartsbezug und wohlverstandener Tradition. Sie erscheinen ewig und zeitlos, wertkonservativ, perfekt, maßvoll, immer ausgewogen im Gleichgewicht, anmutig und wegen ihrer gesuchten Materialien und deren Farbigkeit von intensivem und natürlichem Ausdruck. Kurz gesagt: Sie erscheinen klassisch.

Sorgsam geprüfte Typologien und Formen der Architekturgeschichte werden in einer ästhetisch fundierten Auswahl einer Revision und Vervollkommnung unterzogen und alle Einzelformen in Hinsicht auf das Ganze harmonisiert.[6] Die mit dem Klassischen verbundene Zeitlosigkeit kann im negativen Sinne aber auch die Bau-

two, institutionalized factions or was this an expression of the conflict of architecture in the 21st century? There has never been such a strong tilt towards the *avant-garde*, on the one side, and towards conservative views, on the other side, as is the case today. Or is this merely a reflection of the completely normal reality of building in the Federal Republic of Germany? Is it not generally true that phases of preservation and of the less spectacular are relieved by phases of the experimental and the breath-taking and vice-versa? Perhaps, however, we are being confronted with a situation similar to the one at the start of the 19th century when one thought one knew everything about the history of architecture and had this history at one's free disposal. Ullrich Schwarz recently described the paths taken by modernity and called for a renewed revision of modernity, that presupposes three certainties, and in a way one is reminded of the discussion two hundred years ago.

»Today's architecture no longer follows a dominant style. It has many styles at its disposal.

Today's architecture is sceptical of all large programmes. It does not seek the new at all costs nor does it become nostalgic. A new quality for the contemporary is emerging.

Modernity today is enlightened. It is also enlightened about itself and no longer has self-delusions. Nevertheless, it does not become cynical, opportunistic or discouraged. It constructively develops its creative potential in a challenging, open situation. It ascertains possibilities within an uncertain space. It knows that completely simple solutions and the dogma of a single path are no longer possible«.[5]

Although Schwarz certainly did not have the architecture of Hilmer & Sattler und Albrecht expressivly in mind when he wrote these words – perhaps it did not come to mind at all – the words certainly apply to this architecture. For if a new quality for what is contemporary is emerging, then the solid, unspeculative architecture carried out by the offices in Munich and Berlin also belongs to this process. The architects in Munich and Berlin do not follow a style that is instantly recognizable and that functions as a sort of trademark. It is far more the case that they follow certain deliberately chosen typologies. They do not seek the new, neither are they nostalgic out of a romantic yearning for a need for an ideal world. And Hilmer & Sattler und Albrecht are enlightened, for they know exactly where to place themselves within both modern and historic architecture. Because they have a very broad knowledge of architectural history in its entirety and above all are at ease with dif-

6. Hilmer & Sattler und Albrecht, Bronzetafel, Beisheim-Center, Berlin-Tiergarten, 2003. (Photo: Stefan Müller.)

6. Hilmer & Sattler und Albrecht, bronze plaque, Beisheim-Center, Berlin-Tiergarten, 2003. (Photo: Stefan Müller.)

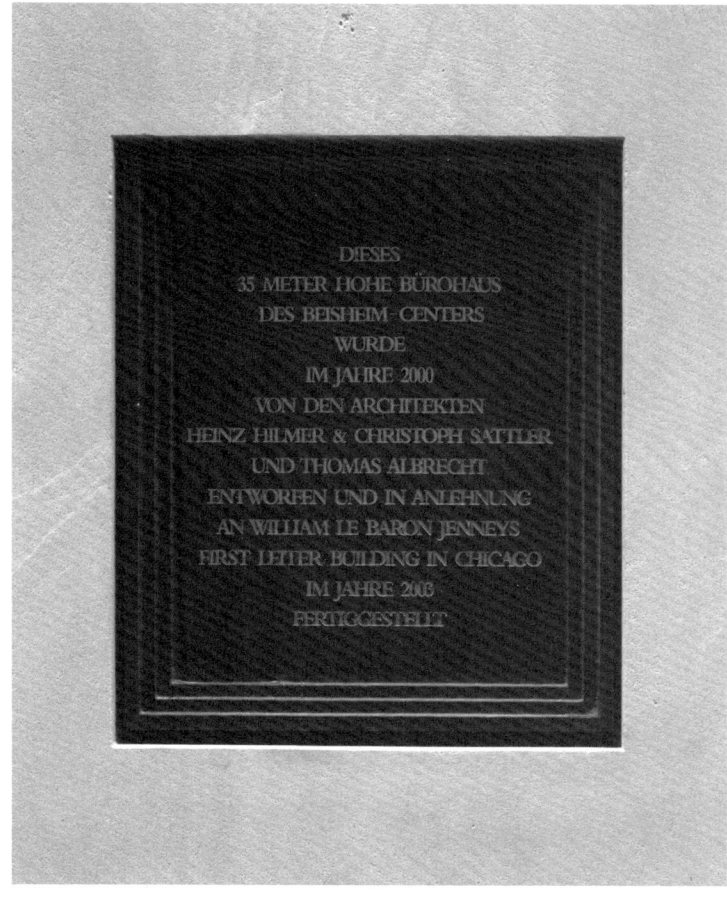

ten ihres Charakters als historisch deter-
minierte Produkte berauben, obwohl sie
natürlich immer auch eine aktuelle Bot-
schaft transportieren. Schon Karl Marx
sah hier eine unauflösbare Schwierigkeit, die nicht darin läge, »zu verstehen,
daß griechische Kunst und Epos an
gewisse gesellschaftliche Entwicklungs-
formen geknüpft sind. Die Schwierigkeit
ist, daß sie uns heute noch Kunstgenuß
gewähren und in gewisser Beziehung als
Norm und unerreichbares Muster gelten.«[7] Wie kann uns etwas gefallen, so
Marx' Problem, das in einer Sklavenhal-
tergesellschaft aus einer ganz besonderen gesellschaftlichen Situation entwickelt worden war? Auf die von Hilmer
& Sattler und Albrecht benutzten historischen Typologien angewendet, lautet
das Problem, wie uns etwas gefallen könne, daß zum Beispiel in der Ausbeuter-
gesellschaft der Gründerzeit entstanden
ist, die wir mit unserer Vorstellung von
Demokratie doch überwunden haben.

Können wir trotzdem dieselben Typologien weiterführen? Die Antwort lautet »ja«,
denn das einigende Band ist die lebendige Tradition der europäischen Stadt, so wie
sie im 19. Jahrhundert entwickelt worden war und bis heute Bestand hat. Natürlich
wissen die Architekten auch, daß es auch andere Auffassungen von Stadt gegeben
hat und noch gibt. Am Kulturforum in Berlin, wo das Büro die beziehungsreiche
Architektur der Gemäldegalerie geplant und ausgeführt hat, galt es, ganz verschie-
dene städtebauliche Haltungen – offen und frei bei Hans Scharoun und seinem
Landschaftsarchitekten Hermann Mattern, gebunden bei Friedrich August Stüler
und Ludwig Mies van der Rohe – einander zuzuführen und zu einer neuen Einheit
zu bringen. In dem zusammen mit Christoph und Donata Valentien 1998 gewonne-
nen Wettbewerb antworten Landschaftsgestaltung und Architektur auf diese verschiedenen Haltungen. Von der Philharmonie strahlen Pflasterbänder in einen
regelmäßig gepflanzten Hain mit Götterbäumen aus: »Das ›Regelmäßige‹ wird frei-
er, das ›Freie‹ regelmäßiger, je mehr sie sich einander nähern. So ergibt sich durch
die Begegnung eine Versöhnung zwischen den beiden Architekturauffassungen,
wenn man will, auch zweier Wahrnehmungen der gesellschaftlichen Realität, deren
jeweilige Anhänger sich so unversöhnlich gegenüberstehen. Was kann man mehr
von einer landschaftsarchitektonischen Gestaltung des Kulturforums verlangen.«[8]
So begründet und so gehandhabt, können die Projekte und Bauten von Hilmer &
Sattler und Albrecht als Botschafter einer zwischen Tradition und Moderne vermit-
telnden und hin- und herschwingenden Baukultur verstanden werden.

ferent types of architecture and typologies of town planning, they can interpret themselves and are also their own historians. They have taken away the illusion of the hidden citation of Post-Modern architecture, so rich in associations, by acknowledging and naming what has stimulated them and clearly voicing their own references. Contrary to the oft-noted, fast-moving pace of modern life and its continuous state of change, the nomadism of modern society, longed for or feared and since 40 years sworn to by the Modernists, Hilmer & Sattler und Albrecht have decided for constancy.

For example, these architects have rediscovered the inscription on buildings. On the neo-Renaissance façade of the editorial offices for the *Frankfurter Allgemeine Zeitung* in Berlin-Mitte the lintel over the entrance, originally meant for an inscription, had been left empty. The opportunity was taken to chisel the name »Frankfurter Allgemeine« on this lintel in the Gothic script typical to the newspaper. On the upper storey of the Beisheim tower, not only does a metal point, gleaming in the light, reach to the skies, on the front facing the square the initials of the Beisheim-Center – »BC« – have been engraved into the stone, while on both sides of the building the full name has been inscribed. In the same way, the inscription »Stadtbibliothek« (city library) graces the new library in Pforzheim. Whoever puts such distinguishing marks on his buildings is not expecting a change in the owners or in the building's function in the foreseeable future. It is far more the case, that it is being clearly said: this building is »forever«.

Hilmer & Sattler und Albrecht cannot be lumped together, however, with the dull revisionists and historicists. The level of their architecture is too high for this. And what they build is modern architecture with modern materials, economically and ecologically up-to-date. Their clients can be sure of the technical reliability of their buildings. Their buildings oscillate between the contemporary world and a well-understood tradition. They seem to be eternal and timeless, well-proportioned, perfect, temperate, always balanced, graceful and because of their carefully chosen materials and their colourfulness they have an intense and natural expression. In short, they appear classical.

Carefully tested typologies and forms from architectural history are revised and perfected in an aesthetically based selection process and all separate forms are brought into harmony with the whole.[6] The timelessness connected to classic architecture can also have negative implications insofar as the buildings can be robbed of their character as historically determined products, although they of course always carry a contemporary message. Karl Marx already saw an insoluble problem in this. This problem did not lie in the »understanding that Greek art and epos were connected to certain forms of development within society. The difficulty lies in the fact, that they still provide us with aesthetic pleasure and in a certain way are the norm and the unreachable model.«[7] Marx's problem was that something that was developed in a slave-holding society within a specific social situation appeals to us so strongly. If one applies this argument to the historic typologies used by Hilmer & Sattler und Albrecht the problem is as follows: how can something appeal to us that, for example, emerged during a time of economic and social exploitation in the last decades of the 19th century. Surely we have overcome this with our idea of democracy. Can we, nevertheless, renew these typologies again? The answer is »yes«. The unifying link here is the living tradition of the European city as it was developed in the

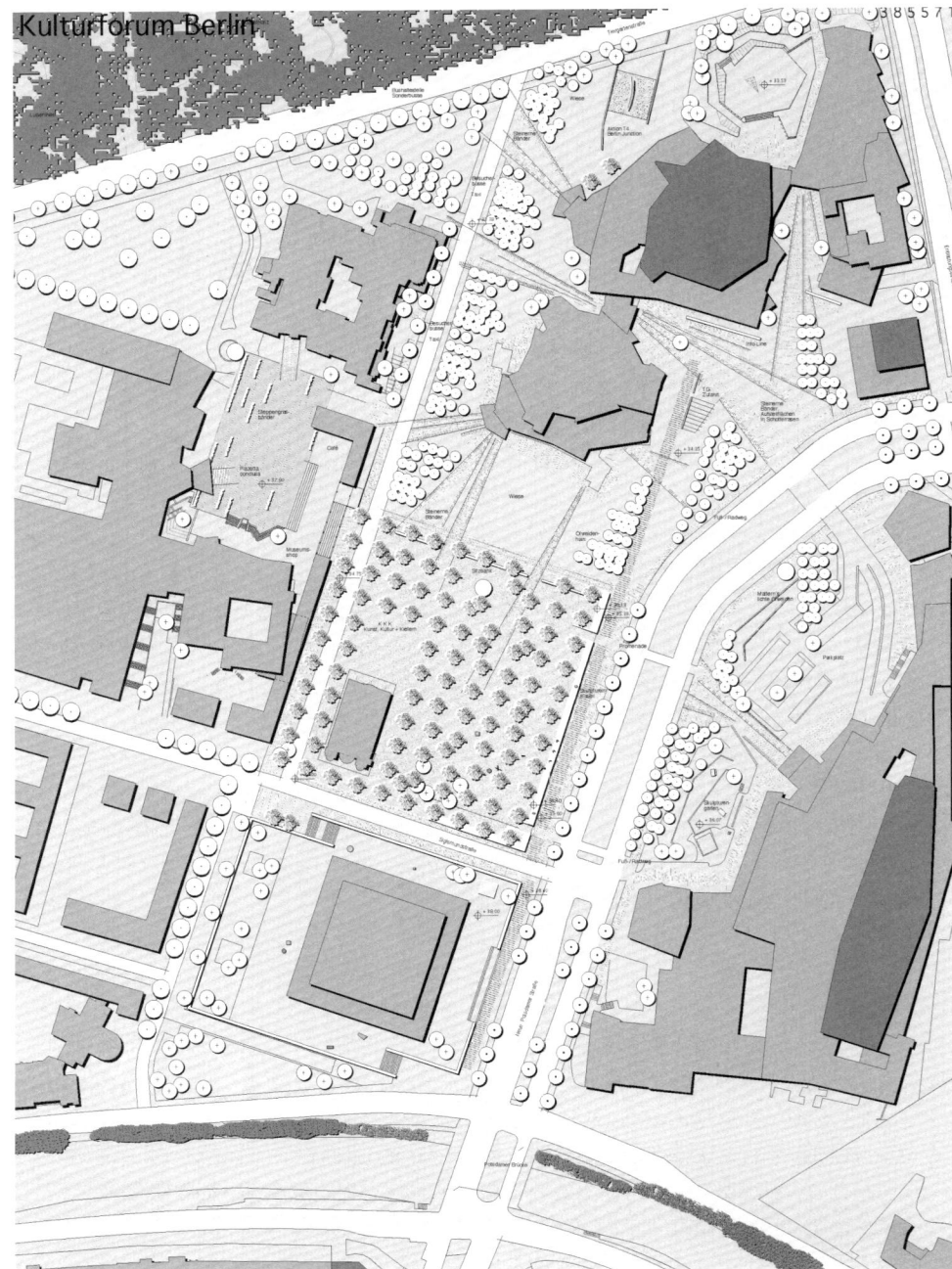

8, 9. Valentien + Valentien + Partner und Hilmer & Sattler und Albrecht, Neugestaltung des Kulturforums, Berlin-Tiergarten, 1998, Wettbewerbsprojekt (1. Preis).

8, 9. Valentien + Valentien + Partner and Hilmer & Sattler und Albrecht, remodelling of the Kulturforum, Berlin-Tiergarten, 1998, competition project (1st prize).

Konvention

Eine Grundfrage der Architektur ist heute wieder diejenige nach der Notwendigkeit einer neuen formalen Ordnung. Genügt das traditionelle Repertoire, oder brauchen wir etwas Neues, um unsere demokratische Ordnung darzustellen und eine dieses System repräsentierende und widerspiegelnde Architektur herzustellen? Günter Behnisch ist auf der Seite der Modernen, die sich sicher sind, daß eine solche neue Ordnung vonnöten ist und daß diese nicht die Ordnung der Klassik sein kann. Statt dessen wird die neue Ordnung demokratische Werte darstellen: »Die tendenzielle Freiheit des Einzelnen, seine Individualität, sein Sichfügen in eine Gesellschaft«.[9] Wie diese neue Ordnung aussieht, welcher formalen Mittel sie sich bedient, braucht dabei zunächst gar nicht zu interessieren. Grundsätzlich ist zunächst die Entscheidung darüber, ob die alten Formen noch ausreichen oder in der heutigen Zeit nicht mehr tauglich sind. Nun ist diese Frage alles andere als neu: Sie bewegt Architekten bereits seit über 200 Jahren, und vielleicht hat Karl Friedrich Schinkel in seinen späten Lebensjahren bereits die einzig gültige Antwort gefunden.

19th century and still exists today. Of course the architects are well aware that there were and still are also other ideas of how the city should be. At the Kulturforum in Berlin, where the firm planned and carried out the architecture for the Gemälde-galerie (picture gallery) that is so rich in associations, one of the aims was to bring completely different ideas about town planning – those of Hans Scharoun and his landscape architect Hermann Mattern being open and free, those of Friedrich August Stüler and Ludwig Mies van der Rohe being more restrained – in contact with each other and thereby create a new unity. In the competition that was won with Christoph and Donata Valentien in 1998 the layout of the landscape and architecture responds to these different ideas. Bands of paving radiate from the Philhar-monie into a grove with trees-of-heaven planted at regular intervals. »The closer they come to each other, that which is ›regular‹ becomes more free and that which is ›free‹ becomes more regular. This encounter reconciles the two understandings of architecture, one could even say, that these are two perceptions of social reality whose respective proponents are sharply opposed to each other. What more could one ask of the layout of the landscape and architecture of the Kulturforum?«[8] Looked at in this way the projects and buildings of Hilmer & Sattler und Albrecht can be understood as mediating between tradition and the modern age, within a building culture that swings back and forth.

Convention

A fundamental question posed by contemporary architecture is once again that of the necessity of a new formal order. Is the traditional repertoire adequate or do we need something new in order to depict our democratic order and should we pro-duce architecture that will represent and reflect this system? Günter Behnisch is on the side of those Modernists who are sure that such a new order is required and that this cannot be the order of classical architecture. Instead, the new order will

Schinkel notierte um 1835 seine Vorstellung der Nachahmung der Alten, die ja seit Winckelmann ein Generalthema des Kunstdiskurses war. Er wendet sich vehement gegen »trivial-treue« Beziehungen zu anerkannten Autoritäten und fordert »geistige Freiheit und spekulative Phantasie«. Wahrhaft »historisches Bauen«, so Schinkel, könne nur dort stattfinden, wo auf irgendeine Weise »ein Mehr, ein neues Element in die Welt« eingeführt würde, »aus dem sich eine neue Geschichte erzeugt und fortspinnt«. Nur so könne ein Kunstwerk entstehen, daß gänzlich durchgebildet ist, »in einem einfachen großartigen Sinne und einem Guße, wie es nur aus der Genialität hervorzugehen vermag«.[10]

Genialität wollen wir heute gar nicht verlangen, ein guter Standard reicht schon aus. Gern stimmen wir ein in die »Hymne auf die Kultur des guten Standards«, die der Publizist Christian Marquart kürzlich angesichts von Einfamilienhäusern sang und fragte, wieso wir immer nur Geniestreiche sehen wollen. Geniestreiche seien bei Genies nichts Besonderes. Die Lorbeeren würden heute ganz im Gegenteil den Architekten gebühren, die für gute Standards sorgen und somit auch für »Baukultur« im besten Sinne des Begriffs. Gibt es sie nicht doch: jene von Marquart vermißten »Bindeglieder zwischen den Sonder- und Spitzenleistungen und dem, was die pure Notdurft an Unansehnlichem gebiert«?[11]

Können wir in den Bauten von Hilmer & Sattler und Albrecht vielleicht diese Bindeglieder erkennen: solide, nicht sensationell, baumeisterlich und von großer Selbstverständlichkeit die Aura des »Immer-schon-Dagewesenen« verströmend? Diese im Herkömmlichen verankerte Architektur gewinnt in jüngster Zeit immer mehr Anhänger, die eher im Bewahrenden den Königsweg suchen als in der Erfindung von Neuem: So hat etwa Peter Eisenman im Mai 2000 in der Helmholtz-Vorlesung an der Humboldt-Universität in Berlin den Abschied vom Konzept der Originalität verkündet. Das Diktat des Neuen dürfe nicht länger die Architektur bestimmen, vielmehr müsse man sie als »eine veränderte Kombination des schon Existierenden« verstehen. Wie andere, die gleich zu Wort kommen, bezieht sich Eisenman auf die Postmoderne, die die erzählerischen, die sprechenden Qualitäten der Architektur in den Vordergrund gestellt habe: das Spiel mit Gegebenem, die Collage von Versatzstücken, den bewußten Umgang mit der Tradition.[12]

Hier knüpft auch Hans Kollhoff, Nachbararchitekt von Hilmer & Sattler und Albrecht am Potsdamer Platz, an. Für den Exponenten einer traditionsorientierten Architektur ist Architektur schlechtweg Konvention. Überraschenderweise bezieht er sich dabei auf die Pop-Kultur der sechziger Jahre des vergangenen Jahrhunderts: So wie man damals Kunst und Leben, Architektur und Alltagskultur zusammenführen wollte, so sei auch heute wieder ein Rückbezug mit einer freilich anderen Stoßrichtung notwendig: Heute gehe es nicht um die Ästhetisierung des Banalen, sondern um die »Herausbildung eines breiten Gefühls für das konventionell Schöne«, und dies in der vielleicht blauäugigen Hoffung »auf eine Eigendynamik der Verfeinerung«.[13] Setzt Kollhoff hier auf die aufklärerische Forderung und Hoffnung, daß gut geformte Architektur auch gute Menschen forme? Er bezeichnet es selbst als ein »klassisches Architekturverständnis«, wobei Klassik für ihn die Lösung einer Aufgabe bedeutet, »die sich an menschenmöglichen Zielen orientiert, welche schließlich mehr oder weniger erfolgreich erreicht werden«. Mit dieser Definition allerdings ließe sich jede Architektur gleich welchen Stils, gleich welchen Materials und gleich ob konventionell oder unkonventionell verteidigen.

present democratic values: »the basic freedom of the individual, his individuality, his place in a society«.[9] The question of what this new order will look like or the formal means which it will use, is not of immediate concern here. The fundamental question is whether the old forms are still adequate or are today no longer suitable. This question is by no means new. It has been posed by architects for over 200 years and during the last years of his life Karl Friedrich Schinkel possibly found the only valid answer.

Around 1835 Schinkel made note of his idea of the emulation of antiquity, an emulation that since Winckelmann had been a general subject in the discourse about art. Schinkel was vehemently opposed to making »trivial-loyal« connections to acknowledged authorities and called for »intellectual freedom and speculative imagination«. For Schinkel, »historical architecture« could really only occur when »something more, a new element« had been introduced in some way. It was from this that »a new history would be created and developed«. It was only in this way that a work of art could be created, that would be complete in its form, »in a simple, wonderful sense and of a kind that can only arise from genius«.[10]

Genius is something that we do not demand today, a good standard is enough. We are more than willing to join in the »hymn to the culture of the good standard«, which the journalist Christian Marquart, prompted by single-family housing, recently sang. He asked why we always wanted to see strokes of genius. Strokes of genius are nothing special for geniuses. In fact, quite the opposite is the case. Today, the accolades go to the architects who ensure the good standard and thereby also the »culture of building« in the best sense of the word. Do they perhaps exist after all, those architects that Marquart cannot find? »The connecting links between the special and top performances and the unsightliness produced by pure neediness«.[11]

Are these connecting links perhaps to be seen in the buildings of Hilmer & Sattler und Albrecht? They are solid, not sensational, emanating a matter-of-fact air of having »always been there«. Recently , architecture that is anchored in the conventional has won an ever greater number of supporters who look for the ideal solution in the tried and tested rather than in discovering something new. For example, in the Helmholtz Lecture at the Humboldt University in Berlin in May of 2000 Peter Eisenman took leave from the concept of originality. Architecture could no longer be determined by the expectation that it would produce something new. It was now much more the case that architecture had to be understood as »a changed combination of the already existing«. As with others, who will soon be cited, Eisenman's point of reference is Post-Modernism. It placed architecture's narrative, rhetorical qualities in the forefront, played with the found object, made a collage out of set pieces and had conscious contact with tradition.[12]

This is also a point taken up by Hans Kollhoff, Hilmer & Sattler und Albrecht's neighbouring architect on Potsdamer Platz. For this exponent of an architecture orientated towards tradition, architecture is the epitome of convention. Surprisingly, his point of reference here is the pop-culture of the 1960s. In the same way that pop-culture wanted to bring together art and life, architecture and the culture of daily life, it is also necessary to revert today, albeit in a different direction. Today, the concern is no longer with the aesthetic qualities of the banal, but rather »with forming a widespread feeling for the conventionally beautiful«. There is a perhaps naive hope here in »the dynamics produced by refinement«.[13] Is Kollhoff relying on the

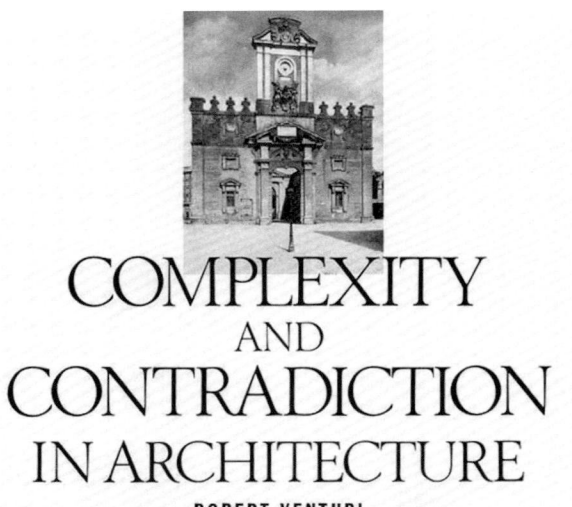

Wichtiger in unserem Zusammenhang ist deshalb Kollhoffs Verweis auf Robert Venturis Begriff von Konvention. Venturi hat in seinem 1966 publizierten Buch *Complexity and Contradiction in Architecture* architektonische Konventionen verteidigt, was damals ein mutiger Schritt war. Der junge amerikanische Architekt empörte sich mit Verve gegen die erdrückende Übermacht der Modernen um Ludwig Mies van der Rohe und dessen Epigonen, und hielt seinen etablierten Kollegen vor, daß sie »in ihrem visionären Eifer, selbst neue Techniken zu erfinden«, ihre Verpflichtung vernachlässigt hätten, »Experten vorhandener Konventionen zu sein«. Für Venturi gibt es keinen linearen Fortschritt, wie er in den USA in den sechziger Jahren im Zuge der Mondlandungseuphorie für real gehalten wurde, sondern viele offene Möglichkeiten: »Architektur ist ebenso evolutionär wie revolutionär. Als Kunst hat sie das bereits Bestehende ebenso ernst zu nehmen wie das, was sein sollte, das unmittelbar Gegebene wie das vielleicht Mögliche«.[14]

Die Positionen von Kollhoff wie auch die von Hilmer & Sattler und Albrecht scheinen gegenüber Venturis »behutsamem Manifest« aus den sechziger Jahren rückschrittlich, da sie das revolutionäre Moment in ihrer Architektur unterdrücken und viel stärker auf die Weiterentwicklung des Tradierten setzen. Aber hat nicht Adolf von Hildebrand schon 1899 recht gehabt, als er bezweifelte, ob es segensreich sei, einen neuen Stil und ein architektonisches »Volapück«, ein Esperanto, zu erfinden: »Als braucht man eine neue Sprache, um etwas Neues zu sagen.« Natürlich brauchten wir eine neue Sprache, würden wir heute aus der Sicht der Moderne der zwanziger Jahre sagen, denn sonst wäre die Architektur vielleicht nie in der Moderne angekommen. Nachdem aber diese Moderne nicht das geleistet hat, was sie leisten wollte, nachdem die schönen Vorstellungen von einer neuen Ordnung durch eine neue Architektur zuletzt an den banalen und öden Kisten des Bauwirtschaftsfunktionalismus gescheitert sind, darf man vielleicht wieder anders denken. Man muß nicht so weit gehen wie 1984 der renommierte Architekturhistoriker Erik Forssmann im Vorwort einer Neuauflage seines inzwischen klassischen Buches *Dorisch, Jonisch, Korinthisch*, das sich mit dem Gebrauch der Säulenordnungen in der Architektur des 16. bis 18. Jahrhunderts auseinandersetzt. Er hat dort zwei Thesen aufgestellt, die hier vor allem deshalb von Interesse sind, weil er sie mit der Moderne verknüpft. Seine erste These lautet, daß sich mit den drei klassischen Säulenordnungen fast alles ausdrücken ließe, »was ein Bauwerk dem Betrachter sagen sollte«. Und er führt aus: »Die Ordnungen lieferten die Vokabeln einer allgemein verständlichen Architektursprache über alle Stilgrenzen hinweg: Ein dorisches Zeughaus, ein jonisches Rathaus, ein korinthischer Palast – sie stellten sich selber dar, da gab es keine Zweifel und keine Profilierungsprobleme.« Seine zweite These betrifft die moderne Architektur – im Unterschied zu den Architekten, die in Rückbezug auf die zehn Bücher zur Architektur von Vitruv die Sprache der Säulenordnungen verstanden. Forssmann schreibt: »Heutige Architekten, die das ausdrucksarme Esperanto des International Style sprechen müssen, werden die Architekten des Vitru-

10. Robert Venturi, *Complexity and Contradiction in Architecture*, Buchtitel, 1966.

10. Robert Venturi, *Complexity and Contradiction in Architecture*, book title, 1966.

enlightened demand and hope, that well-formed architecture also forms good people? He himself calls it a »classical understanding of architecture«, by which he means that it offers a solution to the task »which orientates itself towards goals that are humanly possible to achieve more or less successfully«. This definition could, however, be used to defend every type of architecture, no matter what its style or materials are, no matter whether it be conventional or unconventional.

More important for our purposes is Kollhoff's reference to Robert Venturi's understanding of convention. In his book, *Complexity and Contradiction in Architecture*, published in 1966, Venturi defended architectural conventions, a brave step at the time. With great verve the young American architect vented his indignation at the suffocating domination of the type of modern architecture practiced by Mies van der Rohe and his imitators and reproached his established colleagues that »in their visionary compulsion to invent new techniques« they have »neglected their obligation to be experts in existing conventions«. For Venturi there was no linear progress of the type that seemed more possible in the USA in the 1960s as a consequence of the post-moon-landing euphoria. For Venturi there were many open possibilities. »Architecture is evolutionary as well as revolutionary. As an art it will acknowledge what is and what ought to be, the immediate and the speculative.«[14]

With respect to Venturi's »gentle manifesto« from the 1960s, the positions of Kollhoff as well as those of Hilmer & Sattler und Albrecht seem retrograde, for they suppress the revolutionary moment in their architecture and are far more concerned with further developing the traditional. But was not Adolf von Hildebrand already right in 1899 when he questioned the benefits of discovering a new style, an architectural Esperanto. »As if one needed a new language to say something new.« From the perspective of the 1920s, we can say today, of course we need a new language, for otherwise architecture might never have become modern. But now that this modernity has not achieved all that it should have, now that the nice ideas about a new order through a new architecture have failed because of the banal and dreary box like buildings demanded by the functionalism of the building industry, perhaps it is possible to think differently. One does not have to go far as the well-known architectural historian, Erik Forssmann did in 1984 in a foreword to his book, which since publication had become a classic: *Dorisch,*

11. Die Säulenordnungen, aus: Vincenzo Scamozzi, *L'Idea della architettura universale*, Teil II, Buch 6, Venedig 1615.

11. The classical orders, from: Vincenzo Scamozzi, *L'Idea della architettura universale*, part II, book 6, Venice, 1615.

vianismus wahrscheinlich um deren markige Sprache und unmißverständliche Artikulationsmöglichkeiten beneiden.«[15]

Für Hilmer & Sattler und Albrecht sind es nicht die Säulenordnungen, die ihnen die Vokabeln liefern, auch nicht ein streng begrenztes formales System, wie es Ungers vertritt, sondern es sind feinfühlig und sinnreich aufgegriffene Typologien. Bezüge werden ohne starren Zwang gesucht, sind einmal formal, einmal inhaltlich begründet, einmal einfach aus der Begeisterung für eine gute Lösung, einer schönen Anmutung heraus gewählt.

»Diktatur der Gestalt«?

Die schärfste, aber auch die bedenkenswerteste Kritik an den Planungen und Bauten von Hilmer & Sattler und Albrecht hat 1992 Dieter Hoffmann-Axthelm formuliert, nachdem das Büro den Wettbewerb für den Potsdamer Platz für sich entschieden hatte. Der Entwurf war für Hoffmann-Axthelm ein »Menetekel der Moderne«.[16] Zwar sei der Entwurf ein »Ordnungsangebot« und »an keiner Stelle willkürlich, subjektiv, aufgeregt oder exaltiert«. Aber der Preis, der für diese neue Ordnung bezahlt wird, sei hoch: Es sei nämlich die Stillstellung des Stadtgefüges, ein Bewegungsverbot. Die »konservative Strategie der Gestaltordnung« sei unfähig, »Stadtwachstum in kleinen autonomen Einheiten zu denken, als Modell zerstreuter Verantwortungen«. Das Grundproblem aber sei die Verwechslung von Gestalt und Struktur: »Es gibt zuviel Gestalt, zu wenig Struktur, zuviel öffentlichen Ausdruck (Straße, Platz, Achse usw.), zu wenig praktische öffentliche Eigenschaften.« Letztlich gipfelt die Kritik in dem Vorwurf, daß die Planung von dem real Vorhan-

12. Leipziger Platz, Berlin-Mitte, Luftaufnahme 1. Drittel 20. Jahrhundert. (Photo: Bildarchiv Foto Marburg.)

12. Leipziger Platz, Berlin-Mitte, aerial photogaph 1st third of the 20th century. (Photo: Bildarchiv Foto Marburg.)

denen losgelöst sei und die Geschichte und Aura des Platzes nicht beachten würde. Durch ihre Gestaltung würde den Baumassen die »völlig deplazierte Würde des Notwendigen verpaßt«, was Hoffmann-Axthelm schließlich zu dem auf jeden Fall deplazierten Vergleich mit Albert Speers Berliner Nord–Süd-Achse führt, wo alles »wie lauter Tempel und Ruhmeshallen« aussehen sollte, obwohl es bloß »Konzernverwaltungen für Tausende von Angestellten« waren.

Zehn Jahre später müßte Hoffmann-Axthelms Kritik ganz anders ausfallen, denn das Menetekel, das er an die Wand malte, ist so nicht eingetroffen. Die meisten der bis heute ausgeführten Bauten und Planungen folgen dem Entwurf. Nur die ersten Investoren debis und Sony bauten ihre Einkaufshallen, die das Leben von der Straße in die klimatisierten Konsumzonen abziehen. Da, wo die Straße mit den Fuß-

Jonisch, Korinthisch. This book dealt with the column orders in architecture between the 16th and 18th centuries. Forssmann, expounds upon two theses, which are above all of interest here, because he links them to the modern age. His first thesis is that the three classic column orders expressed almost everything »that a building should say to the observer.« He continues, »the orders were the words of a common architectural language that could be understood beyond stylistic borders. A Doric guard house, an Ionic town hall, a Corinthian palace presented themselves, there was no uncertainty here and no problem arising from the architect's desire to ›leave his mark‹.« His second thesis concerns modern architecture. In contrast to those architects, who understood the language of the column orders as laid out in the *Ten Books of Architecture* by Vitruvius, Forssmann writes that contemporary architects who have to use the feeble expressions of the Esperanto of the International Style probably envy the architects of Vitruvianism for their vigorous language and clear possibilities of articulation.[15]

For Hilmer & Sattler und Albrecht it is not the column order that provides them with words, nor is it a clearly bordered formal system, as expounded by Ungers, but rather typologies that are used in a sensitive and meaningful way. References are sought but not compulsively. Their justification is sometimes of a formal nature, sometimes the justification arises from the content, and sometimes the enthusiasm for a good solution, for a good effect, suffices as justification.

»Dictatorship of form«?

The strongest criticism of the plans and buildings carried out by Hilmer & Sattler und Albrecht, but one that also provides food for thought, was made by Dieter Hoffmann-Axthelm in 1992, after the firm had won the competition for the Potsdamer Platz. For Hofmann-Axthelm the design was an »ominous prediction of modernity«,[16] for while it »presented an order« and was »in nowhere arbitrary, subjective, agitated or exalted«, the price for this new order was high. The price was nothing less than the immobilization of the urban structure, a ban on movement. The »conservative strategy« behind the ordering of the buildings was incapable of conceiving of urban growth in small, autonomous units; as a model of disparate responsibilities. The fundamental problem, however, was the confusion of form and structure. »There is too much form, not enough structure; too many spaces for public expression (street, square, axis etc.) and not enough practical, public features«. The criticism peaked in the reproach that the planning was removed from that which actually existed and paid no attention to the history and aura of Potsdamer Platz. Its buildings, performing necessary functions, would be given an inappropriate value. This even led Hoffmann-Axthelm to draw an entirely unsuitable comparison to Albert Speer's north–south axis for Berlin, where »everything had to look like temples and halls of fame«, when in reality they were »only companies with thousands of employees«.

Ten years later Hoffmann-Axthelm would have to take back his criticism, for the prediction that he had foreseen did not transpire. Most of the buildings and plans that have been carried out up to now follow the design. It was only the first investors, debis and Sony, who built shopping malls, that pulled life from the street

wegen sich immer mehr belebt und nicht nur für Touristen zu einem Treffpunkt geworden ist, entsteht tatsächlich ein neues städtisches Leben, das durchaus mit einer gewissen Würde auftreten darf. Und je dichter das Viertel wird, desto deutlicher wird die Idee der Stadt, die Hilmer & Sattler und Albrecht hier verfolgten. Mit jedem Meter mehr an Fassaden am Leipziger Platz, dem nun vor der Vollendung stehenden Beisheim-Center, mit der gegenüber 1991 leicht veränderten städtebaulichen Planung, dem Potsdamer Platz mit den nun vor den fünf Hochhäusern in »richtiger« Proportion erscheinenden Eingangspavillons des Bahnhofs, der stark belebten Potsdamer Straße und dem Übergang zum Kulturforum, das ebenfalls immer attraktiver wird, entsteht hier immer mehr ein wirklich städtisches Gefüge mit praktischen öffentlichen Eigenschaften, ohne ein Zuviel an öffentlichem Ausdruck mit wechselnder Gestalt und einem noch lange nicht aufgebrauchten Potential an Variabilität. Sind es doch zuweilen gerade die strengen Auflagen, die zu kreativen Leistungen anstacheln. Frank O. Gehry hat es mit der DG-Bank am Pariser Platz vorgeführt, wie man trotz solcher Auflagen eine begeisternde Architektur gestalten kann. Und am Leipziger Platz findet zur Zeit ein wahrer Wettkampf darum statt, wie man bei vorgegebener Gleichheit aller Häuser allein durch Variationen und Verfeinerung des Fassadenreliefs sich unterscheiden kann. Wie bei dem Seniorenwohnhaus in Berlin-Schöneberg entschieden sich die Architekten auch hier für eine geschwungene Fassade; in diesem Fall führt der Schwung der einzelnen Felder nach innen, und erst dort, wo die Wohnetagen beginnen, sind leicht nach außen gewölbte, schmale bronzene Austritte angebracht, die auf die Wohnnutzung hindeuten.

Es wäre übertrieben und sogar falsch, Hilmer & Sattler und Albrecht wegen solcher handwerklich präzise durchgeführter gestalterischer Ideen zur aktuellen Avantgarde zu rechnen. Ganz im Gegenteil, sie haben jeder Form von Avantgardismus oder gar Exzentrik abgeschworen. Ihre Qualitäten liegen in der präzisen Auswahl und Verwendung qualitätvoller Materialien, sie verkörpern den Typus des Baumeisters, wie er eigentlich verloren geglaubt war. Denn heute geht es im Baugewerbe doch nicht mehr um lange Haltbarkeit und hohe Qualität, sondern um schnelle Profitmaximierung bei möglichst minimalem Einsatz. Hilmer & Sattler und Albrechts Architektur hingegen steht für Dauerhaftigkeit, sowohl im Materiellen als auch im Formalen – keine Experimente!

Bauen in der großen Stadt

»Je größer die Stadt, desto größer und breiter werden Plätze und Straßen, desto höher und umfangreicher alle Gebäude, bis deren Dimensionen mit den zahlreichen Stockwerken und unabsehbaren Fensterreihen kaum mehr künstlerisch wirksam gegliedert werden können. Alles dehnt sich ins Maßlose und die ewige Wiederholung derselben Motive allein schon stumpft die Empfänglichkeit so ab, daß nur ganz besondere Krafteffekte noch einige Wirkung erzielen vermögen. Auch das läßt sich nicht ändern und der Städtebauer muß wie der Architekt sich für die moderne Millionenstadt seinen eigenen Maßstab zurechtlegen.«[17] Was der wichtigste Städtebaulehrer des ausgehenden 19. und beginnenden 20. Jahrhunderts, der Wiener Camillo Sitte, hier 1889 in so klaren Worten zusammengefaßt hat, gilt heute noch

to air-conditioned consumer zones. The streets with their pedestrian paths are becoming ever more vibrant and are not just a meeting-point for tourists but also an indication that a new urban life of a certain value is really emerging. And as this quarter becomes denser, the idea of the city that Hilmer & Sattler und Albrecht had becomes clearer. Every new metre of façade on Leipziger Platz, the almost completed Beisheim-Center with small alterations in comparison with the urban development plan of 1991, the Potsdamer Platz with the entrance pavilions to the train station now in »proper« proportion to the five towers, the busy Potsdamer Straße and the crossing to the Kulturforum that is also becoming ever more attractive, all make clear that there is a real urban structure emerging here with ever more practical, public features, without too much public expression, with changing form and a potential for variability that is far from being used up. Occasionally the strict conditions even serve to spur on creative efforts. With the DG-Bank on Pariser Platz, Frank O. Gehry showed how despite such conditions one can create an architecture that elicits enthusiasm. And on Leipziger Platz there is real competition going on at the moment to show that despite the stipulated uniformity of the buildings, they can differ greatly through the variations and refinements of their façade reliefs. As with the retirement home in Berlin-Schöneberg, the architects also decided on a curved façade here. In this case the curve is concave and it is only at the point where the residential storeys begin and the small bronze balconies are attached, indicating residential use, that there is a slight curve to the outside.

It would be an exaggeration and even incorrect to place Hilmer & Sattler und Albrecht amongst the contemporary *avant-garde* because of the craftsmanship and precision with which they have carried out such creative ideas. On the contrary, they have renounced all forms of the *avant-garde* and certainly of eccentricity. Their qualities lie in the precise selection and use of materials of a high quality. They embody that type of architect who was believed gone. Today's building industry is no longer concerned with durability and high quality, but with a fast and maximum profit with as low expenditures as possible. In contrast, in both its material and in formal terms, the architecture of Hilmer & Sattler und Albrecht represents permanency. No experiments!

Building in the big city

»The bigger the city, the larger and broader will be its squares and streets, the higher and more spacious will be its buildings, until their dimensions with the many storeys and incalculable rows of windows can almost not be structured anymore in an artistic way. Everything becomes extreme and the constant repetition of the same motifs already dulls one's receptivity to such an extent that only extraordinary displays of strength still have some effect. This too cannot be changed and like the architect, the town planner must set his own standards for dealing with the modern, big city.«[17] The clear words that Camillo Sitte uttered in 1889 – Sitte was a Viennese and the most important teacher of town planning in the late 19th and early 20th centuries – are still valid today. The scale has to be accommodated to the size of the city and does not have to refer to the human being. A different frame of reference can certainly be chosen. This frame obeys other laws. Its scale basis are broad streets

immer. Der Maßstab muß auf die Größe der Stadt abgestimmt und nicht unbedingt auf den Menschen bezogen sein, sondern kann durchaus einen anderen Bezugsrahmen wählen. Dieser Rahmen gehorcht anderen Gesetzen; Bezugsgrößen sind breite Straßen und Plätze, und auf deren Größe antworten Türen und Fenster der Bauten. Dabei muß es nicht zu einem Widerspruch zwischen Fassadenästhetik und Nutzerbedürfnissen kommen, wie sie Wilhelm Busch als Kritik an der Münchener Maximilianstraße und dem »Maximilianstil« geübt hat. Die ästhetischen Ansprüche des Planers stimmen hier nicht mit den praktischen Ansprüchen des Benutzers überein. Was von vorn so gemütlich aussieht, erweist sich von hinten betrachtet als gar nicht auf den Menschen bedacht.

Auch die Portale, wie man besser statt Türen sagen sollte, die Hilmer & Sattler und Albrecht an die privaten und öffentlichen Bauten vor allem in Berlin anbringen, scheinen für den Menschen einfach zu groß. Ihre Proportion entspricht aber den Bauwerken und ihrer

13. Hilmer & Sattler und Albrecht, Ritz-Carlton Hotel und Apartment-Tower, Beisheim-Center, Berlin-Tiergarten, 2003. (Photo: Stefan Müller.)

13. Hilmer & Sattler und Albrecht, Ritz-Carlton Hotel and apartment tower, Beisheim-Center, Berlin-Tiergarten, 2003. (Photo: Stefan Müller.)

Stellung in der Straße oder am Platz selbst und auch der Bedeutung des Bauwerks und seiner Bewohner. Wer am Leipziger Platz sein Studio oder im Beisheim-Apartment-Tower seine 600 m² große Luxuswohnung bezieht, der will seine Gäste nicht an einer genormten Tür aus dem Baumarkt begrüßen, sondern eben an einem Portal, dessen Größe und Materialität (Bronze) auf die tatsächliche oder vermeintliche Bedeutung des Hausherrn verweist. Dies ist keine übertriebene Geste, sondern einerseits ein Rückbezug auf eine Tradition des 19. Jahrhunderts, und andererseits ist diese Geste angemessen allein deshalb, weil in diesem Turm oder in diesem Haus nicht irgendwer wohnt, sondern eine Klientel, die sich zumindest über ihre Kaufkraft vom »normalen« Bürger deutlich abhebt. Denn die Preise für die Wohnungen an diesen Adressen liegen auf Weltmarktniveau.

Spätestens nachdem Hilmer & Sattler und Albrecht 1991 den Wettbewerb um den Bebauungsplan für den Bereich des Potsdamer und des Leipziger Platzes in Berlin-Mitte gewonnen hatten, hat sich in ihrem Œuvre die Leitvorstellung von der kompakten, räumlich komplexen europäischen Stadt festgesetzt. Zu dieser Leitvorstellung gehören in Berlin großräumliche Elemente wie Freiräume, Raumfolgen, Grünbereiche und ein zusammenhängendes Straßennetz. Das Raumprofil dieser Straßen hat die Proportion 2:1 (35 m Gebäudehöhe, 17,5 m Straßenbreite). Die 35 m Höhe werden auch am Leipziger Platz entgegen der sonst im Stadtgebiet geltenden Traufhöhe von 22 m beibehalten, um den gewaltigen Proportionen des Plat-

and squares and the doors and windows of buildings are a response to the dimensions of their size. This does not mean that there has to be a contradiction between the aesthetics of the façade and the needs of the user, something that Wilhelm Busch criticized about Munich's Maximilianstraße and the »Maximilian style«. The aesthetic standards of the planner do not correspond here with the practical demands of the user. Seen from the back, that which looks so pleasant from the front, is not concerned with the human being.

The portals – a more fitting term than doors – that Hilmer & Sattler und Albrecht have above all placed on their private and public buildings in Berlin, also seem to be too big for a human being. Their proportion corresponds, however, to the buildings and their position on the street or square as well as to the significance of the building and its residents. If one has a studio-apartment on Leipziger Platz or has moved into a luxury apartment of 600 m^2 in the Beisheim apartment tower, one does not want to greet one's guests at a standardized door from the do-it-yourself store, but rather at a portal whose material (bronze) indicates the real or assumed significance of the owner. This is not an exaggerated gesture, for it not only recalls a tradition of the 19th century, but it is also appropriate, for the resident of this building or tower is not a nonentity. At least in what it can afford, the clientele that lives here is quite clearly a step above the »normal« person. The prices for the apartments at these addresses are at the level of the world market.

It was at the latest, once Hilmer & Sattler und Albrecht won the competition in 1991 for the development of Potsdamer Platz and Leipziger Platz in Berlin-Mitte, that the determining idea of the compact, spatially complex European city established itself firmly in their work. In Berlin this idea includes large, spatial elements such as open spaces, urban structure, green areas and an inter-connected network of streets. The spatial profile of these streets has the proportion of 2:1 (35 m building-height, 17,5 m street width). In contrast to the city's usual eaves' height of 22 m, the height of 35 m has also been used at Leipziger Platz, thereby furnishing the huge proportions of this square with an appropriate border. The apartment tower of the Beisheim-Center at Potsdamer Platz rises a further 40 m and regulates the scale of the entrance pavilions to the Potsdamer Platz train station, for without this background, they would appear enormous. Independent of the formal structuring of the façades of these buildings at Potsdamer Platz and Leipziger Platz, at the Beisheim-Center and at the newly built square where Hans-von Bülow-Straße and Auguste-Hauschner-Straße meet, where there will be diverse office buildings with an eaves' height also measuring 35 m, and before any stylistic classification is made one should recognize that Hilmer & Sattler und Albrecht have created a compact, urban situation. Kurt Tucholsky's observation, that Berlin combined the disadvantages of a big American city with those of a German provincial town, while the merits of the city could be read about in Baedecker, is at least no longer relevant for this area. What has emerged here is neither a miniature version of an American sky-

14. Wilhelm Busch, Karikatur einer Eingangstür in der Münchner Maximilianstraße.

14. Wilhelm Busch, caricature of an entrance door in the Maximilianstraße, Munich.

zes einen angemessenen Rand zu geben. Nochmals 40 m höher ragt der Apart-ment-Tower des Beisheim-Centers am Potsdamer Platz auf und gibt dem ohne die-sen Hintergrund riesig erscheinenden Eingangspavillon zum Bahnhof Potsdamer Platz einen regulierenden Maßstab. Unabhängig von der formalen Gestaltung der Fassaden dieser Bauten am Potsdamer und Leipziger Platz, am Beisheim-Center und an dem neu entstehenden Platz im Kreuzungspunkt der Achsen der Hans-von-Bülow-Straße und der Auguste-Hauschner-Straße mit verschiedenen Bürohäusern mit einer Traufhöhe von ebenfalls 35 m ist Hilmer & Sattler und Albrecht vor aller stilistischen Zuordnung eine kompakte urbane Situation zu verdanken. Kurt Tu-cholskys Bonmot, daß Berlin die Nachteile einer amerikanischen Großstadt mit denen einer deutschen Provinzstadt vereine, während die Vorzüge der Stadt im Baedeker stünden, gilt jetzt zumindest für diesen Bereich nicht mehr. Denn hier ist weder eine Miniaturausgabe einer amerikanischen Hochhaus-City noch eine auf-geblasene Kleinstadt entstanden, sondern eine urbane Situation, die mit den ande-ren Hauptstädten Europas konkurrieren kann.

Nicht nur wegen der verwandtschaftlichen Beziehungen, die Christoph Sattler mit dem Bildhauer Adolf von Hildebrand verbinden, sondern angesichts der grundsätzlichen Bedeutung von dessen 1899 geäußerten Leitsätzen sei an dieser Stelle noch einmal die Frühgeschichte künstlerischer Stadtplanung bemüht. In sei-nem Aufsatz »Einiges über die Bedeutung von Größenverhältnissen in der Architek-tur« hat Sattlers Urgroßvater das künstlerische Moment architektonischer Gestal-tung hervorgehoben: »Das Schaffen in Verhältnissen, die innere Formkonsequenz, das Schalten und Walten mit Gegensätzen, Richtungen etc. ist ein künstlerischer Vorgang und Inhalt, welcher unabhängig vom Stil zu betrachten ist und in der Hauptsache schon vollständig feste Gestalt annehmen kann. Ohne überhaupt noch in eine bestimmte Stilart ausgelaufen zu sein oder überhaupt auszulaufen.«[18] Oh-nehin, so Hildebrand an gleicher Stelle weiter, hänge das »Gute oder Schlechte« in der Architektur nicht von der Stilart ab, sondern von Dingen, die viel allgemeinerer Natur seien. So etwa »räumliche Disposition, in der das Einzelne zueinander und zum Ganzen steht, indem es aus dem Ganzen einen einfachen oder komplizierten Gegenstand macht«.[19] Diese vor einhundert Jahren formulierten Leitsätze gelten heute für Hilmer & Sattler und Albrecht sowohl bei städtebaulichen Planungen als auch im Hochbau, sowohl im Großen als auch im Kleinen. Dabei läßt sich die Stil-frage, und das heißt heute meist die Frage nach der Fassadengestaltung, nur inner-halb einer akademischen Analyse von der allgemeinen Konzeption ablösen. Denn stilistische Haltung und Suche nach den angemessenen Referenzen bedingen und erwarten zugleich eine Entscheidung für eine bestimmte städtebauliche Ausgangs-situation, die selbst wiederum abhängig von der Stilwahl ist.

Die feinen Unterschiede

Die präzise baumeisterliche Ausarbeitung von Details, die ausgesuchten Materia-lien und deren Farbigkeit und die baukünstlerische Sorge um das Relief der Fassa-den gehört zu den besonderen Qualitäten des Büros. Die Architekten setzen viel Zeit und Ehrgeiz daran, Details zu entwickeln, die die Wirkung der Räume oder der Fassaden zu steigern helfen. Wie bei ihren Bauten überhaupt geht dies so zurück-

scraper city nor an inflated small town, but rather an urban situation that can compete with Europe's other capital cities.

It is not only the familial ties between Christoph Sattler and the sculptor Adolf von Hildebrand, that lead us here to take another look at the early history of artistic town planning but above all the fundamental significance of principles laid down by Hildebrand in 1899. In his essay »Einiges über die Bedeutung von Größenverhältnissen in der Architektur«, Sattler's great-grandfather emphasized the artistic moment in architectonic structuring: »Creation within relationships, the internal consistency of form, a free hand with opposites, directions etc. is an artistic process and has artistic content that is to be viewed independently of the style and in the main it can take on a complete solid form. This, without having made use of a specific style.«[18] In any case, Hildebrand continues, the »good or bad« in architecture does not depend on the type of style, but on things which are of a much more general nature. For example, »spatial disposition, in which the individual elements are in relation to each other and to the whole and can make the whole a simple or complicated thing«.[19] These principles, laid out a century ago, are valid today for Hilmer & Sattler und Albrecht in both their town planning and in their buildings, in both large terms and in small. Only an academic analysis would remove the question of style – and today that usually means how the façade has been fashioned – from the overall concept. A stylistic position and the search for appropriate references both demand and anticipate a decision for a definite point of departure in town planning, which is itself again dependent on the style that is chosen.

The fine distinctions

The firm is especially distinguished by its precise elaboration of details, by its careful choice of materials and their colours and by the architectural care taken with the façade's relief. The architects spend a lot of time and effort in developing details that will help to emphasize the architectural effect made by the rooms or the façades. As is the case with their buildings in general, this occurs so quietly and with such restraint, that the uninitiated will feel the effect, but not know from where it comes. For example, the new lamps in the central hall of the Gemäldegalerie in Berlin create a completely new effect, but – word of honour – who knew, without being informed beforehand that this new atmosphere was due to the capital-like wreath made of cast elements around the spotlights.

Other elements, such as the window and door reveals, stepped two to three times, that can be found almost everywhere, the fluting on the pilasters, the profiled parapets and not least the unceasing endeavour to develop contemporary capitals, are indications of the ambition to create façades that are as lively and differentiated as those on the 19th century buildings that have been taken as a reference. This is not copying. On the contrary, the modern element can be seen in the aim of achieving similar effects with the means provided by contemporary building technology.

Their approach to the effect made by their building materials is of a similar nature. The expressiveness of different types of stone, from clinker brick to concrete, from plaster to terra cotta, as well as diverse types of sandstone, is taken carefully into account when these stones are examined and selected. If the building

haltend und leise vor sich, daß der Uneingeweihte zwar die Wirkung spürt, aber gar nicht weiß, woraus sie resultiert. So hat die zentrale Halle der Gemäldegalerie in Berlin durch die neuen Leuchten plötzlich eine ganz neue Wirkung, aber – Hand aufs Herz – wer wüßte, ohne informiert zu sein, daß diese neue Atmosphäre dem kapitellartigen Kranz aus Gußelementen um die Strahler herum zu verdanken ist?

Andere Elemente, wie die fast allgegenwärtigen zwei- bis dreifach gestuften Faschen, die Kannelierungen von Wandpfeilern, die profilierten Brüstungen und nicht zuletzt die andauernden Versuche, zeitgenössische Kapitelle zu entwickeln, zeugen von dem ambitionierten Bestreben, ähnliche lebhafte und wechselvolle Fassaden zu entwickeln, wie sie etwa die Referenzbauten des 19. Jahrhunderts auszeichnen. Auch hier wird nicht kopiert, sondern das moderne Element besteht darin, mit den Mitteln der heutigen Bautechnik ähnliche Effekte zu erzielen.

In dieselbe Richtung zielt ihre Auseinandersetzung mit der Anmutungsqualität der Baumaterialien. Die Ausdruckskraft verschiedenster Steinsorten vom Klinker über Beton, Putz und Terrakotta bis zu diversen Sandsteinen werden für den jeweiligen Zusammenhang geprüft und ausgesucht. Wenn nicht die Bauaufgabe eine eher dunkle Farbigkeit vorgibt, wie im Fall der U-Bahnstation Mendelssohn-Bartholdy-Park, bevorzugen Hilmer & Sattler und Albrecht eine helle Farbigkeit. Spanischer Bateig begeistert die Architekten wegen seines an die menschliche Haut erinnernden Farbtons, ein heller, beiger Kalkstein aus Portugal bezaubert die drei Partner wegen seiner »optimistischen Leichtigkeit«. Auch sonst sind es helle, Heiterkeit verströmende Steinsorten und Verputze, weshalb einem in Berlin und München zuweilen das farbliche Flair der Toskana umweht.

Die andere Lieblingsfarbe der Partner ist ein kräftiges Rot; rot leuchtet nachts die 925 Lounge Bar am Gendarmenmarkt in Berlin. Rot ist die Wand entlang der langen, drei Geschosse überwindenden Treppe im Picasso-Museum in Münster. Und wem dies noch nicht rot genug ist, der möge in die Stadtbibliothek nach Pforzheim kommen. Alle Regale, Tische und Stühle in dem riesigen, durch eine Freitreppe zugänglichen Bibliothekssaal sind rot. Zuerst irritiert, versteht man erst nach und nach, daß es dieses Rot ist, das dem Raum seine homogene, ruhige und würdevolle Wirkung verleiht, denn die sonst aufdringlich bunten Buchrücken verschwinden optisch unter der allgegenwärtigen Farbe.

Die Geschichte als Steinbruch

Hilmer & Sattler und Albrecht benutzen die Geschichte als schier unerschöpflichen Steinbruch, der für jede Gelegenheit das passende Vorbild mitsamt den passenden Materialien und der geschmacksvollsten Farbigkeit liefert. Aber die Auswahl aus dem großen Buch der Baugeschichte ist keineswegs beliebig wie in der Architektur des 19. Jahrhunderts, sondern sowohl an der jeweiligen Bauaufgabe, dem jeweiligen regionalen und lokalen Umfeld und schließlich an der von den Architekten oder ihrem Bauherrn gewünschten Intention und Wirkung ausgerichtet. Es handelt sich also um einen sehr konkreten, intellektuell begründeten und von einem umfassenden historischen Wissen von den Typologien, den Bauformen und den sozialen Hintergründen von Architektur getragenen Eklektizismus. Wenn etwa beim Beisheim-Center am Potsdamer Platz der Typus der Geschäftshochhäuser im

itself does not require a darker colour – as with the underground station Mendelssohn-Bartholdy-Park – then Hilmer & Sattler und Albrecht prefer to use lighter colours. The architects are enthusiastic about Spanish Bateig , because its different hues of colour remind them of human skin. A light, beige limestone from Portugal appeals to the three partners because of its »optimistic lightness«. This repeated use of light-coloured types of stone and plasterwork, radiating good cheer, means that sometimes in Berlin and Munich one encounters colours that recall Tuscany.

The partners' other favourite colour is a strong red. The 925 Lounge Bar on Gendarmenmarkt in Berlin shines red at night. The wall beside the staircase covering three storeys in the Picasso Museum in Munster is red. And if this is not red enough for some, then they should go to the city library in Pforzheim. All of the shelves, tables and chairs in the huge library room, entered from a free-standing staircase are red. Confused at first, one slowly understands that it is this red that lends the room its homogenous, calming and dignified effect, for the manifold colours of the books, which would be otherwise obtrusive, disappear amongst this omnipresent colour.

15. Hilmer & Sattler und Albrecht, Leuchtenverkleidungen aus Gußaluminium, Gemäldegalerie, Berlin-Tiergarten, 2003. (Photo: Stefan Müller.)

15. Hilmer & Sattler und Albrecht, light fittings in cast aluminium, Gemäldegalerie, Berlin-Tiergarten, 2003. (Photo: Stefan Müller.)

History as a quarry

Hilmer & Sattler und Albrecht use history as a virtually inexhaustible quarry that provides the appropriate model for every occasion along with the appropriate materials and the most tasteful colours. But the selection made from the big book of architectural history is by no means arbitrary as in the architecture of the 19th century, rather it is directed towards the building task at hand, towards the regional and local context and finally, towards the intention and effect aimed for by the client or by the architects themselves. This is an eclecticism that is very concrete and intellectual. It demands a comprehensive knowledge of typologies, architectural forms and the social backgrounds of architecture. For example, the Beisheim-Center at Potsdamer Platz follows in the tradition of office skyscrapers in Chicago or New York of the late 19th century, translating this into a modern use of forms, not only with a town planner's view of the use of extremely dense urban space, but also with a view of the social history behind the genesis of these American buildings. In the same

16. Holabird and Roche, Erweiterung des Monadnock Building (Burnham und Root, 1891), Chicago 1893. (Aus: John Zukowsky, *Chicago Architektur,* München 1987, S. 366.)

16. Holabird and Roche, extension of the Monadnock Building (Burnham and Root, 1891), Chicago 1893. (From: John Zukowsky, *Chicago Architektur,* Munich 1987, S. 366.)

Chicago oder New York des ausgehenden 19. Jahrhunderts aufgegriffen und in eine moderne Formensprache übersetzt wird, so geschieht dies nicht nur im Hinblick auf die städtebauliche Typologie der hochverdichteten City, sondern auch im Hinblick auf die sozialen Entstehungsgründe dieser Bauten. So wie Chicago damals einen Höhepunkt seiner Wirtschaftskraft erreichte und sich dieser in den Hochhausbauten dokumentierte, so soll das Berliner Stadtzentrum eine solche Kraft (selbst wenn sie zur Zeit nicht tatsächlich vorhanden ist) ausstrahlen.

Barocke Bibliotheken standen im Hintergrund der Überlegungen zur Stadtbibliothek in Pforzheim. Das zur Hauptstraße ausgerichtete große Kastenfenster prägt die Wirkung des Innenraums, der mit seiner Galerie und seinem gewaltigen Volumen tatsächlich barocke Maßstäbe wiederaufleben läßt. Nur sind jetzt nicht Mönche oder Fürsten, sondern Bürger der Stadt Pforzheim die Nutzer dieser repräsentativen Räume. Im Kontrast zur roten Möblierung stehen die grünen Leuchten an den Leseplätzen, die ebenfalls auf eine alte Bibliothekstradition verweisen.

Im Wohnungsbau, den das Büro in den letzten Jahren vor allem für eine gehobene Klientel errichtet, sind die formalen Anlehnungen ebenfalls breit gestreut. So lassen sich die Stadthäuser am Olympiapark in München, die um einen halböffentlichen Freibereich mit Wasserbassins angeordnet sind, mit den »gated communities« in den USA vergleichen. Bei den zwei Wohnhäusern an der Außenalster werden für Hamburg typische gründerzeitliche Gebäude- und Wohnkonzepte neu interpretiert. Im Herzen der Wohnbauten am Tiergartendreieck in Berlin befindet sind ein sogenannter »Pocket-Park«, den es bislang nur in Paris und einige Male in England gab. Der Park liegt auf privatem Grund, ist aber dennoch tagsüber öffentlich zugänglich. Nur nachts und zu besonderen Anlässen werden die Tore geschlossen. Die asymmetrisch angeordneten fünf- bis sechsgeschossigen Wohnkomplexe strahlen eine noble Gediegenheit aus, wozu die Rahmung der Fenster mit Profilen und Faschen, die horizontale Gliederung durch Gesimsbänder und die durch Wiener Sprossen verfeinerten Fenster ihren Teil beitragen. Aber auch hier erfährt der Besucher gleich beim Eintritt in die großzügige Lobby, wo ihn nach amerikanischen Muster ein »doorman« begrüßt, daß er einen Wohnbau für herausgehobene Menschen betritt.

Wesentlich kleiner als die bis zu 200 m² großen Wohnungen im Tiergartendreieck sind die Wohnungen in den achtgeschossigen Wohnhochhäusern auf der The-

way that Chicago at this time had reached a pinnacle of its economic strength and documented this in the construction of skyscrapers, Berlin's city centre should also radiate such a strength (even if it is at the moment not present).

Baroque libraries formed the background to the considerations for the design of the city library in Pforzheim. The huge double-skin glazing element looking out to the main street defines the effect made by the interior, whose great volume and gallery really does revive Baroque proportions. This time, however, it is not monks or princes but the citizens of Pforzheim who are using these grand rooms. The green reading lamps are in contrast to the interior's red furnishings and are also a reminder of an older tradition in libraries.

In the residential architecture, that the firm has been carrying out in the last years primarily for a prosperous clientele, the formal references also cover a broad spectrum. For example, the townhouses at the Olympiapark in Munich, arranged around a semi-public, open area with ponds can be compared to American »gated communities«. The two residential buildings on the banks of the Außenalster in Hamburg are a new interpretation of architectural and residential concepts typical of this city in the late 19th century. In the middle of the residential buildings in the Tiergartendreieck in Berlin there is a so-called »pocket park«, which until now could only be found in Paris and occasionally in England. While the park is on private property, it is open to the public during the day. It is only at night and on special occasions that the gates are locked. The five-to-six-storey residential complexes have been arranged asymmetrically. Contributing to their aura of stylishness, of high-quality, is the way that the windows have been framed with profiles and borders, the horizontal structuring through ledges and the refinement of the widows through special mullions. But here too, the visitor is aware as soon as he enters the lobby – where, following the American model, he is greeted by a doorman – that he is in a residential building for people of a special status.

The apartments in the eight-storey residential towers on the Theresienwiese in Munich are much smaller than the apartments in the Tiergartendreieck, which can measure up to 200 m². The broadly extending balconies on buildings that have been constructed according to the stipulations for subsidised housing as laid out in Otto Steidle's master plan – the architects are friends

17. Bibliothekssaal, ehemalige Benediktinerabtei, Wiblingen, 1744. Aufnahme 1950er Jahre. (Photo: Bildarchiv Foto Marburg.)

17. The library room in the former Benedictine abbey, Wiblingen, 1744. Photograph from the 1950s. (Photo: Bildarchiv Foto Marburg.)

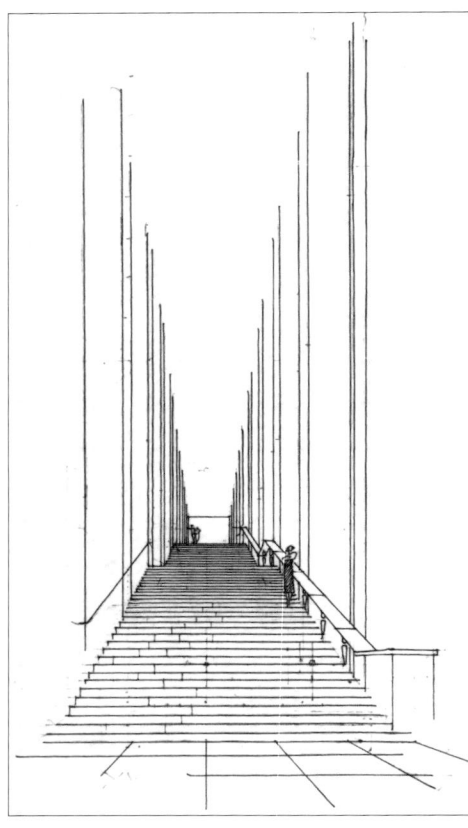

18. Hans Döllgast, Treppenhaus, Alte Pinakothek München, Zeichnung, 1956. (Architekturmuseum, TU München.)

18. Hans Döllgast, Stairway, Alte Pinakothek Munich, Drawing, 1956. (Architecture Museum, TU Munich.)

resienwiese in München. Die weit ausladenden Balkone der unter Maßgaben des sozialen Wohnungsbaus auf dem Masterplan von Otto Steidle, mit dem die Architekten befreundet sind, errichteten Bauten nehmen Bezug auf die schwungvollen Balkone der Wohnbauten der fünfziger Jahre, freilich mit dem Unterschied, daß mit heutiger Bautechnik sich wahrlich terrassenartige Dimensionen dieser einstigen Austritte auch im Geschoßwohnungsbau bewerkstelligen lassen.

Gezielt gesetzt ist die Referenz an den Treppenraum der von Hans Döllgast renovierten Alten Pinakothek in München beim hinter historischen Fassaden verborgenen Picasso-Museum in Münster. Die Treppe, die in dem schmalen zur Verfügung stehenden Raum die einzig denkbar gute Lösung für die Erschließung war, ist eben nicht nur irgendeine Treppe in einem Museum, sondern eine veritable »Museumstreppe«. Das schwebende Dach über dem Tresen der 925 Lounge Bar erinnert an Soffitten in der Theaterarchitektur und wurde direkt durch den französischen Art-Déco-Architekten Robert Mallet-Stevens angeregt.

Beim neuen Globushaus in Schloß Gottorf, Schleswig, sind es andere architektonische Pathosformeln, die formale wie inhaltliche Anregungen abgaben: das ebenso berühmte wie rätselhafte, um 1730 entstandene Jantar Mantar in Jaipur. Bereits Le Corbusier hatte sich von dieser Stern- und Sonnenbeobachtungsstation bei seinen Bauten und Skulpturen in Chandigarh inspirieren lassen. Und 1962 regte es Myron Goldsmith zu dem Kitt Peak National Observatory bei Tucson in Arizona an; zu diesen ikonographischen Bezügen kommt die persönliche Bekanntschaft Christoph Sattlers als auch Thomas Albrechts mit dem Mies-Schüler Myron Goldsmith. Beide studierten – freilich um zwei Jahrzehnte versetzt – bei ihm am IIT in Chicago.

In anderen Fällen sind die Referenzen lokal begründet oder resultieren aus lokalen Bauvorschriften, die als kreativitätsanregende Vorgaben gern aufgenommen werden. So nimmt das Haus der Bayerischen Wirtschaft in München die Pavillontypologie der Max-Joseph-Straße auf und setzt sie mit modernen Mitteln fort. Ebenso verfuhren die Architekten am Karl-Scharnagl-Ring, wo die mit Terrakottasteinen verkleideten und dynamisch reliefierten Fassaden des Büro- und Geschäftskomplexes sich als mächtige Gewinner in den Glasfassaden der gegenüberliegenden Straßenseite spiegeln und zeigen, welche Bautradition in München am rechten Platz ist. Beim U-Bahnhof Mendelssohn-Bartholdy-Park in der Nähe des Potsdamer Platzes haben Hilmer & Sattler und Albrecht sich vollkommen auf die lange Berliner Tradition verlassen und Klinker mit Stahl zu einer zeitlosen Architektur kombiniert, die selbst scharfe Berliner Architekturkritiker zu dem außergewöhnlichen Lob hinrissen, daß hier ein Nutzbau entstanden sei, »der sich nach den gestalterischen Verirrungen der sechziger bis achtziger Jahre endlich wieder dem architektonischen Niveau der U-Bahn-Vergangenheit eines Alfred Grenander gewachsen zeigt«.[20]

19. Robert Mallet-Stevens, Bühnenbild zu Marcel L'Herbiers L'Inhumaine, 1923. (Aus: Archives d' Architecture Moderne, Rob Mallet-Stevens, Brüssel.)

19. Robert Mallet-Stevens, set for Marcel L'Herbier's L'Inhumaine, 1923. (From: Archives d' Architecture Moderne, Rob Mallet-Stevens, Bruxelles.)

of Steidle – refer back to the sweeping balconies on the apartment houses of the 1950s, although admittedly with the difference that contemporary technology allows for terrace-like dimensions for what were formerly balconies on multi-storeyed apartment houses.

The stair-hall behind the historic façade in the Picasso Museum in Munster is a deliberate reference to the stair-hall in the Alte Pinakothek in Munich, renovated by Hans Döllgast. This staircase – the only good solution to the question of how to open up the available narrow space – is not simply a staircase in a museum but rather a veritable »museum staircase«. The roof that hangs over the bar in the 925 Lounge Bar reminds one of the soffits of stage architecture and is directly inspired by the French Art-Déco architecture of Robert Mallet-Stevens.

The new globe house at Schloß Gottorf in Schleswig was indebted to a different architectonic model for inspiration both in formal terms and those of content. The model was the famous but enigmatic Jantar Mantar built in Jaipur in 1730. This stellar and solar observatory had already inspired Le Corbusier in his buildings and sculptures for Chandigarh and in 1962 it would be a source of stimulation for Myron Goldsmith in his design for the Kitt Peak National Observatory near Tucson, Arizona. In addition to this iconographic reference, is the acquaintance of both Christoph Sattler and Thomas Albrecht with Myron Goldsmith, who had been a student of Mies. Sattler und Albrecht were Goldsmith's students – albeit two decades apart – at the ITT in Chicago.

In other places the references spring from local conditions or result from local building regulations that have been greeted as a stimulus to creativity. For example, the Haus der Bayerischen Wirtschaft (centre for the Bavarian economy) in Munich

20. Das große Samrat Yantra, Jantar Mantar, Jaipur, Indien, um 1730. (Photo: Andreas Volwahsen.)

20. The great Samrat Yantra, Jantar Mantar, Jaipur, India, c. 1730. (Photo: Andreas Volwahsen.)

21. Otto Wagner, Post-
sparkasse, Wien, 1904
to 1906. Luftauslässe.

21. Otto Wagner, Postal
Savings Bank, Vienna,
1904–06. Ventilation
outlets.

An anderen Orten sind es eher rein formal begründete Anleihen aus der Geschichte der Architektur: so Mediensäulen in der Halle des Gebäudes für die *Frankfurter Allgemeine Zeitung*, die aus massivem Stahl scharfkantig herausgearbeitet wurden und deren Vorbild die Luftauslässe der Postsparkasse in Wien von Otto Wagner
sind. Oder zuweilen scheinen es private Vorlieben zu sein, die Ideengeber waren:
so etwa im zentralen Saal der Gemäldegalerie Berlin die »Lampenschirme« aus
feingliedrigen Gußelementen mit frei geschwungenen Linien, für die ein ähnliches
Motiv von Antoni Gaudí in der Kathedrale von Palma de Mallorca Pate stand. Ebenfalls allein aus ästhetischen Gründen wurde der großzügige, fast 7 m hohe Eingangsbereich des Bürohauses des Beisheim-Centers in Berlin nach der Anregung
einer Moschee aus Kairo dreifarbig in Weiß, Rot und Grün mit Marmor verkleidet.

Es muß noch einmal hervorgehoben werden, daß all diese Bezüge von den Architekten selbst benannt worden sind, und im Falle des Bürohauses im Beisheim-
Center ist der Bezug zum First Leiter Building von William Le Baron Jenney gar auf
der Bronzeplakette zusammen mit den Namen der Architekten fest eingraviert.; es
ist also nicht die Leistung des Architekturhistorikers, diese Referenzbauten und
Zitate aufzuspüren und zu interpretieren. Wenn Hilmer & Sattler und Albrecht
sagen würden, daß sie alles selbst erfunden hätten, dann hätte der Kritiker leichtes
Spiel, ihnen die Anlehnungen und Zitate nachzuweisen und sie gleichsam des Pla-
giats zu bezichtigen. Indem sie aber selbst auf ihre Quellen verweisen, wird dem
Kritiker die Luft abgeschnitten. Und da die Quellen auch noch so sinnfällig ausge-
wählt sind, machen sich die Architekten nahezu unangreifbar. Es geht hier aber
nicht um ein intellektuelles Spiel zur Geschichte der Architektur, sondern um qua-
litätvolle Baukunst. Die Gestalt der Bauten von Hilmer & Sattler und Albrecht birgt
kein Risiko, es werden erprobte Systeme und Details verwendet. Das Neue dieser
Bauten ist aber ebenso unverkennbar, denn es sind nie bloße Kopien anderer Bauten, und an allen spürt man die immer wieder angestrengte Suche nach neuen
Lösungen, die tatsächlich Baukultur entstehen lassen. Sieger in einem Spiel, die
Referenzen und Zitate zu erkennen, wäre nicht derjenige, der die meisten Verweise
identifiziert, sondern es sind all die Menschen, die mit offenen Augen durch Berlin
oder München gehen und sich tagtäglich an solch solider, freundlicher und anspruchsvoller Architektur erfreuen können.

22. Alfred Grenander,
U-Bahnhof Gesund-
brunnen, Berlin-Wed-
ding. Aufnahme 1930er
Jahre. (Photo: Bildar-
chiv Foto Marburg.)

22. Alfred Grenander,
underground station
Gesundbrunnen,
Berlin-Wedding. Pho-
tograph from the
1930s. (Photo: Bild-
archiv Marburg.)

takes up and continues the pavilion typology of Max-Joseph-Straße through the use of modern means. The architects are also persuasive at Karl-Scharnagl-Ring, where the office and commercial complexes, with terracotta cladding and dynamic reliefs, are reflected as powerful victors in the glass façades on the other side of the street and make clear which architectural tradition belongs to Munich. With the underground station at Mendelssohn-Bartholdy-Park close to Potsdamer Platz, Hilmer & Sattler und Albrecht based their work on a long Berlin tradition, combining clinker brick and steel to create a timeless architecture, which moved one of Berlin's usually sharp-tongued architecture critics, to voice the unusual praise, that a functional building was built here »that after the architectural confusion in the years between the 1960s and 1980s matched architectural standard of underground stations of the past by Alfred Grenander«.[20]

Elsewhere, architectural history has provided stimuli in more purely formal terms, such as with the media columns in the lobby of the building for the *Frankfurter Allgemeine Zeitung*. Sharp-edged, they are made of solid steel and have been modelled on the ventilation outlets in Otto Wagner's Postal Savings Bank in Vienna. Sometimes personal predilections provided the idea, such as in the central room of the Gemäldegalerie in Berlin where the »lampshades« out of finely structured mouldings with curved lines, are similar to a motif to be found in Antoni Gaudí's cathedral in Palma de Mallorca. It was also purely for aesthetic reasons that the expansive entrance area in the office building of the Beisheim-Center in Berlin, measuring almost 7 m in height was clad in white, red and green marble. The inspiration for this was a mosque in Cairo.

It must be again emphasized here that all of these references have been named by the architects themselves and in the case of the office building in the Beisheim-Center the reference to the First Leiter Building by William Le Baron Jenney has even been engraved onto the bronze plaque alongside the names of the architects. It is, therefore, not the achievement of the architectural historian to uncover and interpret these references and citations. If Hilmer & Sattler und Albrecht were to contend that they discovered everything themselves, then it would be easy for the critic to point out their borrowings and citations and accuse them of plagiarism. Because they themselves point towards their sources, however, the wind is taken out of the critic's sails. And since these sources are always selected with great care, they are almost unassailable. What this is all about in the end, however, is not simply an intellectual game about the history of architecture, but rather about quality architecture. In the shape they give their buildings, Hilmer & Sattler und Albrecht do not take risks. Systems and details which have been tried and tested are used. It is also undeniable, however, that there is something new about these buildings, for they are never just copies of other buildings. Looking at each building, one feels that great effort has been expended in seeking new solutions that would allow for the emergence of a real building culture. The winner in a game of recognizing the references and citations would not be the one who recognizes the most, but rather all those people who walk with open eyes through Berlin or Munich and daily take pleasure in this solid, friendly and sophisticated architecture.

23. Mausoleum in der Medrese-Moschee des Sultans Barquq, Kairo, 1384–86. (Photo: Katharina Sattler.)

23. Mausoleum in the Medrese Mosque of the Sultan Barquq, Cairo, 1384–86. (Photo: Katharina Sattler.)

1
Ich danke den Architekten für Gespräche und Hilfen; unter den Mitarbeitern des Büros sei besonders Alexander Waimer hervorgehoben. Anregend waren die Interviews von Klaus-Dieter Weiss mit Heinz Hilmer und Christoph Sattler, veröffentlicht als »Abstraktion und Gegenständlichkeit«, *Werk, Bauen und Wohnen*, 1991, Nr. 6, S. 2–9, und »Der Stadt die Tradition, der Architektur die Individualität«, *Deutsche Bauzeitung*, 1992, Nr. 3, S. 351–358, sowie das mit einer Einführung von Stanislaus von Moos versehene Buch *Hilmer & Sattler, Bauten und Projekte*, Stuttgart/London 2000.

2
Winfried Nerdinger, »Erfinden, erschauen oder erarbeiten: Positionen des architektonischen Entwerfens«, *Thesis, Wissenschaftliche Zeitschrift der Bauhaus-Universität Weimar*, 1999, Heft 2, S. 28–34, hier S. 33.

3
Amber Sayah, »So einfach wie Ikea: In Bonn hat der erste Konvent Baukultur getagt«, *Stuttgarter Zeitung*, 7. April 2003, S. 8; Andreas Rossmann, »Schrumpfen als Chance: In Bonn ist die Stiftung Baukultur auf den Weg gebracht worden«, *Frankfurter Allgemeine Zeitung*, 8. April 2003, S. 42.

4
Michael Bienert, »Schinkel und seine Jünger: Neue Pläne für den Wiederaufbau der Berliner Bauakademie«, *Stuttgarter Zeitung*, Kultur, 15. März 2003.

5
Ullrich Schwarz, »Wege der Moderne«, Einleitung zur Broschüre zum Hamburger Architektur Sommer 2003, S. 11; zur Stildiskussion um 1800 vgl. Klaus Jan Philipp, »Die Anfänge der Stildiskussion in Deutschland«, in: Winfried Nerdinger (Hrsg.), *Zwischen Glaspalast und Maximilianeum: Architektur in Bayern zur Zeit Maximilians II. 1848–1864*, Eurasburg 1997, S. 52–63.

6
Vgl. Manolis Korres, in: *Die griechische Klassik – Idee oder Wirklichkeit: eine Ausstellung im Martin-Gropius-Bau*, Berlin, 1. März – 2. Juni 2002, Mainz 2002, S. 364.

7
Karl Marx, »Grundrisse«, 1857, zitiert nach: Salvatore Settis, »Der Klassizismus und das Klassische«, in: *Die griechische Klassik*, a.a.O., S. 51.

8
Gabi Dolff-Bonekämper und Almut Jirku, »Kulturforum zum vierten – und zum letzten?«, in: *Architektur in Berlin, Jahrbuch 1999*, S. 158–165, hier S. 165; Thies Schröder, »Wettbewerb Kulturforum Berlin«, *Garten + Landschaft*, Heft 4, 1998, S. 23–27.

9
Günter Behnisch, »Triumph der Form, Glanz der Dauer«, *Werk, Bauen und Wohnen*, Heft 1/2, 1992, S. 6–9, hier S. 9.

10
Zitiert nach: Goerd Peschken, *Karl Friedrich Schinkel: Das architektonische Lehrbuch*, München 1979, S. 149.

11
Christian Marquart, »Wieso immer nur Geniestreiche? Hymne auf die Kultur des guten Standards«, *Architektur + Wettbewerbe*, Heft 189, 2002, S. 64/65.

12
Ralf Hertel, »Das Diktat der Originalität«, *Berliner Zeitung*, Feuilleton, 27. Mai 2000.

13
Hans Kollhoff, »Architektur ist Konvention«, *archithese*, Heft 2, 2003, S. 92–94.

14
Robert Venturi, *Complexity and Contradiction in Architecture*, 2. Auflage, New York 1977, S. 41ff.

15
Erik Forssmann, *Dorisch, Jonisch, Korinthisch: Studien über den Gebrauch der Säulenordnungen in der Architektur des 16.–18. Jahrhunderts*, Reprint der 1. Auflage von 1961, Braunschweig 1984, S. 6.

16
Dieter Hoffmann-Axthelm, »Menetekel der Moderne: Das Scheitern zweier Entwürfe am Potsdamer Platz«, *Werk, Bauen und Wohnen*, Heft 1/2, 1992, S. 49–60, hier S. 51 und S. 60.

17
Camillo Sitte, *Der Städtebau nach seinen künstlerischen Grundsätzen*, Reprint der 4. Auflage von 1909, Braunschweig 1983, S. 117.

18
Adolf von Hildebrand, »Einiges über die Bedeutung von Größenverhältnissen in der Architektur«, in: ders., *Gesammelte Schriften*, Straßburg 1909, S. 9–21, hier S. 17. (Der Aufsatz erschien zuerst 1899 in *Pan*.)

19
Ebd., S. 20.

20
Bernhard Schulz, in: *Baumeister*, Heft XI, 1998, S. 12.

40

1

I would like to thank the architects for discussions and help. Amongst the firms's employees I am especially grateful to Alexander Waimer. The interviews that Klaus-Dieter Weiss held with Heinz Hilmer and Christoph Sattler were stimulating. See »Abstraktion und Gegenständlichkeit«, *Werk, Bauen und Wohnen*, 1991, no. 6, p. 2–9, and »Der Stadt die Tradition der Architektur die Individualität«, *Deutsche Bauzeitung*, 1992, no. 3, p. 351–358, as well as the monograph with an introduction by Stanislaus von Moos, *Hilmer & Sattler, Bauten und Projekte*, Stuttgart/London, 2000.

2

Winfried Nerdinger, »Erfinden, erschauen oder erarbeiten: Positionen des architektonischen Entwerfens«, *Thesis, Wissenschaftliche Zeitschrift der Bauhaus-Universität Weimar*, 1999, no. 2, p. 28–34, here p. 33.

3

Amber Sayah, »So einfach wie Ikea: In Bonn hat der erste Konvent Baukultur getagt«, *Stuttgarter Zeitung*, April 7, 2003, p. 8; Andreas Rossmann, »Schrumpfen als Chance. In Bonn ist die Stiftung Baukultur auf den Weg gebracht worden«, *Frankfurter Allgemeine Zeitung*, April 8, 2003, p. 42.

4

Michael Bienert, »Schinkel und seine Jünger: Neue Pläne für den Wiederaufbau der Berliner Bauakademie«, *Stuttgarter Zeitung*, »Kultur«, March 15, 2003.

5

Ullrich Schwarz, »Wege der Moderne«, introduction to the brochure for the *Hamburger Architektur Sommer 2003*, p. 11. On the discussion of style around 1800, see Klaus Jan Philipp, »Die Anfänge der Stildiskussion in Deutschland«, in: Winfried Nerdinger,

ed., *Zwischen Glaspalast und Maximilianeum: Architektur in Bayern zur Zeit Maximilians II. 1848–1864*, Eurasburg, 1997, p. 52–63.

6

See Manolis Korres, in: *Die griechische Klassik – Idee oder Wirklichkeit: eine Ausstellung im Martin-Gropius-Bau*, Berlin, March 1 – June 2, 2002, Mainz 2002, p. 364.

7

Karl Marx, »Grundrisse«, 1857, cited from: Salvatore Settis, »Der Klassizismus und das Klassische«, in: *Die griechische Klassik*, loc. cit. p. 51.

8

Gabi Dolff-Bonekämper and Almut Jirku, »Kulturforum zum vierten – und zum letzten?« in: *Architektur in Berlin, Jahrbuch 1999*, p. 158–165, here p. 165; Thies Schroeder, »Wettbewerb Kulturforum Berlin«, *Garten + Landschaft*, no. 4, 1998, p. 23–27.

9

Günter Behnisch, »Triumph der Form, Glanz der Dauer«, *Werk, Bauen und Wohnen*, no. 1/2, 1992, p. 6–9, here p. 9.

10

Cited in: Goerd Peschken, *Karl Friedrich Schinkel: Das architektionische Lehrbuch*, Munich 1979, p. 149.

11

Christian Marquart, »Wieso immer nur Geniestreiche? Hymne auf die Kultur des guten Standards«, *Architektur + Wettbewerbe*, no. 189, 2002, p. 64/65.

12

Ralf Hertel, »Das Diktat der Originalität«, *Berliner Zeitung*, »Feuilleton«, May 27, 2000.

13

Hans Kollhoff, »Architektur ist Konvention«, *archithese*, no. 2, 2003, p. 92 to 94.

14

Robert Venturi, *Complexity and Contradiction in Architecture*, 2nd edition, New York, 1977, p. 41ff.

15

Erik Forssmann, *Dorisch, Jonisch, Korinthisch: Studien über den Gebrauch der Säulenordnungen in der Architektur des 16.–18. Jahrhunderts*, reprint of the 1st edition of 1961, Braunschweig, 1984, p. 6.

16

Dieter Hoffmann-Axthelm, »Menetekel der Moderne: Das Scheitern zweier Entwürfe am Potsdamer Platz«, *Werk, Bauen und Wohnen*, no. 1/2, 1993, p. 49–60, here p. 51 and p. 60.

17

Camillo Sitte, *Der Städtebau nach seinen künstlerischen Grundsätzen*, reprint of the 4th edition of 1909, Braunschweig 1983, p. 117.

18

Adolf von Hildebrand, »Einiges über die Bedeutung von Größenverhältnissen in der Architektur«, in: the same, *Gesammelte Schriften*, Strasbourg 1909, p. 9–21, here p. 17. (The essay first appeared in *Pan* in 1899.)

19

Ibid, p. 20.

20

Bernhard Schulz, in: *Baumeister*, no. XI, 1998, p. 12.

Bauten und Projekte
Buildings and Projects

Umbau der Neuen Wache zur Zentralen Gedenkstätte der Bundesrepublik Deutschland, Berlin-Mitte, 1993

Die Neue Wache von Karl Friedrich Schinkel wurde im Jahr 1818 als Gebäude für die königlichen Wachsoldaten eingeweiht. Sie war einer der letzten Bausteine seines städtebaulichen Gesamtkonzepts für einen Abschnitt von Unter den Linden, den er als preußische »Via triumphalis« in Gedenken an die Befreiungskriege gestaltete. Der Entwurf mit seinem annähernd quadratischen Grundriß und seinen vier massiven Ecktürmen ist einem römischen Castrum nachempfunden, vor die Hauptfassade ist ein Portikus mit zehn dorischen Säulen gestellt.

Mit Ende des Ersten Weltkriegs und dem Niedergang der Monarchie verlor das Gebäude seine ursprüngliche Funktion. Nach kontroversen Diskussionen führte man einen Architektenwettbewerb zur Umgestaltung der Neuen Wache als Ehrenmal für die Opfer des Ersten Weltkriegs durch, in dem Heinrich Tessenow den ersten Preis erhielt.

Sein Entwurf sah eine vollständige Entkernung vor, so daß ein einziger Innenraum in den Abmessungen von 19 m Breite, 16 m Tiefe und 9 m Höhe entstand. Zur Belichtung wurde eine kreisförmige Öffnung mit 4 m Durchmesser durch das Dach gebrochen und mit einem Ring aus Bronze eingefaßt. Darunter, im Mittelpunkt des Raumes, wurde ein schwarzer monolithischer Granitblock aufgestellt. Der Fußboden wurde abgesenkt und mit einem Mosaik aus mit Blei verfugten Basaltsteinen

Conversion of the Neue Wache (New Guard House) to the Central Memorial for the Federal Republic of Germany, Berlin-Mitte, 1993

Karl Friedrich Schinkel's Neue Wache (New Guard House), completed in 1818, was designed as a building for the royal sentries. It was one of the last elements in his larger plan for the design of a part of Unter den Linden. In memory of the Wars of Liberation, Schinkel saw this part of the boulevard as Prussia's »via triumphalis«. The design, with a ground-plan that is an approximate square and its four massive turrets is reminiscent of a Roman castrum. In front of its main facade there is a portico with ten Doric columns.

With the end of World War One and the demise of the monarchy, the building's original function disappeared. After some controversy, an architectural competition was held for remodelling the Neue Wache into a memorial for the victims of World War One. First prize was won by Heinrich Tessenow.

His design called for a complete gutting of the interior, thereby creating a single, inner room 19 m wide, 16 m deep and 9 m high. Light was obtained through a circular opening in the roof, 4 m in diameter and enclosed by a bronze ring. Underneath was the room's focal point, a black, monolithic block of granite. The newly sunken floor was covered with a mosaic of basalt stones with lead joints and the walls clad in panels of muschelkalk.

Tessenow also made substantial changes to the outside of the building.

1. Innenraum mit der durch den Berliner Bildhauer Harald Haacke geschaffenen Vergrößerung der Plastik *Trauernde Mutter mit totem Sohn* von Käthe Kollwitz. (Photo: Stefan Müller.)

1. Interior with sculpture *Mother with her Dead Son* by Käthe Kollwitz, enlarged by Berlin sculptor Harald Haacke. (Photo: Stefan Müller.)

2. Ansicht der Neuen Wache von Unter den Linden. (Photo: Stefan Müller.)

2. View of the Neue Wache from Unter den Linden. (Photo: Stefan Müller.)

Umbau der Neuen Wache zur Zentralen Gedenkstätte der Bundesrepublik Deutschland, Berlin-
Mitte, 1993

3. Verlegen des Mo-
saikpflasters. (Photo:
Peter Dörrie.)

3. Laying the mosaic
paving. (Photo: Peter
Dörrie.)

4. Rekonstruktions-
zeichnungen der zwei
Mosaikmuster des
Fußbodens von Tesse-
now.

4. Reconstruction
drawings of the two
mosaic patterns of
Tessenow's floor.

belegt, die Wände mit Platten aus Muschelkalk verkleidet.

Wesentliche Eingriffe nahm Tessenow
auch an der äußeren Bausubstanz vor:
alle Fenster in den seitlichen Fassaden
wurden zugemauert. Von den fünf
Wandöffnungen hinter dem Portikus
ließ er die beiden äußeren verschließen
und die drei mittleren auf drei Viertel
ihrer Höhe reduzieren.

Gegen Ende des Zweiten Weltkriegs
wurde die Neue Wache bei einem Bom-
benangriff stark beschädigt. Die Wieder-
aufbauarbeiten der DDR als »Mahnmal
für die Opfer des Faschismus und des
Militarismus« orientierten sich zunächst
weitgehend an der Raumgestaltung
Tessenows. Den von den Spuren des
Krieges gezeichneten Gedenkstein be-
ließ man vorerst an seinem Standort.

Im Jahr 1969 erfolgte dann eine völlige Neugestaltung des Innenraums:
Anstelle des Granitblocks wurde ein pris-
matisch geschliffener Glaswürfel als Trä-
ger der »ewigen Flamme« in einer dafür geschaffenen Vertiefung plaziert.
Das Tessenowsche Fußbodenmosaik, das
durch die Umbauarbeiten in Teilen zer-

All of the windows on the side façades
were walled up. He had the two outer
openings in the wall behind the portico closed up and the remaining three
openings reduced to three-quarters of
their height.

Towards the end of World War Two
the Neue Wache was seriously damaged
by bombs. The reconstruction work carried out by the GDR was intended as a
»memorial for the victims of fascism and
militarism« and was initially largely orientated towards Tessenow's interior
design. For the time being, the memorial
stone bearing marks of the war was left
in place.

In 1969 the interior was given a completely new design. Instead of the granite
block, a prismatic, polished glass cube
now held the »eternal flame« and was
placed in a hollow specially created for
this purpose. Tessenow's floor-mosaic,
partially damaged through the renovation work, was covered in Bulgarian marble. Somewhat later the wall cladding
was changed.

With the end of the GDR a new discussion arose over the use of the Neue
Wache. Making use of the personal idea
of Helmut Kohl, the German Chancellor
at the time, it was decided at the beginning of 1993, that this building would be
converted into the Central Memorial
for the Federal Republic of Germany.
Tessenow's work should provide the
basis for this endeavour, however, a
sculpture by Käthe Kollwitz, *Mother with
Dead Son* would be quadrupled in size
and placed in the middle of the room.

There was only half a year for the
restoration and convertion. After the
marble floor had been cleared away,
parts of Tessenow's basalt mosaic reap-
peared for which no plans exist. The
only thing that was known was that the
mosaic was put together out of stones of
four different sizes. Proceeding from the

stört wurde, überdeckte man mit einem neuen Belag aus bulgarischem Marmor. Etwas später wurde die Wandverkleidung ausgetauscht.

Mit dem Ende der DDR entstand eine erneute Diskussion um die Nutzung der Neuen Wache. Auf eine persönliche Idee des damaligen Bundeskanzlers Helmut Kohl zurückgehend, wurde Anfang 1993 der Umbau zur Zentralen Gedenkstätte der Bundesrepublik Deutschland beschlossen. Grundlage sollte der Entwurf Tessenows sein, jedoch mit der um das Vierfache vergrößerten Skulptur *Trauernde Mutter mit totem Sohn* von Käthe Kollwitz in der Mitte des Raumes.

Für den Rück- und Umbau stand lediglich ein halbes Jahr zur Verfügung. Nach dem Abtragen des Marmorfußbodens kamen Teile des Tessenowschen Basaltmosaiks wieder zum Vorschein, über das keinerlei Planunterlagen existierten. Bekannt war lediglich, daß es aus vier verschiedenen Steinformaten zusammengesetzt war. Anhand von zwei regelmäßig wiederkehrenden Steinen gelang schließlich die Rekonstruktion des Verlegemusters. Auch die Wandverkleidung wurde in Material und Fugenschnitt exakt entsprechend dem Tessenowschen Zustand wiederhergestellt. Darüber hinaus waren umfangreiche Sanierungsmaßnahmen an der inneren und äußeren Bausubstanz erforderlich.

Parallel zu den Bauarbeiten fertigte der Bildhauer Harald Haacke die Vergrößerung der Kollwitz-Plastik an. Am 14. November 1993, 175 Jahre nach ihrer Fertigstellung als Wachgebäude, wurde die Neue Wache als Zentrale Gedenkstätte der Bundesrepublik Deutschland eingeweiht.

Projektleiter: Peter Dörrie

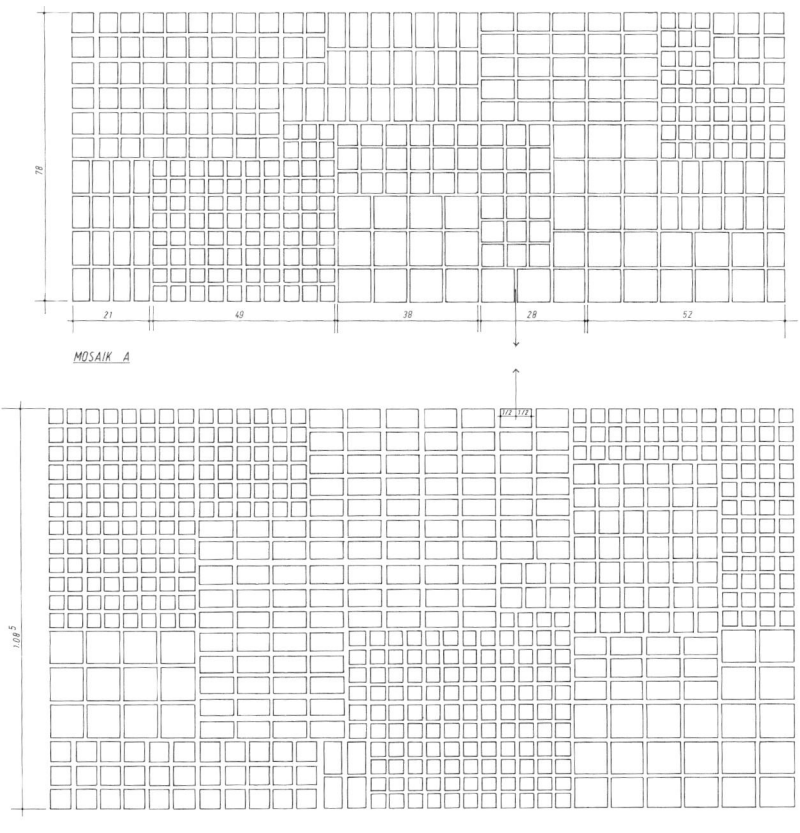

MOSAIK A

MOSAIK B

regular recurrence of two stones, we were finally able to reconstruct the pattern that had been used. In both its material and joint-shape the wall cladding was also restored to exactly what it had looked like for Tessenow. In addition, extensive renovation measures were necessary both inside and outside.

At the same time as this construction work was being carried out, the sculptor Harald Haake enlarged the Kollwitz sculpture. On November 14, 1993, 175 years after the completion of the guard house, the Neue Wache was officially declared to be the Central Memorial for the Federal Republic of Germany.

Project architect: Peter Dörrie

Bahnhof Potsdamer Platz, Berlin-Tiergarten, 1995–2006

Der Potsdamer Platz bildete bereits 1838 den Ausgangspunkt für das Berliner Eisenbahnnetz. Auch beim Wiederauf- und Ausbau des Bahnnetzes nach 1989 wurde es an dieser Stelle erheblich erweitert: Vom Tiergarten kommend, kreuzt ein viergleisiger Tunnel den Potsdamer Platz in Nord–Süd-Richtung, verläuft dabei unter den Hochhäusern des Beisheim-Centers und dem Delbrück-Haus und weitet sich dann zu einem 50 m breiten, 250 m langen und 18 m tiefen, unterirdischen Bahnhofsbauwerk aus.

Auf dem Potsdamer Platz befinden sich die beiden Eingangsgebäude als halboffene Stahl-Glas-Pavillons. Sie erinnern in mehreren Aspekten an die Neue Nationalgalerie von Ludwig Mies van der Rohe, die nur wenige hundert Meter westlich davon liegt.

Die minimalistisch verfeinerten Stahlbauten bestehen jeweils aus einem orthogonalen Trägerrost, der auf vier Stützen ruht. Die schwarz gestrichene Konstruktion ist aus dickwandigen, geschweißten Stahlprofilen zusammengefügt, die Kubatur ist auf die erforderlichen Mindestmaße von 26 m mal 26 m Grundfläche und 10 m Höhe reduziert.

Trotz der geringen Baumasse entwickeln die beiden ruhenden kubischen Körper durch ihre Dualität und ihre strenge axiale Anordnung eine deutliche Präsenz auf dem durch die umstehenden Hochhäuser definierten Stadtraum des Potsdamer Platzes.

Potsdamer Platz station, Berlin-Tiergarten, 1995–2006

In 1838 Potsdamer Platz was already the starting point for Berlin's railway network. During the reconstruction and enlargement of this network after 1989 this point was considerably expanded. Coming from the Tiergarten a four-track tunnel crosses Potsdamer Platz in a north–south direction, runs under the towers of the Beisheim-Center and the Delbrück-Haus and then broadens to become an underground train station construction 50 m in width, 250 m in length and 18 m in depth.

Both of the entrance buildings on Potsdamer Platz are semi-open, steel and glass pavilions. In a number of ways, they are a reminder of Ludwig Mies van der Rohe's National Gallery, which is only a few hundred meters to the west.

The steel buildings, refined along minimalist lines, each consist of an orthogonal beam grid that rests on four supports. The construction, painted black, has been fabricated out of welded thick-section steel profiles. The volume has been reduced to the mandatory minimum of 26 m by 26 m for the base and 10 m for the height.

Despite this small mass, their duality and exact axial placement means that the two stationary cubic bodies have a clear presence on Potsdamer Platz, an urban space defined by the surrounding towers.

The sign »Bahnhof Potsdamer Platz« (Potsdamer Platz train station) has been designed as an integrated part of the

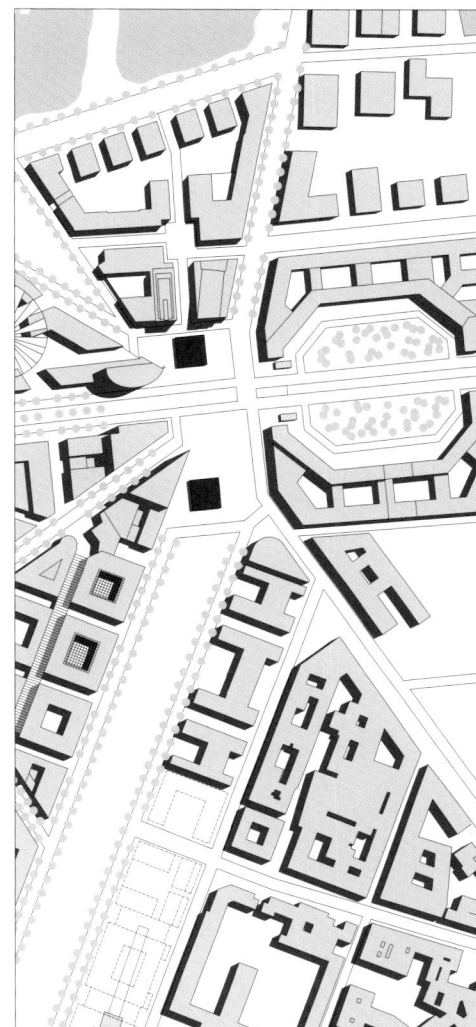

1. Ansicht des südlichen Pavillons vom Potsdamer Platz. (Photo: Stefan Müller.)

2. Lageplan.

2. Site plan.

1. View of the southern pavilion from Potsdamer Platz. (Photo: Stefan Müller.)

Bahnhof Potsdamer Platz, Berlin-Tiergarten,
1995–2006

3. Blick aus dem süd-
lichen Pavillon zum
Beisheim-Center. (Pho-
to: Stefan Müller.)
4. Die Treppenanlage
im südlichen Pavillon.
(Photo: Stefan Müller.)

3. View from the south-
ern pavilion towards
the Beisheim-Center.
(Photo: Stefan Müller.)
4. The stairway in the
southern pavilion.
(Photo: Stefan Müller.)

5. Blick auf beide Pavil-
lons von Süden. (Pho-
to: Stefan Müller.)

5. View of both pavil-
ions from the south.
(Photo: Stefan Müller.)

Der Schriftzug »Bahnhof Potsdamer Platz« ist als integraler Bestandteil der Fassade entworfen. Die Schrift ist in einzelnen Leuchtbuchstaben auf den Stahlträger aufgesetzt.

Um die untere Ebene großzügig mit Tageslicht zu versorgen, sind das Dach und die Wände der Pavillons vollständig verglast. An den Wänden sind einzelne, rahmenlose Glasscheiben schuppenförmig übereinander angeordnet, durch die offenen Fugen wird auf einfache Weise die erforderliche Luftzirkulation hergestellt.

In Zusammenarbeit mit Modersohn & Freiesleben sowie Hermann + Öttl

façade. The neon letters have been put on a steel beam.

In order to provide the lower levels with generous portions of daylight, the roof and the walls of the pavilions have been completely glazed. Single, unframed glass plates have been placed scale-like on the walls, thereby providing for the necessary circulation of air through these openings through simple means.

In cooperation with Modersohn & Freiesleben and Hermann + Öttl

U-Bahnhof Mendelssohn-Bartholdy-Park, Berlin-Tiergarten, 1996–98

Der neue Haltepunkt Mendelssohn-Bartholdy-Park, an der zum Landwehrkanal orientierten Seite des Potsdamer Platzes gelegen, wurde an eine bestehende Hochbahntrasse zwischen den Stationen Gleisdreieck und Potsdamer Platz eingefügt. Dieser Streckenabschnitt hat eine traditionsreiche, aber auch wechselhafte Geschichte: Er war schon Bestandteil des allerersten Berliner U-Bahnnetzes, das im Jahr 1902 eingeweiht wurde. Nach starken Beschädigungen im Zweiten Weltkrieg und anschließender Wiederherstellung war er Teil einer durchgehenden Verbindung zwischen Ost und West, die trotz der Teilung der Stadt in den 50er Jahren zunächst aufrechterhalten wurde, dann aber mit dem Bau der Mauer 1961 ein abruptes Ende fand.

Nach dem Mauerfall waren umfangreiche Instandsetzungs- und Wiederherstellungsarbeiten erforderlich, bis 1993 der Lückenschluß erfolgte und der Bahnbetrieb zwischen den Stadtzentren in Ost und West wiederaufgenommen wurde. Das Streckenviadukt im Bereich des neuen Bahnhofgebäudes wurde im Zuge dieser Maßnahme als moderne Stahlkonstruktion neu errichtet. Die Streckenführung mußte zur Einrichtung des neuen Haltepunktes, der damals schon im Zusammenhang mit den Planungen zum Potsdamer Platz konzipiert, aber noch nicht ausgeführt wurde, geringfügig verändert werden. Eine Überbauung des nördlichen Gebäudeteils mit einer 28 m hohen Blockstruktur ist im Bebauungsplan vorgesehen.

Mendelssohn-Bartholdy-Park underground station, Berlin-Tiergarten, 1996–98

The new underground station Mendelssohn-Bartholdy-Park, located on the Landwehrkanal side of Potsdamer Platz, was added to the already existing elevated railway line between the Gleisdreieck and Potsdamer Platz stations. This stretch of the line is rich in tradition but has also seen many changes. It belonged to Berlin's very first subway network, completed in 1902. After heavy damage in World War Two and subsequent reconstruction, it was part of a direct connection between East and West that was maintained despite the division of the city in the 1950s, but then came to an abrupt end with the construction of the Wall in 1961.

After the fall of the Wall a comprehensive overhaul and refurbishment had to be carried out, so that it was not until 1993 that there was a resumption of the underground train service between the city centres in the East and the West. A part of this work was the new steel construction for the overhead railway at the new train station. The new station was included in the plans for the development of Potsdamer Platz, but it was not yet carried out. The construction of this new stop meant that the route had to be slightly modified. The development plan envisages a superstructure at the north of the building with an urban structure 28 m in height.

The building for the train station can be divided into three parts. The cubic like front building lies opposite the steel

1. Ansicht des südlichen Eingangspavillons vom Reichpietschufer. (Photo: Stefan Müller.)

2. Lageplan.

2. Site plan.

1. View of the southern entrance pavilion from Reichpietschufer. (Photo: Stefan Müller.)

53

U-Bahnhof Mendelssohn-Bartholdy-Park,
Berlin-Tiergarten, 1996–98

3. Ansicht des Brü-
ckenbauteils von der
Köthener Straße. (Pho-
to: Stefan Müller.)

3. View of the elevat-
ed building part from
Köthener Straße. (Pho-
to: Stefan Müller.)

4. Ansicht des nörd-
lichen Eingangsbau-
werks von der Köthe-
ner Straße. (Photo:
Stefan Müller.)
5. Fassadenschnitt
durch das nördliche
Eingangsbauwerk.

4. View of the north
entrance from Köthe-
ner Straße. (Photo:
Stefan Müller.)
5. Section through the
façade of the north
entrance building.

Das Bahnhofsgebäude gliedert sich
in drei Teile. Gegenüber der Fachwerk-
brücke am Landwehrkanal erhebt sich
ein kubischer Kopfbau. Von den anderen Gebäudeteilen setzt er sich durch
das auf 18 Stahlstützen ruhende, flache
Dach in Form einer 1 m starken Platte
ab. Das Dachtragwerk besteht aus einem
quadratischen Trägerrost aus geschweißten Vollwandträgern. Zwei Kaskadentrep-
pen führen zu den Seitenbahnsteigen
nach oben.

An den südlichen Eingangspavillon
schließt sich ein langgestrecktes Brückenbauteil an. Die Dachform ändert
sich hier in eine flache Segmenttonne,
die aus biegesteifen Stahlrahmen kon-
struiert ist. Über den Gleisen ist ein
durchgehendes Oberlichtband angeordnet, das die Bahnhofshalle zusätzlich zu
den seitlichen Fensterbändern großzügig mit Tageslicht versorgt.

Das nördliche Eingangsbauwerk ver-
breitert sich zur Aufnahme der Treppen-
anlagen. Eine Passage durchquert das

lattice bridge over the Landwehrkanal.
A flat roof in the form of a slab 1 m thick
and resting on 18 steel supports sets this
front building apart from the other
building elements. The roof beam construction consists of a grid made out of
welded plate girders. Two cascading
stairs lead up to the platforms on the
sides.

The southern entry pavilion connects
to a long bridge construction. The form
of the roof changes here, becoming
flat, segmented and barrel-shaped, constructed out of rigid steel frames. Above
the tracks is a continuous skylight that is
a source of light in addition to the strips
of windows on the sides. The train station's concourse is thereby ensured a
generous supply of daylight.

The northern entry construction
broadens for the stairway. An arcade
runs through the building, opened at
both sides by large entrance portals.
From here, there is a short pedestrian
connection to Potsdamer Platz.

Gebäude und öffnet sich nach beiden Seiten mit großen Eingansportalen. Von hier ist eine kurze Fußgängeranbindung zum Potsdamer Platz gegeben.

Entsprechend der Typologie der Berliner Hallenbahnhöfe ist der untere Teil des Bauwerks ein geschlossener Massivbau. Hier sind die Eingangshallen und die technischen Betriebsräume untergebracht. Die Bahnhofshalle im oberen Teil wird dagegen von einer reinen Stahlkonstruktion überspannt und kann dadurch gut belichtet werden.

Die einheitliche Behandlung der Fassaden faßt alle drei Bauteile zu einem Ganzen zusammen und gibt dem Gebäude eine homogene Erscheinung. Als Fassadenmaterialien werden Klinker und Stahl kombiniert, was bei Berliner Verkehrsbauwerken Tradition hat. Dabei kommt dem Mauerwerk im Kontrast zur kühlen Strenge des Stahlbaus eine entscheidende Bedeutung zu: Die Wirkung der Fassade wird wesentlich geprägt durch seine Plastizität und die Flächen-

Corresponding to the typology of Berlin's train stations with a hall type of enclosure, the lower part of this construction is closed and solid. The entrance halls and rooms for diverse mechanical purposes have been placed here. In contrast, the hall above is spanned by construction made only of steel and can therefore be well lit.

The façades of the three building parts are all the same, making a whole out of these parts and lending the building a homogenous appearance. As is traditional for Berlin's transport buildings, a combination of clinker bricks and steel was used as the material for the façade. The masonry – in contrast to the cool severity of the steel construction – plays an important role in the effect made by the façade, which is in large part defined by its plasticity and the surface effect of its material, brick bond and natural colours.

A further subdivision of the façade into separate areas results from the visi-

6. Ansicht des Gebäudes von Nordwesten.
(Photo: Stefan Müller.)

6. View of the building from the northwest.
(Photo: Stefan Müller.)

wirkung von Material, Verband und natürlicher Farbigkeit.

Eine weitere Gliederung in einzelne Fassadenfelder ergibt sich durch die sichtbare Anordnung der Stahlstützen in den Hauptkonstruktionsachsen. Diese Stützen sind ihrerseits beidseitig durch Mauerwerkslisenen eingefaßt. Als Binder gemauert, treten sie jeweils zweifach gestaffelt nach vorne. Ein durchlaufender Binderverband tritt in jeder siebten Lage um 2,5 cm aus der Fläche hervor und führt dadurch eine zusätzliche horizontale Gliederung ein. Die zweifach nach vorne gestaffelten Mauerwerkslisenen, die horizontalen Binderschichten sowie die eigentliche Fassadenfläche liegen in insgesamt vier verschiedenen Ebenen. Das Fassadenrelief hat eine Gesamttiefe von 10 cm.

Das Mauerwerk aus hartgebranntem Klinker zeichnet sich durch ein intensiv changierendes Farbenspiel aus. Das Spektrum der gewählten blau-bunten Sortierung reicht dabei von Rot- und Brauntönen über Blau und Violett bis hin zu einem silbrig-grauen Glanz. Auch die einzelnen Steine weisen in sich starke Farbverläufe auf und sind sichtbar vom Vorgang des Brennens gezeichnet. Die Farbintensität wird noch gesteigert durch die Wahl einer anthrazitfarbigen Mörtelfuge. Die horizontalen Bänder heben sich zusätzlich zu ihrem plasti-

ble arrangement of the columns on the main grid lines. These columns are bordered on both sides with protruding brickwork. Built as brick headers they are staggered twice outwards. A continuous header course projects 2,5 cm forwards of the wall surface at every seventh course, thereby introducing an additional horizontal structuring. The masonry protrusions staggered twice, the horizontal header courses as well as the actual surface of the façade are on a total of four different levels. The relief on the façade has a total depth of 10 cm.

The masonry of hard-baked clinker bricks is distinguished by strong changes in the play of colours. The spectrum of the chosen colours ranges from red and brown hues to blue and violet to a silvergrey sheen. The individual stones also demonstrate strong differences in their colouring and have been clearly marked by the firing process. The intensity of the colours is further emphasized by the choice of a charcoal-grey mortar jointfiller. In addition to the plasticity in the way in which they protrude from the façade, the different colour of the horizontal strips to the underlying façade is a further contrast. They are made of a full brick in a reddish colour that differs in the nuances of its brightness from the blue-coloured brick sorting. Before exe-

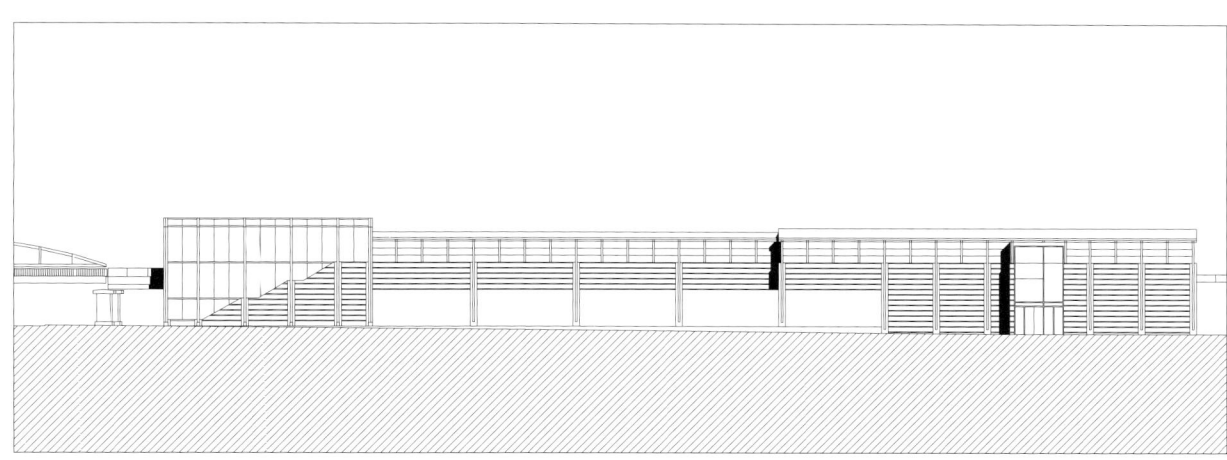

7–9. Ansicht des Ge-
bäudes von Osten
und Grundrisse.

7–9. Elevation of the
building from the east
and floor plans.

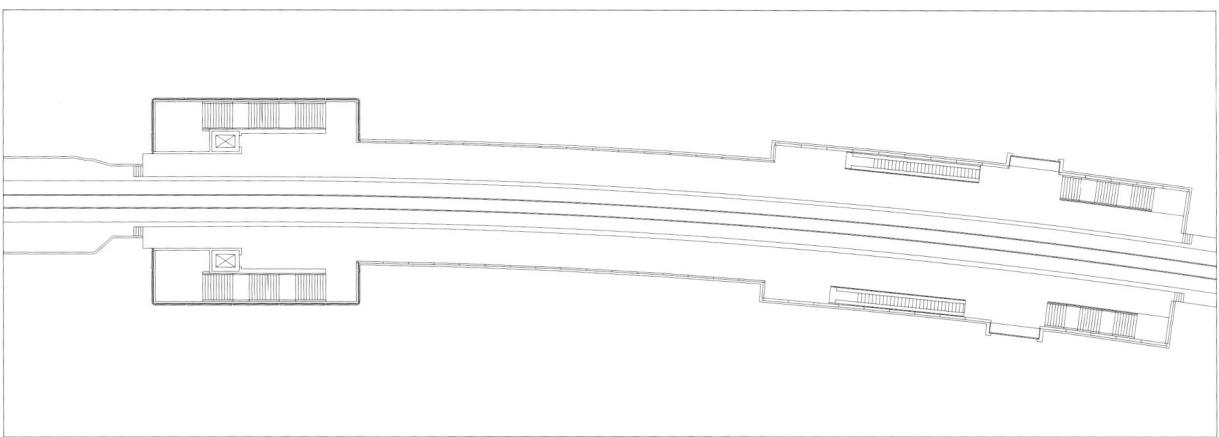

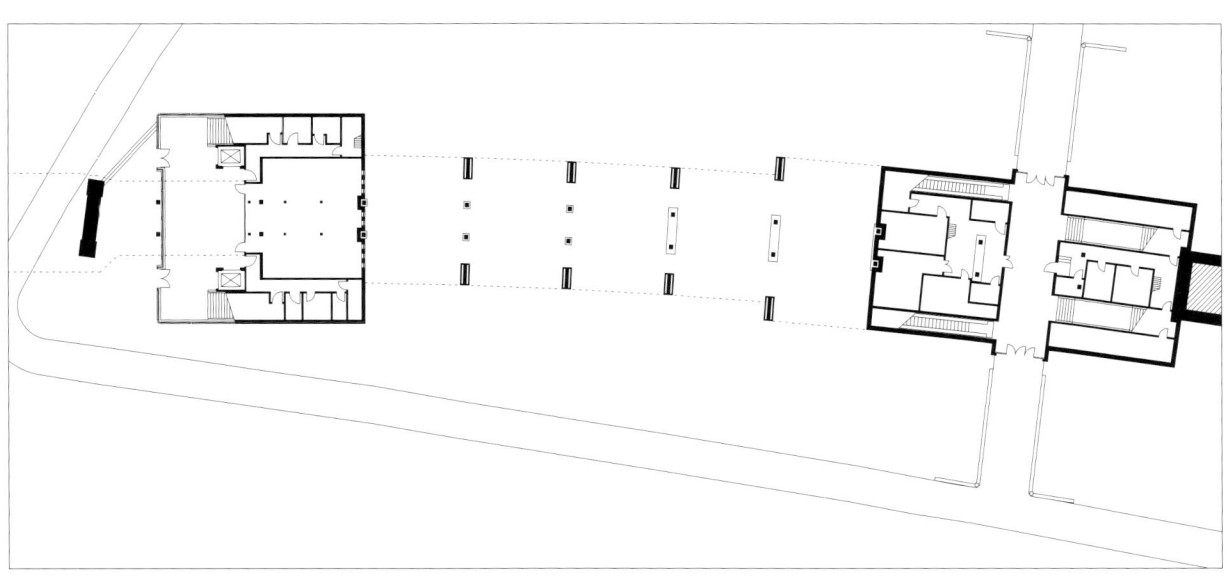

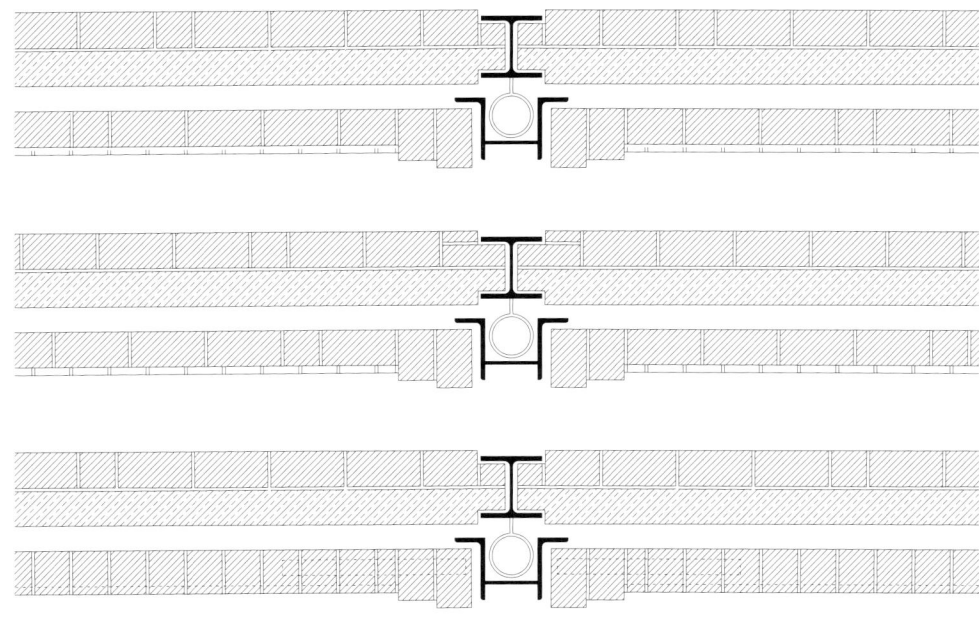

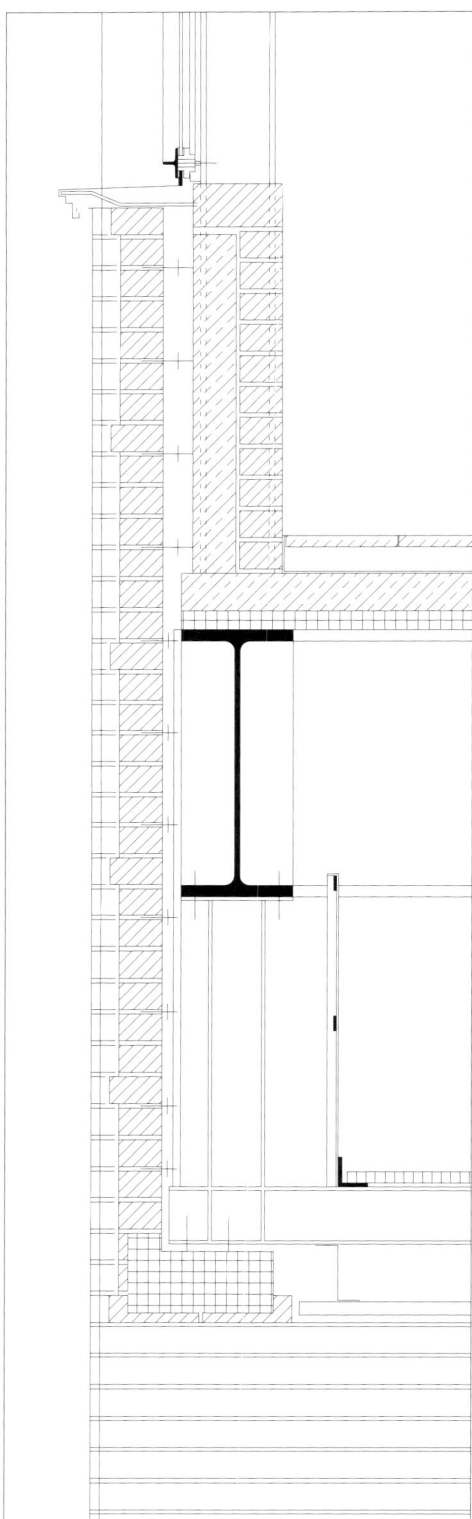

schen Hervortreten aus der Fassaden-
ebene durch eine andere Farbigkeit von
der Fläche ab. Sie sind aus Vollsteinen in
einer roten Brennfarbe hergestellt, die
sich um Nuancen in der Helligkeit von
der blau-bunten Sortierung unterscheiden. Die Wirkung wurde vor der Ausführung anhand mehrerer Musterwände
erprobt.

Bei der Hochbahnstation Mendelssohn-Bartholdy-Park handelt es sich seiner Funktion als Verkehrsbauwerk entsprechend um ein einfaches Bauwerk
mit klarer Struktur. Erst bei näherem
Herantreten erschließen sich die Fein-
heiten der Fassade. Viel von der Wirkung
beruht auf einer Gestaltung, welche bewußt die Ausdruckskraft des handwerk-
lichen Mauerwerksbaus zur Geltung
kommen läßt. Dieses Gestaltungsmittel
wurde in verschiedenen Stilformen der
Architektur, wie z. B. im Expressionis-
mus, eingesetzt, ist aber letztendlich dem
Material selbst zu eigen und somit zeitlos. Der Aspekt der Zeitlosigkeit unter-
scheidet das Gebäude deutlich von einigen der Neubauten am Potsdamer Platz
in unmittelbarer Umgebung, bei denen
dem Mauerziegel verwandtes Fassadenmaterial, Terrakotta, in industrieller Bau-
weise ausgeführt wurde.

Projektleiter: Alexander Waimer
*Ausführungsplanung: Architekturbüro Hans-
Peter Störl*

cution, this effect was first tried out on
a number of sample walls.

In accordance with its function as a
transport building, the elevated train station Mendelssohn-Bartholdy is a simple
building with a clear structure. It is only
by closer inspection that the refinements
of the façade become apparent. Much
of its effect comes from the conscious
choice of allowing the craftsmanship of
the masonry building to express itself.
This sort of choice has been made in
different architectural styles, such as
Expressionism. In the end, however, this
is a quality that belongs to the material
and is therefore timeless. The aspect of
timelessness clearly distinguishes this
building from some of the new buildings
in its immediate vicinity on Potsdamer
Platz, where the terracotta cladding of
the façades – a related material – has
been used in the manner of an industrial method of construction.

Project architect: Alexander Waimer
*Working drawings: Hans-Peter Störl Archi-
tects*

Mendelssohn-Bartholdy-Park underground station, Berlin-Tiergarten, 1996–98

10. Vertikaler Detail-
schnitt durch das
Brückenbauteil.
11. Horizontale Detail-
schnitte durch das
Brückenbauteil.

12. Bahnsteighalle.
(Photo: Stefan Müller.)
13. Treppenanlage im
südlichen Eingangs-
pavillon. (Photo: Ste-
fan Müller.)

10. Vertical detailed
section through the
elevated building part.
11. Horizontal detailed
sections through the
elevated building part.

12. Station hall. (Photo:
Stefan Müller.)
13. Stairway in the
southern entrance
pavillon. (Photo: Stefan
Müller.)

Haus der Bayerischen Wirtschaft, München, 1993–98

Das Haus der Bayerischen Wirtschaft ist ein Verwaltungsgebäude mit integriertem Konferenzzentrum, für dessen Entwurf wir in einem Architektenwettbewerb den ersten Preis erhielten. Es befindet sich in hervorragender Lage zwischen Carl von Fischers konzentrischem Karolinenplatz mit dem Obelisken als Mitte und den Parkanlagen des Maximiliansplatzes.

Die Pavillontypologie der Max-Joseph-Straße war bestimmend für die Gliederung in zwei Baukörper mit einem mittleren Verbindungsglied, in dem der Eingang und die Treppenanlage entwickelt sind. Die sechsgeschossigen Häuser haben einen zweigeschossigen Sockelbereich.

In der doppel-T-förmigen Baukörperfigur sind die Straßenfassaden mit Terrakottasteinen verkleidet, während die hofseitigen Bauteile in einfacher Weise verputzt sind.

Die Terrakottaverkleidung erfährt nur eine Modellierung im Flächenrelief, indem alle Vertikalen der Fassadenteile abgerundet und alle Horizontalen scharfkantig profiliert sind. Als einzige Unregelmäßigkeit treten die Penstergesimse aus der sonst planen Fassade hervor. Da der Fensteranteil bei diesem Gebäude sehr hoch ist, wirken die Wände fast schon wie in Stützen und Brüstungen aufgelöst. Die Straßenfassade des Eingangsbaukörpers hat aus dem gleichen Grund vertikal gestaltete Terrakottaelemente, die, nur 12,5 cm breit – ähnlich gotischen Kirchenbauten – das

Haus der Bayerischen Wirtschaft (House of Bavarian Economy), Munich, 1993–98

The Haus der Bayerischen Wirtschaft fulfils administrative functions and has a conference centre. We won first prize in an architectural competiton for the design of this building. It has an excellent location between Carl von Fischer's concentric Karolinenplatz with an obelisk at its centre and the park area of Maximiliansplatz.

The pavilion typology to be found on Max-Joseph-Straße determined the subdivision of this building into two parts with a central, connecting section in which the entrance and the staircase can be found. The six-storey buildings have a two-storey base.

The street façades of the buildings – a double T-shape – are clad with terracotta panels while the façades facing the courtyard have a simple plaster finish.

The surface of the terracotta cladding has been modelled in such a way that all the vertical façade elements have been rounded and all of the horizontal elements have been given sharp-cornered profiles. The only irregularity is that the windowsills project forward of the otherwise flat façade. Since there is a very high proportion of windows in this building, the walls give the effect of being reduced to piers and spandrels. For the same reason, the street façade of the entrance has vertically formed terracotta elements, which are only 12,5 cm wide – similar to Gothic churches – thereby further emphasizing the tension between glass and masonry.

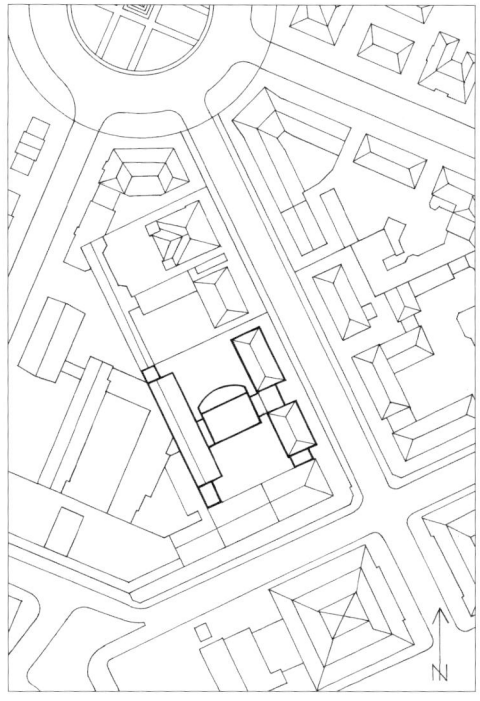

1. Ansicht des Gebäudes von der Max-Joseph-Straße. (Photo: Jens Weber.)

2. Lageplan.

2. Site plan.

1. View of the building from Max-Joseph-Straße. (Photo: Jens Weber.)

61

Haus der Bayerischen Wirtschaft, München,
1993–98

3. Restaurant. (Photo:
Jens Weber.)
4. Foyer mit einem
Wandbild von Imi
Knöbel. (Photo: Jens
Weber.)

3. Restaurant. (Photo:
Jens Weber.)
4. Foyer with a mural
by Imi Knöbel. (Photo:
Jens Weber.)

5, 6. Treppenhaus mit
einem Kunstkonzept
von Ulrich Horndash.
(Photos: Jens Weber.)

5, 6. Staircase with
art concept by Ulrich
Horndash. (Photos:
Jens Weber.)

Spannungsverhältnis Glas / Mauerwerk noch überhöhen.

Integriert in die Gesamtkonzeption waren die Künstler Imi Knöbel und Ulrich Horndash. Imi Knöbel ist mit einem fünfteiligen Wandbild aus mennigefarbigen Aluminiumtafeln im Foyer vertreten, während Ulrich Horndash die unterschiedlichen Farbkonzeptionen zur Raumgestaltung des Treppenhauses und der Konferenzräume geschaffen hat.

Projektleiter: Fritz Treugut
Mitarbeiter: Ulrich Greiler, Johannes Rössler, Barbara Schelle

The artists, Imi Knöbel and Ulrich Horndash were integrated into the concept as a whole. Imi Knöbel is represented in the foyer with a five-piece, red lead-coloured mural of aluminium panels. Ulrich Horndash created the colour concept for the interior design of the stairwell.

Project architect: Fritz Treugut
Collaborators: Ulrich Greiler, Johannes Rössler, Barbara Schelle

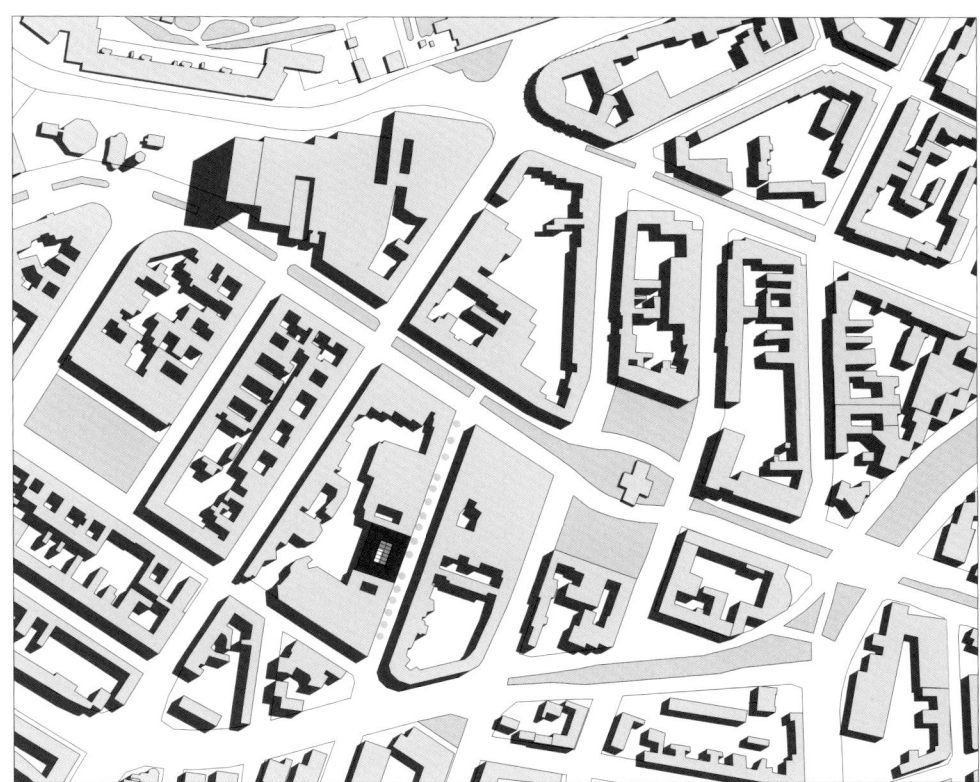

Seniorenwohnhaus in der Passauer Straße, Berlin-Schöneberg, 1996–99

Eine der letzten großen Baulücken in bester Lage – schräg gegenüber dem Kaufhaus des Westens – war der Ort, den sich die Tertianum AG für den Neubau einer ihrer Seniorenwohnhäuser aussuchte.

Die für uns neue Bauaufgabe will sich nicht nur verbal von den früheren »Altersheimen« absetzen: Das Alter wird als dritter, wichtiger Lebensabschnitt interpretiert, man sieht die Bewohner als vitale, jung gebliebene Menschen, die im Zentrum der Großstadt ihr Leben genießen, unweit von Kinos, Restaurants, Theatern. Entsprechend diesem Anspruch ähnelt das Haus eher einem modernen Hotel.

Nach außen stellt es sich mit einer städtischen, optimistischen Fassade dar: Oberhalb einer zweigeschossigen, profilierten Sockelzone sind fünf Wohngeschosse mit einer mehrfach geschwungenen Fassade angeordnet. Die Bewegung wird verstärkt durch zwei Gesimsbänder pro Geschoß, welche die Fenster oben und unten einfassen. Nicht nur aus baukonstruktiven Gründen wurden diese Bänder oben mit Zinkblech verkleidet. Der starke Farbkontrast zwischen dem Dunkelgrau des Metalls und der hellbeigen Putzoberfläche erinnert an Mendelsohnsche Konzepte.

Eine Wellenbewegung über zwei Fensterachsen umfaßt jeweils ein Apartment: Im heraustretenden Teil der Welle befindet sich ein Wintergarten, im Wellental ein dazugehöriger Wohnraum. In Höhe der Berliner Traufe von 22 m

Retirement home in Passauer Straße, Berlin-Schöneberg, 1996–99

For its new retirement home the Tertianum AG chose one of the last big, empty building sites in a choice location directly opposite the Kaufhaus des Westens.

With this building we had to distance ourselves more than verbally from earlier »old peoples' homes«. Age is interpreted here as a third, important stage of life. The residents are seen as vigorous people who have remained young and who want to enjoy life in the centre of the big city, close to cinemas, restaurants and theatres. Accordingly, the residence is similar to a modern hotel.

An urban, optimistic façade is presented to the outside world. Above a two-storey, profiled socle zone, are five residential storeys with a multi-curved façade. The façade's movement is intensified by the two strips of cornices on each storey. They serve to border the windows, both above and below. It was not only for reasons of construction that these strips were covered on the top with sheet-zinc. The strong contrast in colour between the dark grey of the metal and the light beige of the plaster surface is a reminder of Mendelsohn's concepts.

1. Detailansicht der Straßenfassade. (Photo: Stefan Müller.)
2. Gesamtansicht des Gebäudes von der Passauer Straße. (Photo: Stefan Müller.)

1. Detailed view of the street façade. (Photo: Stefan Müller.)
2. General view of the building from Passauer Straße. (Photo: Stefan Müller.)

3. Lageplan.

3. Site plan.

Seniorenwohnhaus in der Passauer Straße,
Berlin-Schöneberg, 1996–99

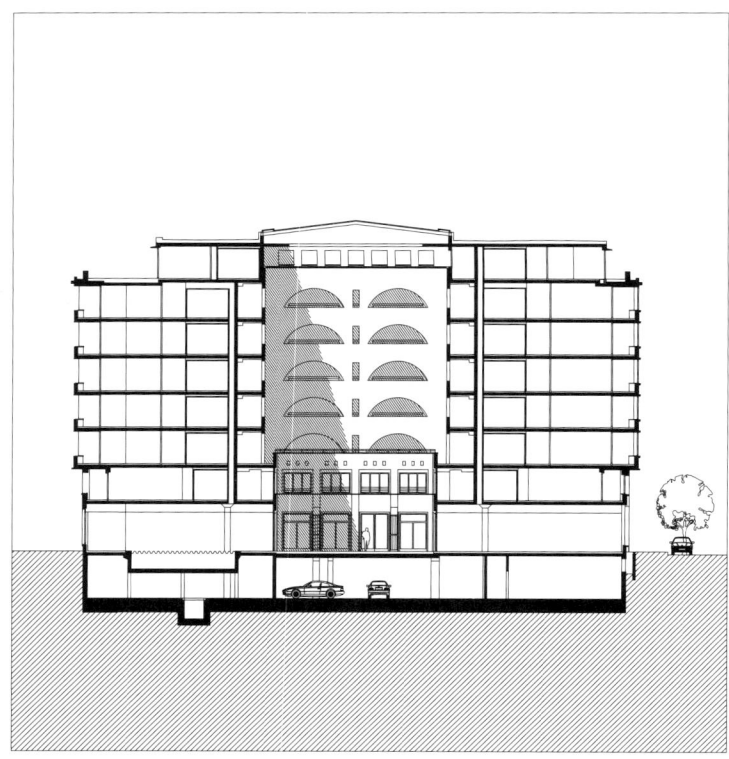

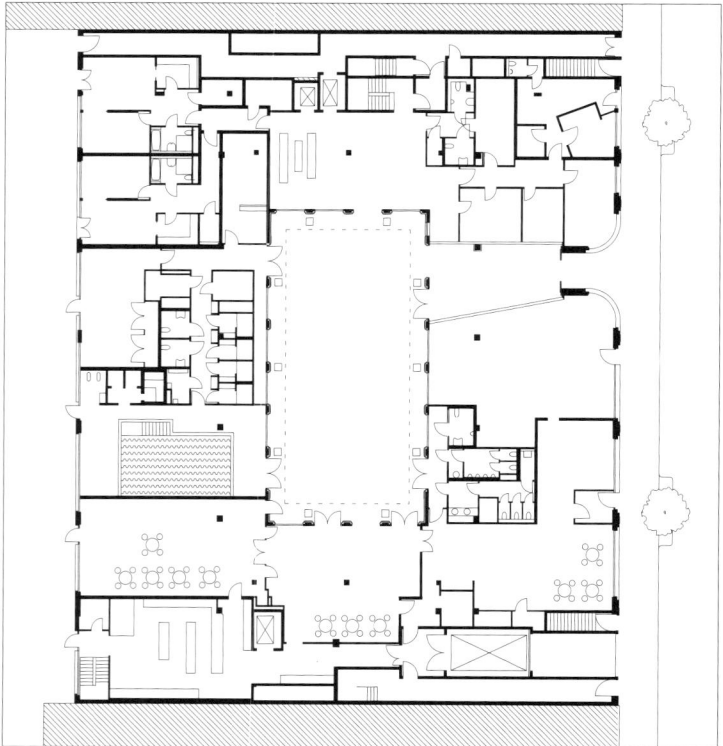

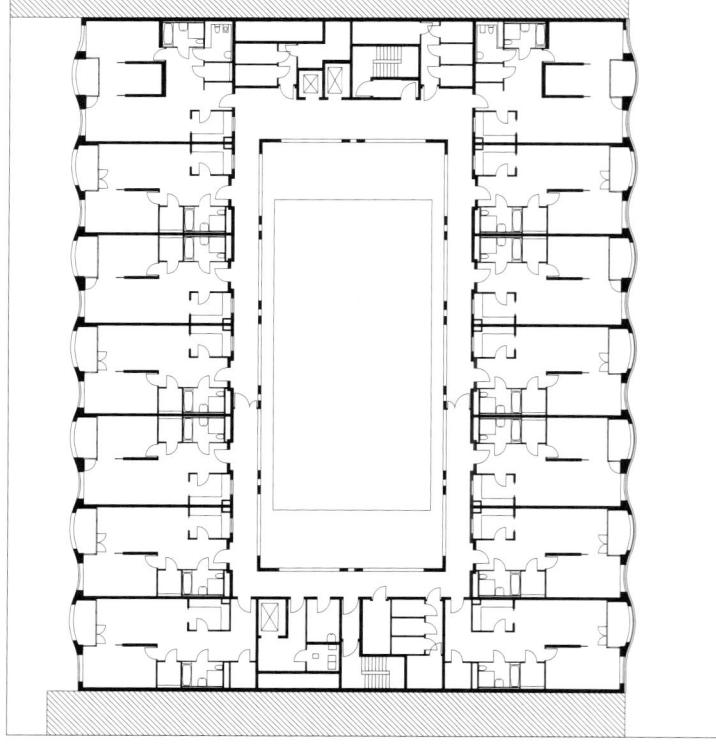

4. Schnitt.
5, 6. Grundrisse (Erd-
geschoß, Normal-
geschoß).

4. Section.
5, 6. Floor plans
(ground floor, typical
floor).

schließt eine auskragende Platte die Fassade ab, auf ihrer Unterseite wird die ungewöhnliche Grundrißfigur der Fassade nachgezeichnet. Das darüber befindliche Dachgeschoß ist mit einer linearen Fassade zurückgestaffelt.

Der mondäne Anspruch generiert ein großzügiges Atrium mit Glasdach, in den Wohngeschossen umschlossen von offenen Arkaden, die direkte optische und akustische Kontakte ermöglichen. Der Bebauungsplan ließ hier nur eine maximale Bautiefe von 18 m zu; im intensiven Dialog mit der Baubehörde wurde aber eine Befreiung erteilt, um den 32 m mal 14 m großen Innenhof realisieren zu können.

Ähnlich einem Hotel gliedert sich das Haus im Inneren: Im Keller sind Garage, Haustechnik und Lagerräume für die privaten Möbel der Bewohner untergebracht. Im Erdgeschoß befinden sich Pförtner, Aufenthalts- und Vortragsräume, ein auch von der Straße aus zugängliches Restaurant, ein Schwimmbad mit Sauna und Massagebereich sowie Arzträume. Der kleine Garten – gestaltet von Regina Poly – orientiert sich zum Blockinneren und bietet den Bewohnern Bewegungsmöglichkeiten, ohne daß sie das Grundstück verlassen müssen.

Das erste Obergeschoß hat 25 einachsige Zimmer für ständig Bettlägerige.

Darüber sind die fünf Regelgeschosse mit jeweils 14 zweiachsigen Apartments angeordnet. Zwei Zimmer, eine zum Atrium orientierte Küche sowie ein Wintergarten bzw. eine Terrasse stehen zur Verfügung. Wohn- und Schlafraum lassen sich durch eine große Schiebetüre zu einem großzügigen räumlichen Verbund zusammenschalten.

In der obersten Etage befinden sich die ganz großen Wohnungen mit 80 m^2 bis 180 m^2. Große Dachterrassen ermög-

There is a wave-like movement above two window modules for each apartment. In the projecting part of the wave is a winter garden and the trough is the living room. At the Berlin eaves' height of 22 m the façade is brought to an end by a projecting overhang on whose underside the façade's unusual plan has been drawn. The attic storey that lies above has a linear façade and is set back.

The demand for elegance occasioned a large atrium with a glass roof that is surrounded by open arcades on all the apartment floors, making direct visual and acoustic contacts possible. The building plan permitted only a maximum depth of 18 m here, but after an intensive dialogue with the building authorities an allowance was made for the inner courtyard, measuring 32 m by 14 m.

The building's interior is divided along the lines of a hotel. The car park, plantrooms and storerooms for the residents' private furniture are in the basement. On the ground floor are the doorman's office, day and lecture rooms, a restaurant that can also be entered from the street, a pool with a sauna and a massage area, as well as doctors' offices. The small garden – designed by Regina Poly – is orientated to the blocks' interior – and provides residents with the opportunity for movement, without having to leave the premises.

The first floor has 25 rooms of one module for the permanently bed-ridden.

Above this are the five typical floors, each with 14 apartments of two modules. These consist of two rooms, a kitchen orientated towards the atrium as well as a winter garden or terrace. The living-room and bedroom are separated by a sliding door that can be opened to provide a large, connected space.

The very large apartments measuring 80 m^2 to 180 m^2 are on the upper floors.

7. Das Atrium. (Photo: Stefan Müller.)
8. Untersicht des Glasdachs. (Photo: Stefan Müller.)

7. The atrium. (Photo: Stefan Müller.)
8. View of the glass roof from underneath. (Photo: Stefan Müller.)

lichen hier einen herrlichen Blick über die Berliner Dächer.

Fasziniert hat uns an diesem Haus ständig das dem *Zauberberg* Thomas Manns nicht unähnliche Szenario von der absurden Spannung zwischen luxuriöser Lebenslust und drohender Todesnähe:

Einerseits gibt es im Keller ein Weinlager, im Erdgeschoß kann der rüstige Bewohner – ohne vom Pförtner oder der staunenden Hausgemeinschaft gesehen zu werden – einen separaten »Geheimausgang« benutzen, um ein diskretes Privatleben außerhalb des Hauses zu führen.

Andererseits gibt es das Pflegegeschoß mit all den heutigen Raffinements der Technik. Hier gelten die – wenn auch leicht abgeschwächten – Vorschriften des Krankenhausbaus.

Zu guter Letzt mußte auch der Abtransport der Verstorbenen aus den Apartments bis ins Detail geplant werden, damit – wie bei Thomas Mann – keiner der Mitbewohner es sieht, wenn der Leichenwagen nachts mit dem Autoaufzug die Tiefgarage unhörbar verläßt.

Projektleiter: Ursula Gonsior, Alexander Waimer
Mitarbeiter: Michael Andreotti, Ulrike Feucht, Britta Greese, Florian Schätz

Large, rooftop terraces provide a marvellous view over Berlin's buildings.

With this building we were constantly fascinated by the tension between the luxurious zest for life and the threat of eminent death. This is a scenario not unlike the one to be found in Thomas Mann's *Magic Mountain*.

In the basement there is a wine cellar. On the ground floor the still sprightly resident can use a separate »secret exit«, without being seen either by the doorman or observant fellow residents. This discretionary measure helps him to lead a private life outside of the building.

On the other hand, the floor with nursing care has all of the current technological refinements. The regulations for hospital buildings – albeit not quite as strict – are valid here.

Finally, the transportation of the deceased out of the apartment also had to be planned down to the last detail. As was the case in Thomas Mann's novel, none of the residents should see the hearse in the car-elevator as it silently leaves the car park at night.

Project architects: Ursula Gonsior, Alexander Waimer
Collaborators: Michael Andreotti, Ulrike Feucht, Britta Greese, Florian Schätz

Seniorenwohnhaus in der Passauer Straße,
Berlin-Schöneberg, 1996–99

9. Ansicht der Fassade zum Atrium. (Photo: Stefan Müller.)
10. Blick von einem Wohngeschoß in das Atrium. (Photo: Stefan Müller.)

11. Flur vor den Apartments. (Photo: Stefan Müller.)

9. View of the façade to the atrium. (Photo: Stefan Müller.)
10. View from an apartment floor towards the atrium. (Photo: Stefan Müller.)

11. Corridor to the apartments. (Photo: Stefan Müller.)

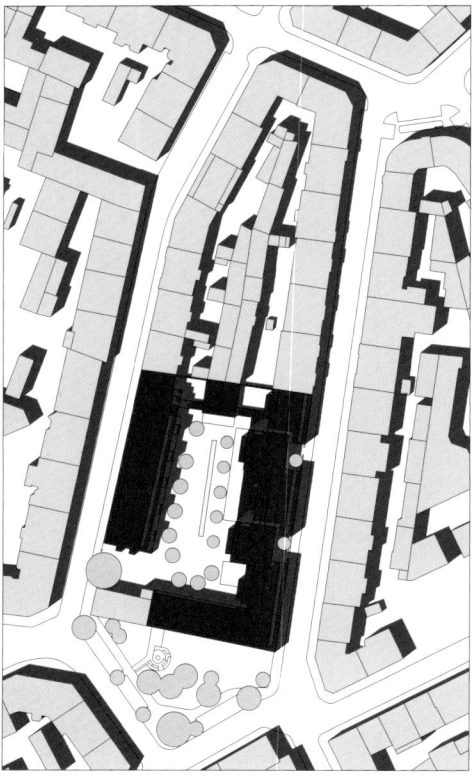

1. Lageplan.

1. Site plan.

2. Ansicht der Anlage von der Klenzestraße. (Photo: Stefan Müller.)

2. View of the complex from Klenzestraße. (Photo: Stefan Müller.)

Seniorenwohnanlage, Jahnstraße/ Klenzestraße, München, 1996–2000

Parallel zum Seniorenwohnhaus in Berlin (siehe S. 64–71) wurde die hier gezeigte Anlage geplant und gebaut. Nicht nur der Bauherr ist derselbe, auch der Denkansatz des innerstädtischen, anspruchsvollen Hauses, das Raumprogramm und die Flächenverteilung sind bei beiden Projekten nahezu deckungsgleich.

Der Bauplatz liegt in einer reizvollen Situation zwischen der historischen Münchner Innenstadt und der Isar. Hier wurde im frühen 19. Jahrhundert eine der ersten Stadterweiterungen angelegt, deren unregelmäßige Blockstruktur das Quartier bis heute prägt.

Die Seniorenwohnanlage besteht aus drei Bauteilen; zwei ca. 80 m lange Baukörper liegen an den Außenseiten des Blockes an der Straße, in nord–südlicher Richtung, während ein dritter Baukörper im Blockinneren die beiden verbindet. Er bildet den südlichen Schlußpunkt der für diese Gegend typischen »Hinterhofbebauung«, die im südlichem Teil des Blockes – wie heute allgemein üblich – weggelassen wurde.

Im Süden des Blockes errichteten wir zeitgleich mit der Seniorenwohnanlage ein Wohn- und Geschäfthaus für einen anderen Bauherrn.

Das Stadtquartier gibt Traufhöhe und Putzfassade vor. Rücksprünge in den langen Fassaden bilden begrünte Eingangssituationen, um Maßstäblichkeit zu erzeugen. Die Straßenfassaden der Seniorenwohnanlage und des Wohn- und Geschäftshauses sind ähnlich gegliedert: Natursteinsockel im Erdgeschoß mit großen Fensterformaten als liegende Rechtecke, darüber farbige Putzfassaden mit senkrechten Fenstern. Horizontale Bänder gliedern die einzelnen Geschosse.

Retirement home, Jahnstraße/Klenzestraße, Munich, 1996–2000

The complex that is shown here was planned and built at the same time as the retirement home in Berlin (see p. 64–71). Not only is the investor the same for both projects but the idea behind this discerning building in the inner city, the spatial organization and the area requirements are virtually the same for both projects.

The building is at an attractive location between Munich's historic old city and the Isar river. In the early 19th century one of the earliest expansions of the city was undertaken here and its irregular structuring of the blocks has shaped this quarter to the present day.

The retirement home is made up of three parts. Two of the building parts, c. 80 m in length lie in a north–south direction towards the street, at the outer sides of the block, while a third part in the interior of the block connects them. This third part, towards the south, rounds off the »courtyard construction« common to this area. As is generally the case today, this type of construction was not carried out in the southern part of the block.

In the southern part of the block we built a residential and commercial building for a different investor at the same time as we were building the retirement home.

The city quarter is the guideline for the eaves' height and the plaster for the façades. Returns in the long façades form entrances with greenery and create a sense of proportion. The street façades of the retirement home and of the residential and commercial building are similar in their structure. The ground floor is a base of natural stone with windows of a large format at reclining rectangles. Above this are coloured

Seniorenwohnanlage, Jahnstraße/Klenzestraße,
München, 1996–2000

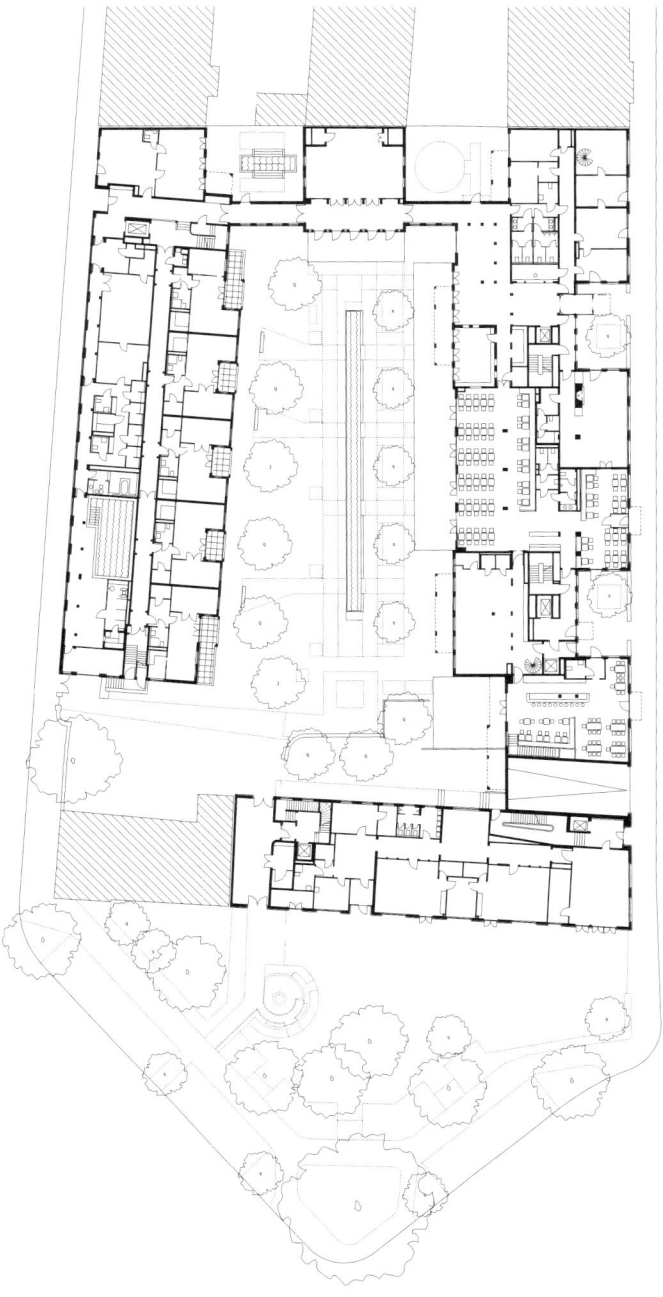

Während das Wohn- und Geschäftshaus nach Süden Wintergärten aufweist, zeigt die Seniorenwohnanlage mit ihren französischen Fenstern, Schiebeläden und Austritten, daß hier keine Wohnungen liegen, sondern einzelne Menschen unabhängig voneinander leben.

Über den ortsüblichen fünf Geschossen befindet sich bei beiden Haustypen ein zurückgesetztes Dachgeschoß. Ein aufwendig detailliertes Geländer weist auf die großzügigen Terrassen hin.

Alle Putzkanten des Hauses sind rechtwinklig ausgebildet; die Stahlgeländer sind dagegen alle gerundet ausgeführt. Die Fassaden der Seniorenwohnanlage sind mit einem warmen, italienisch anmutendem, umbrafarbigen Anstrich versehen.

Im Hof sind die Fassaden einfacher gestaltet; hier befindet sich das ruhige Zentrum der Anlage, alle öffentlichen Räume des Erdgeschosses – wie Speiseraum, Kaminzimmer, Bibliothek – orientieren sich auf ihn. In seiner Mitte ist ein flaches Wasserbecken angeordnet. Im

plaster façades with vertical windows. The individual storeys are separated by horizontal bands.

While there are winter gardens towards the south in the residential building, the retirement home with its French windows, sliding shutters and balconies indicates that there are not apartments here but rather individuals who live independently of each other.

Above the local customary five storeys, the roof storey has been set back. A finely detailed railing indicates the presence of the large terraces.

The building's plaster edges are all rectangular; in contrast the steel railings have all been rounded. The façades of the retirement home have been painted a warm, umber colour that reminds one of Italy.

In the courtyard the façades are simpler. This is where the quiet centre of the complex is located and all of the ground floor's public spaces – such as the dining room, the recreation room and the library – are orientated towards it. There

3. Ansicht der Anlage von Klenzestraße Ecke Baumstraße. (Photo: Stefan Müller.)
4. Detailansicht der Fassade. (Photo: Stefan Müller.)

3. View of the complex from the corner of Klenzestraße and Baumstraße. (Photo: Stefan Müller.)
4. Detailed view of the façade. (Photo: Stefan Müller.)

5. Grundriß (Erdgeschoß).
6. Blick in den Garten. (Photo: Stefan Müller.)

5. Floor plan (ground floor).
6. View of the garden. (Photo: Stefan Müller.)

Seniorenwohnanlage, Jahnstraße/Klenzestraße,
München, 1996–2000

7. Der Gemeinschafts-
bereich. (Photo: Stefan
Müller.)
8. Flur vor dem Veran-
staltungsraum. (Photo:
Stefan Müller.)

9. Flur vor der Biblio-
thek. (Photo: Stefan
Müller.)

9. Hallway in front of
the library. (Photo:
Stefan Müller.)

7. The communal area.
(Photo: Stefan Müller.)
8. Hallway in front of
the functions room.
(Photo: Stefan Müller.)

Norden begrenzt der zweigeschossige Veranstaltungsraum den Hof, der mit verglasten Gängen an die beiden angrenzenden Trakte anbindet.

Das Wohn- und Geschäftshaus setzt sich durch seine Details und seine Farbgestaltung deutlich ab; im Erdgeschoß ist ein Kindergarten mit der dazugehörigen Freifläche untergebracht. In den Geschossen lassen von außen die regelmäßig wiederkehrenden Wintergärten die Anordnung der Wohnungen erkennen.

Projektleiter: Christian Winter, Philipp Althammer
Mitarbeiter: Veronica Barth, Janka-Karita Guhl, Alexandra Stepanienko, Daniel Türcke, Harald Kettner, Ariana Wolf

is a shallow pool in the middle of the courtyard. In the north the two-storey room for events borders the courtyard. Here, there are glazed passageways that lead to the two neighbouring tracts.

In both their details and colours the residential and commercial building sets itself apart. On the ground floor there is a kindergarten with the required open space. From outside, the regularly recurring winter gardens allow one to recognize the arrangement of the apartments on the floor levels.

Project architects: Christian Winter, Philipp Althammer
Collaborators: Veronica Barth, Janka-Karita Guhl, Alexandra Stepanienko, Daniel Türcke, Harald Kettner, Ariana Wolf

Zwei Wohnhäuser im Tiergartendreieck, Berlin-Tiergarten, 1997–2000

Die Wohnbebauung in zentraler Lage – in unmittelbarer Nähe zu Kurfürstendamm, Tiergarten, Regierungsviertel, Potsdamer Platz – ist Teil eines städtebaulichen Gesamtkonzepts, das neben mehreren Botschaften Büro-, Wohn- und Geschäftsnutzungen miteinander verbindet.

Das Tiergartendreieck wurde seit dem Zweiten Weltkrieg als Zirkuswiese genutzt und war somit eine der letzten großen zu beplanenden Flächen in Westberlin. Durch den städtebaulichen Entwurf der Architekten Walter Stepp und Hille Machleidt wurde 1996 ein dem Prinzip des Potsdamer Platzes verwandtes Konzept verwirklicht: Enge Gassen mit nur 6 m Breite bei Gebäudehöhen von 18 m erzeugen eine reizvolle, wirklich städtische Dichte. Gleichzeitig entsteht in der Mitte des Quartiers ein sogenannter halböffentlicher »pocket park« nach englischem Vorbild, der tagsüber öffentlich zugänglich ist. In der Nacht werden die Tore in den Gassen geschlossen, so daß nur die Anwohner Zutritt haben.

Der Komplex des »gehobenen Wohnens« direkt am Landwehrkanal wurde von uns als Ensemble von vier sechsgeschossigen Häusern entworfen, die sich um einen Kreuzgang mit innenliegendem Garten gruppieren – gleichsam als verkleinertes Abbild des Gesamtkomplexes. Zwei der vier Häuser haben wir geplant und realisiert, das mittlere Gebäude an der Straße und das östlich davon liegende.

Two apartment houses in the Tiergartendreieck, Berlin-Tiergarten, 1997–2000

This residential construction in a central location – very close to Kurfüstendamm, Tiergarten, the government quarter and Potsdamer Platz – is part of a larger, urban development concept that will connect a number of embassies, offices, residences and commercial premises.

Since World War Two the Tiergartendreieck was used by circuses and remained as one of the last, big, unplanned areas in West-Berlin. In 1996 the urban development design of the architects Walter Stepp and Hille Machleidt was realized. Their concept was related to the principle underlying Potsdamer Platz: Narrow alleys with a width of only 6 m and a building height of 18 m create an appealing density that is quintessentially urban. At the same time a so-called semi-public »pocket park« along English lines will be developed in the middle of the quarter. During the day it will be open to the public but at night the gates in the alleys will be closed, so that it can only be entered by residents.

We designed the complex of »luxury residences« directly beside the Landwehrkanal as an ensemble of four six-storey buildings grouped around a cloister with a garden. This was also a copy of the entire complex in reduced form. We planned and built two of the four buildings – the middle building on the street and the building lying east of it.

The succinct, canopied entrance is meant to make an impression. Behind the entrance is an office for a round-the-clock doorman. The large foyer is in red-

1. Vogelperspektive.

1. Bird's eye view.

2. Luftbild der Anlage mit Blick Richtung Landwehrkanal. (Photo: Günter Schneider.)

2. Aerial view of the complex looking towards the Landwehrkanal. (Photo: Günter Schneider.)

Zwei Wohnhäuser im Tiergartendreieck,
Berlin-Tiergarten, 1997–2000

3. Grundriß der Wohn-
anlage (Erdgeschoß).
1, 2 Hilmer & Sattler
und Albrecht, 3 Moore
Ruble Yudell, 4 Gesine
Weinmiller.
4. Lageplan.

3. Floor plan of the
housing complexes
(ground floor).
1, 2 Hilmer & Sattler
und Albrecht, 3 Moore
Ruble Yudell, 4 Gesine
Weinmiller.
4. Site plan.

5. Ansicht des Gebäu-
des vom Landwehr-
kanal. (Photo: Stefan
Müller.)

5. View of the building
from the Landwehr-
kanal. (Photo: Stefan
Müller.)

Der Zugang ist prägnant ausgebildet: ein repräsentativer Eingang mit Vordach, dahinter eine Pförtnerloge, die rund um die Uhr besetzt ist. Das großzügige Foyer ist in rötlichem Kirschholz gehalten. Das Vorbild sind amerikanische Luxuswohnanlagen, die nicht nur ein zusätzliches Maß an Sicherheit durch Kameraüberwachung gewährleisten, sondern auch den Bewohnern zahlreiche Serviceleistungen anbieten: Reinigung der Wohnung, Auffüllen des Kühlschranks, Aufbewahren des Schlüssels bei längerer Abwesenheit etc. Über den überdachten, aber seitlich offenen Kreuzgang werden die sechs Treppenhäuser der Wohnanlage angebunden, die dann die 55 verschiedenen Wohnungen in den vier Häusern erschließen.

Alle Wohnungen – von 100 m² bis 200 m² – haben mindestens zwei Bäder, lichte Raumhöhen bis zu 3,30 m und

dish cherry-wood. The model here was the American luxury residential complex that not only provides an additional measure of protection through camera surveillance but also offers residents a variety of services, including apartment cleaning, grocery shopping, keeping the key during longer absences etc. The six stairwells of the complex are connected to the covered cloister that is open at the sides. These stairwells then lead to the 55 different apartments in the four buildings.

All of the apartments – from 100 to 200 m² – have at least two bathrooms, high ceilings of up to 3.30 m and loggias. Some of the apartments have two floors and the apartments on the top of the buildings have rooftop gardens.

The urban planning is not orthogonal and this is also true of most of the buildings. We wanted this unusual form to be

6. Schnitt.
7. Emilio Lancia und
Gio Ponti, Casa Rasini,
Mailand, 1934. (Photo:
Palladium Photo-
design.)

6. Section.
7. Emilio Lancia and
Gio Ponti, Casa Rasini,
Mailand, 1934. (Photo:
Palladium Photo-
design.)

8. Ansicht der beiden
Gebäude vom Atrium.
(Photo: Stefan Müller.)
9. Blick in eine Gasse.
(Photo: Stefan Müller.)

8. View of both build-
ings from the atrium.
(Photo: Stefan Müller.)
9. View into a passage-
way. (Photo: Stefan
Müller.)

Loggien; einige sind zweigeschossig, die
obersten Wohnungen haben Dachgär-
ten.

Der städtebauliche Entwurf ist schräg-
winklig, ebenso die meisten Häuser. Wir
wollten diese ungewöhnliche Form auch
im Inneren der beiden von uns entwor-
fenen Häuser erlebbar werden lassen,
so daß jetzt die meisten Räume keinen
90°-Winkel aufweisen.

Alle Häuser des Wohnkomplexes sind
in hellbeigem bis weißem Farbton gehalten, im Erdgeschoß wurde als Fassaden-
bekleidung Warthauer Sandstein gewählt, die Putzfassade ist in mehrere
Ebenen profiliert. Eine absolute Symmetrie innerhalb der Fassaden wurde ver-
mieden, war hier doch das Turmhaus
Rasini von Emilio Lancia und Gio Ponti
in Mailand aus dem Jahr 1934 das Vorbild.

Projektleiter: Ulrike Flacke, Peter Solhdju
Mitarbeiter: Ayhan Ayrilmaz, Sigurd Hauer,
Michael Maurer, Peter O'Callaghan, Frigga
Uhlisch

Two apartment houses in the Tiergartendreieck, Berlin-Tiergarten, 1997–2000

experienced on the inside of the two buildings that we designed. This means that 90° angles are not to be found in most of the rooms.

The colour of all buildings in the residential complex lies between light beige and white. Warthauer sandstone was chosen for the cladding on the ground floor façade. The plaster façade has multi-levelled profiles. An absolute symmetry within the façades was avoided. In this we followed the example of the tower building Rasini of 1934 in Milan by Emilio Lancia and Gio Ponti.

Project architects: Ulrike Flacke, Peter Solhdju
Collaborators: Ayhan Ayrilmaz, Sigurd Hauer, Michael Maurer, Peter O'Callaghan, Frigga Uhlisch

Zwei Wohnhäuser im Tiergartendreieck,
Berlin-Tiergarten, 1997–2000

10, 11. Das Foyer.
(Photos: Stefan Müller.)

10, 11. The foyer.
(Photos: Stefan Müller.)

12. Blick in eine Wohnung. (Photo: Stefan Müller.)
13. Perspektivische Innenansicht einer Wohnung.

12. View into an apartment. (Photo: Stefan Müller.)
13. Perspective view of an apartment interior.

Umbau des Verlags- und Redaktions- gebäudes der *Frankfurter Allgemeinen Zeitung*, Berlin-Mitte, 1997–99

Das Haus Mittelstraße 2–4 in seiner heutigen Ausformung wurde in den Jahren 1899/1900 von den Architekten Hötzel & Tenner als Bankgebäude errichtet. Das sogenannte Quartier 210 B erlebte in den letzten Jahren des 19. Jahrhunderts eine rege Bautätigkeit, da es eine der begehrtesten Lagen der damaligen Reichshauptstadt darstellte, in der engen stadträumlichen Verbindung zur Prachtstraße Unter den Linden und vor allem durch den 1882 neu eröffneten Bahnhof Friedrichstraße. Dieser bewirkte in seinem Umfeld die Neugründung von Hotels, eleganten Frisiersalons und Einrichtungshäusern.

Nach dem Krieg diente der Bau als Verlags- und Redaktionshaus von verschiedenen Zeitungen.

Exemplarisch weist die Fassade Entwurfselemente und architektonische Stilmittel der Neorenaissance auf:

Dem erhöht gelegenen Erdgeschoß, ausgebildet mit einer stark plastischen Rustika, folgen das erste und zweite Obergeschoß in Kolossalordnung mit Pilastern, ein Kranzgesims im Übergang zum dritten Obergeschoß sowie ein weit auskragendes Traufgesims als Abschluß zum Dachgeschoß. Als Material wurde im Sockel grobkörniger Elbsandstein verwendet.

Die Fassade hat sieben Achsen, streng symmetrisch aufgebaut, die Mitte nimmt völlig selbstverständlich die prächtigst gestaltete Eingangssituation auf, die ein Giebel mit erstaunlicherweise leerem

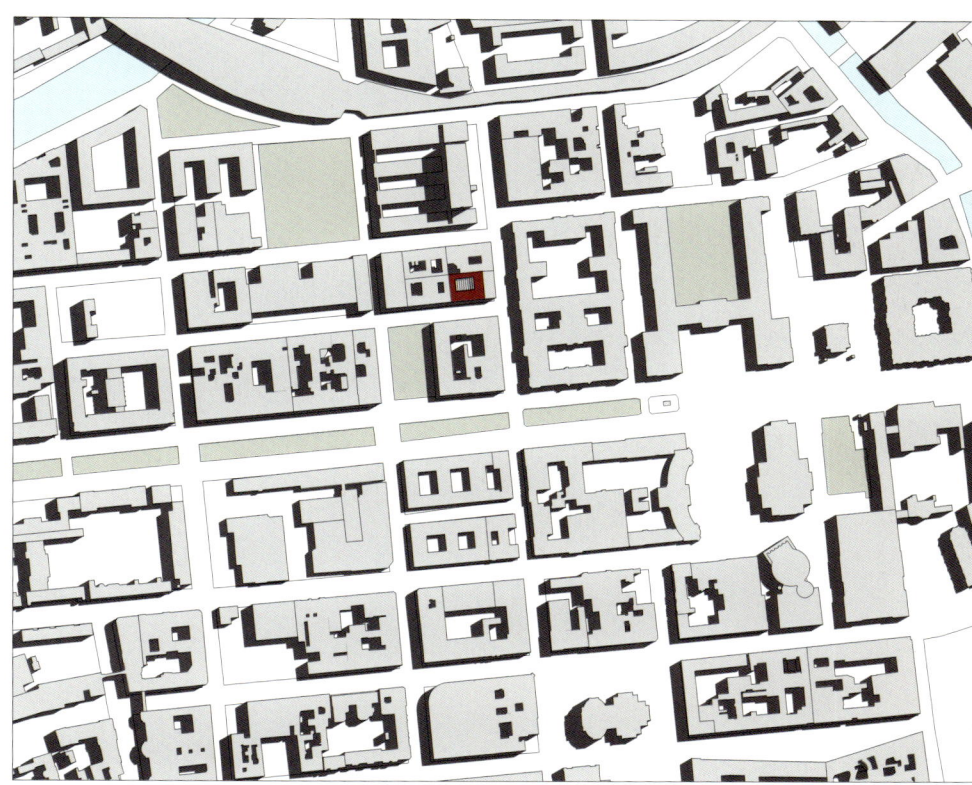

Renovation of the *Frankfurter Allgemeine Zeitung* publishing and editorial offices, Berlin-Mitte, 1997–99

The present-day appearance of the building at 2–4 Mittelstraße was the work of the architects Höltzel & Tenner, who designed a building for a bank in 1899/1900. In the final years of the 19th century there was a great deal of building activity in the so-called Quartier 210 B, as this was one of the most desired locations in the capital of the German Empire. This was partly because of its proximity to the magnificent boulevard, Unter den Linden, but mostly because of the recent opening (1882) of the Friedrichstraße train station, that had been quickly followed by the founding

1. Ansicht des Gebäudes von der Mittelstraße. (Photo: Stefan Müller.)
2. Detailansicht des Haupteingangs. (Photo: Stefan Müller.)

3. Lageplan.

3. Site plan.

1. View of the building from Mittelstraße. (Photo: Stefan Müller.)
2. Detailed view of the main entrance. (Photo: Stefan Müller.)

Umbau des Verlags- und Redaktionsgebäudes
der *Frankfurter Allgemeinen Zeitung*, Berlin-
Mitte, 1997–99

4. Das Atrium. (Photo: Stefan Müller.)
5. Detailansicht einer Mediensäule. (Photo: Stefan Müller.)

6, 7. Schnitt und Grundriß (Erdge-schoß).

6, 7. Section and floor plan (ground floor).

4. The atrium. (Photo: Stefan Müller.)
5. Detailed view of a media column. (Photo: Stefan Müller.)

Giebelfeld oberhalb der Trauflinie noch akzentuiert.

Bei der Restaurierung der Fassade wurde darauf geachtet, daß bei notwendigem Steinaustausch wieder ein sehr homogener Elbsandstein verwendet wurde.

Verändernde Eingriffe wurden nur unter den äußeren Fensterachsen vorgenommen, indem die Felder unter dem Erdgeschoßfenster für einen PKW-Aufzug und notwendig gewordene Fluchttüren geöffnet wurden.

Der Hof ist geprägt von einer gleichmäßigen vierseitigen Umbauung, sie variiert nur im Bereich der beiden Treppenhäuser. Er ist in cremefarbenen, glasierten Verblenderziegeln mit großflächigen Holzfenstern gehalten. Dekorative Lüftungsöffnungen für die alte Heizung unter jedem Zimmerfenster wurden geschickt in das System der Putzlisenen integriert.

Zwar war die Ausbildung des Hauses nach außen zur Straße hin einheitlich, im Inneren, vor allem im Innenhof, um den die vier Büroflügel orientiert sind,

of new hotels, elegant hair salons and furniture stores. After the war the building contained publishing and editorial offices of newspapers.

Design elements and architectural stylistic devices of the neo-Renaissance are evident on the façade.

The raised ground floor with its vividly moulded rustication is followed by the first and second storeys in colossal order with pilasters. In the transition to the third storey there is a crowning cornice and an ending is made on the top storey with a projecting eaves cornice. The material used for the socle was coarse-grained sandstone from the Elbe area.

The façade is made up of seven modules in strict symmetrical order. The magnificent entrance is of course in the middle. Its pride of position is accentuated by a gable which has a surprisingly empty tympanum above the eaves.

During the restoration of the façade, care was taken that for the necessary replacement of the stone a very homogenous sandstone from the Elbe area was once again used.

Changes were only made underneath the exterior window modules. The area underneath the ground floor window was opened for a car elevator and the requisite fire-escape doors.

The courtyard is characterized by a regular four-sided enclosure, that only varies around the two stairwells. The work here has been done in cream-coloured, glazed, facing bricks with large, wooden windows. Ornamental ventilation openings for the old heating system under the windows have been skilfully integrated within the structure of the plaster vertical mouldings.

Although the building was uniform in its development towards the outside street, in the inside, above all in the inner courtyard, around which four office wings are orientated, the parcelling out

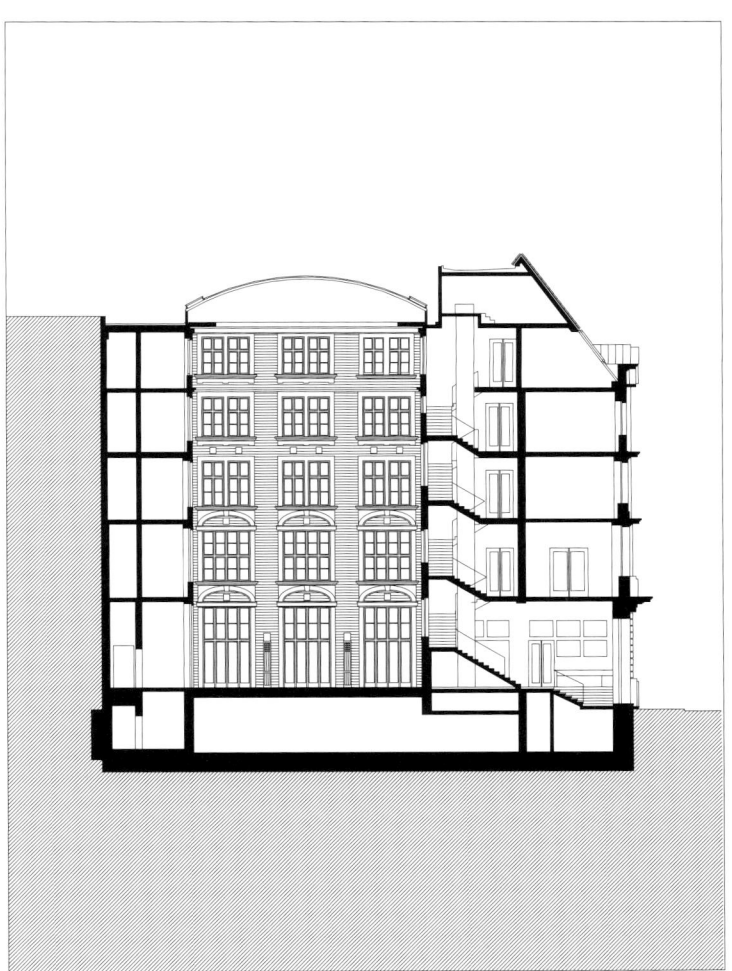

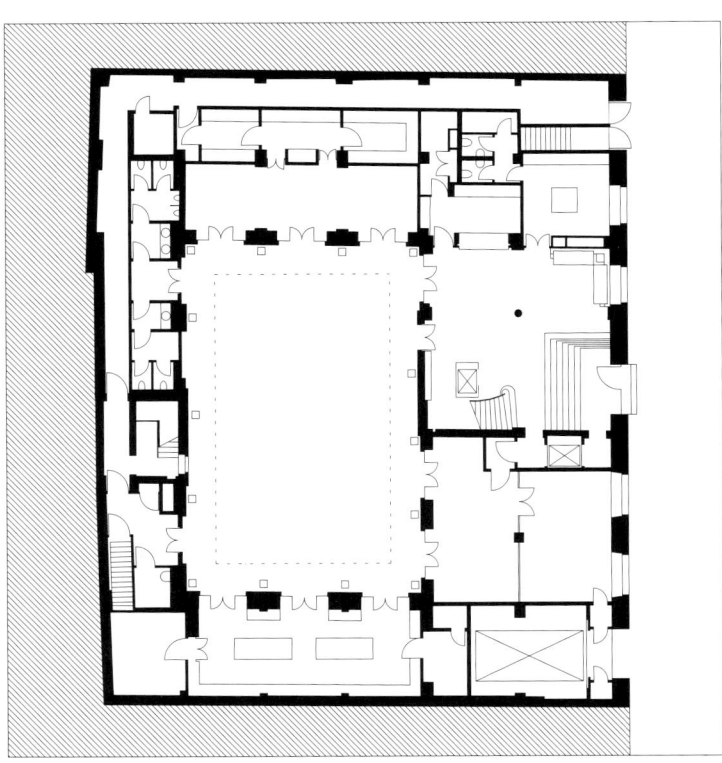

8. Das illuminierte
Atrium. (Photo: Stefan
Müller.)

8. The atrium illumina-
ted. (Photo: Stefan
Müller.)

9. Hauseingang. (Pho-
to: Stefan Müller.)

9. Main entrance. (Pho-
to: Stefan Müller.)

war noch die aus den historischen Haus-
nummern 2–4 ersichtliche Parzellierung
in drei Grundstücke erkennbar: So hatte
der Hof zwei unterschiedliche Niveaus,
der alte Keller unterschiedlich ausge-
prägte Decken, von preußischer Kap-
pendecke bis gemauertem Kreuzgewöl-
be.

Als uns im Frühjahr 1997 die Aufgabe
gestellt wurde, das Haus für die *Frank–
furter Allgemeine Zeitung* herzurichten,
stand für den Bauherrn und uns im Vordergrund, ein modernes Bürohaus mit
den technischen Möglichkeiten des ausgehenden 20. Jahrhunderts zu schaffen,
dies aber mit Rücksicht auf die fast un-
versehrte Bausubstanz zu tun, dergestalt,
daß der Betrachter erst auf den zweiten
oder dritten Blick die doch erhebliche
Veränderungen realisiert.

Die wichtigste Veränderung ist der
jetzt neu überdachte Innenhof, der das
Herz und Zentrum des Hauses darstellt.
Neben der Höhenangleichung des Fußbodens und der Schaffung einer einheitlichen Traufhöhe war uns wichtig, den
Eingriff erkennbar auszubilden.

Zentrale Gedanken dabei waren, die
historische Fassade zu erhalten, eine
klare Trennung zum neuen Glasdach,
sowie die Mediensäulen zur Aufnahme
der Technik als neue skulpturale Elemente zu schaffen.

Als neutrales Trennungselement leis-
tet dies das Passepartout oberhalb der
Innenhoffassaden, eine umlaufende auskragende Platte. Es hat mehrere Funk-
tionen: Erstens reduziert es den lichten
Querschnitt über dem Hof und macht
ihn damit klimatechnisch besser be-
herrschbar. Zweitens ist es allseitig mit
akustisch dämpfendem Material belegt
und bewirkt damit eine geringere Nach-
hallzeit und dadurch eine hervorragen-
de Akustik. Drittens gibt es die Möglichkeit, alle störenden Elemente des Glasdachs wie Entrauchungsöffnungen so

of the building at 2–4 Mittelstraße into
three lots was still perceptible. The courtyard had two different levels, the old cellar's ceilings ranged from Prussian coved
to a brick groin vault.

When we were given the task in 1997
of refurbishing this building for the
Frankfurter Allgemeine Zeitung, we were of
the same mind as the client. Above all,
we wanted a modern office building with
the technical possibilities of the late
20th century, but there would also be
such care taken with the almost intact
building substance, that it would only be
after a second or even third look that
the observer would realize that major
changes had been made.

The major change is the new roof
over the inner courtyard – the building's
heart and centre. As well as aligning the
floor height and creating a uniform

zu kaschieren, daß für den Betrachter lediglich die reine Konstruktion aus den 6 cm breiten gebogenen Stahlträgern und den Glaselementen erkennbar wird. Alle aussteifenden Elemente wurden in den Randbereich der Konstruktion gelegt, so daß, anders als bei vielen neu entstandenen Glasdächern in Berlin, der sichtbare Bereich des Glasdachs nur eine Ebene aufweist und störende Unterspannungen somit entfallen. Der Raum als solcher sollte frei bleiben von jeglichen technischen Einrichtungen.

Die Hoffassaden selbst wurden behutsam restauriert und an einigen Stellen rekonstruiert, lediglich die metallenen Lüftungsöffnungen wurden im ersten Obergeschoß zur Aufnahme von Lautsprechern verändert, im obersten Geschoß beherbergen sie die Beleuchtungskörper.

eaves' height it was important to us that the change was discernible.

The central idea here was to maintain the historic façade, to effect a clear separation from the new glass roof, and to shape the media columns to be used for the technology as new, sculptural elements.

The passepartout above the façade of the inner courtyard, an ongoing, projecting panel, is responsible for a neutral division. It has a number of functions. In the first place, it reduces the opening above the courtyard so that its temperature can be better controlled. Secondly, all of its sides have been insulated with noise reduction material, so that there is almost no echo and therefore excellent acoustics. Thirdly, it allows for the concealment of the unsightly elements of the glass roof, such as the ventilation

10. Das Foyer. (Photo: Stefan Müller.)

11. Perspektive des Kaminzimmers.

10. The Foyer. (Photo: Stefan Müller.)

11. Perspective view of the room with fireplace.

Das Atrium stellt bewußt eine Ambivalenz zwischen Innen- und Außenraum dar, die Ziegelfassaden und Fenster sind klare Außenelemente, während die Untersicht des Glasdachs gefühlsmäßig dem Innenraum zugeordnet wird. Diese Ambivalenz wird nun unterstützt durch den bewußten Einsatz des in zwei Verlegearten gestalteten Afzelienparketts – einem Innenraumelement – und dem Außenelement der Mediensäulen, die aus massivem Stahl scharfkantig herausgearbeitet wurden. Als Vorbild dienten uns die Luftauslässe der Postsparkasse in Wien von Otto Wagner. Technisch haben sie die Funktion der Beleuchtung und Belüftung des Atriums. Da sie eindeutig ein neues Element sind, rücken sie von der Fassade ab.

An das Atrium lagern sich im wesentlichen Bibliothek, Buffetraum und das Foyer an. Das Foyer wurde um eine Gebäudeachse vergrößert, so daß es jetzt in einem angemessenen Größenverhältnis zu dem neuen Hauptraum des Hauses

openings, so that the observer is only aware of the actual construction itself – curved steel beams 6 cm in width and the glass elements. All elements that have had to be structurally braced have been placed at the edge of the construction. This means, that unlike many of the new glass roofs in Berlin, only one level of this glass roof is visible and all of the unsightly elements are concealed. The space as such has remained free of any technical equipment.

The courtyard façades themselves were carefully restored and partly reconstructed. Changes were only made on the first storey to the old metal ventilation openings. These were altered to allow them to hold loudspeakers. In the upper storey there are lights in these openings.

There is a conscious ambivalence in the atrium between interior and exterior space. The brick façades and windows are clearly exterior elements, while one would instinctively place the soffit of the glass roof as belonging to the interior space. This ambivalence is emphasized further by the deliberate use of the hardwood floor (Afzelienparkett), which is laid in two different patterns – an interior element – and the exterior element of the sharp-edged media columns, fashioned out of massive steel. Our model for this were the ventilation columns in Otto Wagner's Postal Savings Bank in Vienna. Their technical function is the lighting and ventilation of the atrium. Since they are clearly a new element, they have been distanced from the façade.

The library, cafeteria and foyer are connected to the atrium. The foyer was enlarged by one module, so that its size is now in proportion to the building's main room. All of the fittings in American cherry-wood are the result of high quality carpentry work.

steht. Alle hierfür entstandenen Einbauten erfolgten als hochwertige Tischlerarbeiten in amerikanischer Kirsche.

Die Büroräume in den Obergeschossen folgen in ihrer Anordnung dem Rhythmus der Fassade. Ein innenliegender, umlaufender Flur erlaubt die durchgehende Erschließung einer Etage. Noch erhaltene originale Innentüren und Zargen wurden aufgearbeitet und in einem Geschoß des Hauses »zusammengelegt«.

Um die Büroräume mit der notwendigen Technik auszustatten, erhielten alle Fensterbereiche eine durchlaufende, handwerklich gefertigte Brüstungsverkleidung, hinter der sich Medienanschlüsse sowie Aggregate zur Kühlung und zum Heizen der Räume befinden. Eine Lüftungsanlage versorgt zusätzlich das Atrium und alle Räume des Hauses mit Zu- und Abluft.

Projektleiter: Sigurd Hauer
Mitarbeiter: Frigga Uhlisch, Peter Westermann

The arrangement of the offices in the upper storeys is in the rhythm of the façade. An inner corridor that runs through the floor makes it everywhere accessible. The original interior doors and frames still in existence were refurbished and »placed together« on one of the storeys.

In order to provide the rooms with the necessary service technology, a continuous, specially made panelling runs beneath all of the windows, behind which various technical outlets, as well as cooling and heating units can be found. In addition, a ventilation system ensures the proper circulation of air in the atrium and all of the building's rooms.

Project architect: Sigurd Hauer
Collaborators: Frigga Uhlisch, Peter Westermann

Graphikmuseum Pablo Picasso, Münster, 1998–2000

Die größte Kollektion von Picassos graphischem Werk, die Sammlung von Gert Huizinga, wurde im Jahr 1997 von der Sparkassenstiftung Pablo Picasso erworben, um sie in Münster auf Dauer der Öffentlichkeit zu präsentieren. Zwei repräsentative Gebäude in der historischen Altstadt wurden zur Verfügung gestellt, nämlich der 1704 erbaute Druffelsche Hof und der direkt angrenzende Hensen-Bau von 1906. Von beiden Gebäuden waren lediglich die historischen Klinkerfassaden im Originalzustand erhalten.

In einem 1998 durchgeführten internationalem Wettbewerb wurde die für Graphik übliche geringe Helligkeit von 50 Lux gefordert, so daß wir für das Museum eine Gliederung in Bereiche mit stark unterschiedlicher Belichtung vorschlugen:

Eine sehr helle Zone mit den Nebenfunktionen Kasse, Garderobe, Vortragsraum und Café im Hochparterre wird

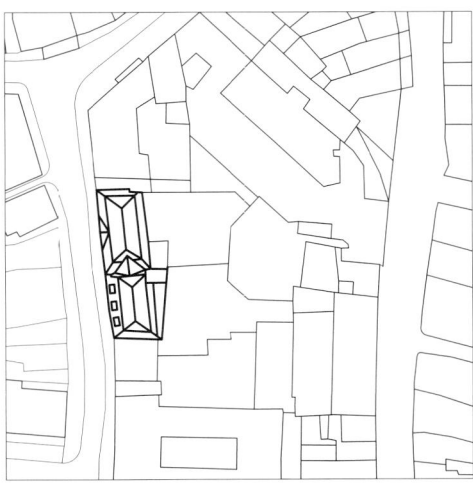

Pablo Picasso Graphics Museum, Munster, 1998–2000

The Gert Huizinga Collection is the largest collection of Picasso's graphic work. It was acquired in 1997 by the Pablo Picasso Sparkassenstiftung (savings bank foundation). This collection was to be placed on permanent, public display in Munster and housed in two prestigious buildings in the historic old town: the Druffelsche Hof built in 1704 and the directly adjoining Hensen Building of 1906. On both buildings the historic clinker façades was all that remained in its original state.

An international competition in 1998 called for a low illumination level of light, 50 lux, common for the display of graphics. We proposed dividing the museum into areas of contrasting strengths of lighting.

A very bright zone for the secondary functions of cash, wardrobe, lecture room, and café on the raised ground floor is lit by large windows to the west

1. Treppenraum. (Photo: Stefan Müller.)
2. Perspektivischer Schnitt.

1. Staircase. (Photo: Stefan Müller.)
2. Perspective section.

3. Lageplan.
4. Ansicht des Druffelschen Hofes und des Hensen-Baus. (Photo: Stefan Müller.)

3. Site plan.
4. View of the Druffelscher Hof and the Hensen-Bau. (Photo: Stefan Müller.)

5. Perspektivische
Zeichnung der Ein-
gangshalle.
6. Eingangshalle. (Pho-
to: Stefan Müller.)

5. Perspective drawing
of the entrance hall.
6. Entrance hall. (Pho-
to: Stefan Müller.)

durch große Fenster im Westen und Osten belichtet. Unmittelbar hinter den historischen Fassaden entwickelt sich ein hoher Treppenraum, der die beiden oberen Etagen erschließt und der durch die Folge unterschiedlicher Fenster vielfältiges Tageslicht erhält. Die Blickverbindung zum öffentlichen Straßenraum ist ebenso gewollt wie die Ähnlichkeit zum Treppenraum in der von Hans Döllgast renovierten Alten Pinakothek in München.

Eher dunkel empfindet man im ersten Augenblick die beiden darüber liegenden Geschosse, welche die künstlich belichteten Ausstellungsflächen beherbergen.

Der Treppenraum vermittelt die ursprüngliche Material- und Detailqualität der Altbauten in abgewandelter Form. Durch die dreigeschossige Wand in roter Farbe, die auch von außen durch die Fenster als modernes Element erkennbar ist, verbindet er die beiden Häuser miteinander.

Pro Etage gibt es sechs Ausstellungsräume, die einfache Proportionen haben. Der Eichenparkettboden und die Decken sind in einen äußeren Rahmen und in ein Innenfeld gegliedert. Dieses Minimum an Detail ist notwendig, um den Einklang mit den dunklen profilierten Bilderrahmen herzustellen, die auch Teil unserer Entwurfsarbeit sind. Die

and east. Immediately behind the historic façades is the high-ceilinged stairhall, that admits a diversity of daylight through different windows and that provides access to the two upper floors. The link to the view of the open street is deliberate, as is the similarity with the stairhall in the Alte Pinakothek in Munich, renovated by Hans Döllgast.

At first the two storeys above, containing the artificially lit exhibition areas, seem quite dark.

The stair-hall conveys the original quality of the materials and details of the older buildings in an adapted form. Through a three-storey red wall, also recognizable from outside as a modern element if one looks through the win-

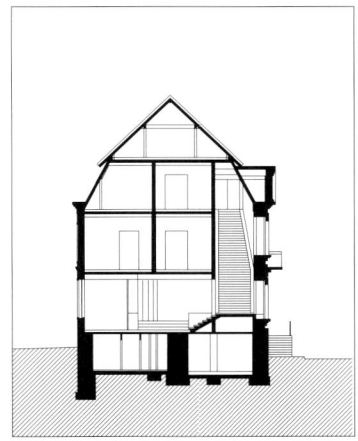

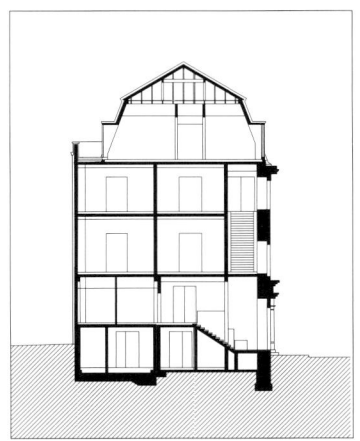

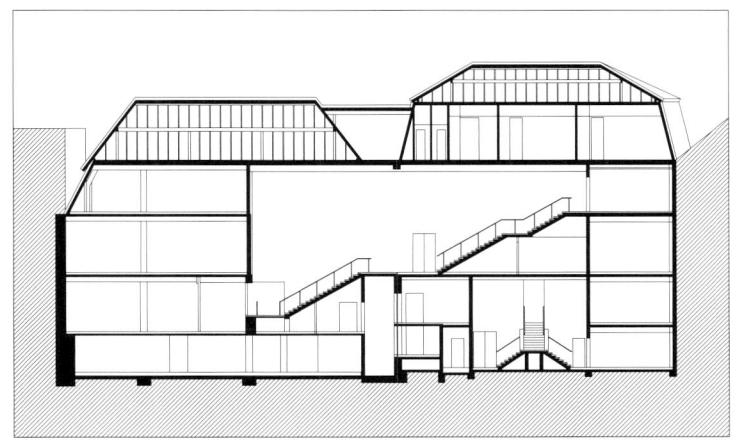

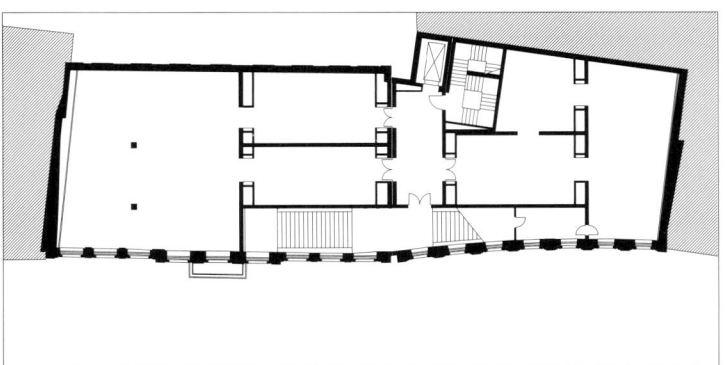

7. Querschnitt Druffel-
scher Hof.
8. Querschnitt Hensen-
Bau.
9. Längsschnitt durch
beide Gebäude.
10, 11. Grundrisse (Erd-
geschoß, Ausstellungs-
geschoß).

7. Cross section Druf-
felscher Hof.
8. Cross section Hen-
sen-Bau.
9. Longitudinal section
of both buildings.
10, 11. Floor plans
(ground floor, exhibi-
tion floor).

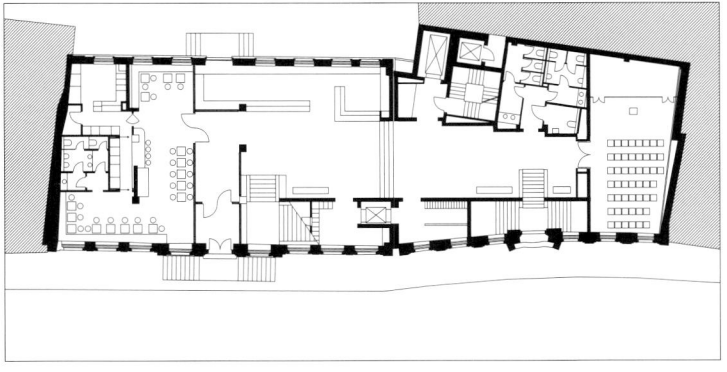

Graphikmuseum Pablo Picasso, Münster,
1998–2000

12, 13. Die Ausstel-
lungsräume. (Photos:
Stefan Müller.)

12, 13. The exhibition
rooms. (Photos: Stefan
Müller.)

14. Das Café. (Photo:
Stefan Müller.)
15. Perspektivische
Zeichnung des Cafés.

14. The Café. (Photo:
Stefan Müller.)
15. Perspective draw-
ing of the café.

künstliche Belichtung erfolgt durch de-
ckenbündige Wandfluter.

Der Zugang durch das Portal des
Druffelschen Hofes erschließt das Museum von der Königsstraße. Hinter dem
Museum im Blockinneren sind Verkaufs-
flächen geplant, ein Verbindungsgang
durch das Museumsfoyer ist vorgesehen.
Das offene Café zur einen Seite und der
Blick in die hohe Treppenhalle auf der
anderen Seite machen die Besonderheit
des Ortes aus.

Projektleiter: Rita Ahlers
Mitarbeiter: Andreas Schindhelm

dows, it connects the two houses with
each other.

There are six exhibition rooms with
simple proportions on each floor. The
oak, hardwood floors and the ceilings
have been divided into an outer frame
and an inner area. This minimum of
detail was necessary in order to achieve
a harmony with the dark profiles of the
pictures frames, that we also designed.
The artificial lighting comes from wall-
washers recessed into the ceiling.

On Königsstraße the museum can be
entered through the portal of the Druffelsche Hof. Behind the museum, in the
interior of the block, an area for stores
is planned, as is a connecting passageway
through the museum's foyer. The open
café, on the one side and the view of the
high-ceilinged stair-hall, on the other
side, make this a special place.

Project architect: Rita Ahlers
Collaborator: Andreas Schindhelm

Zwei Wohnhäuser an der Außenalster, Hamburg, 1998/99

Die zwei Wohnhäuser an der Außenalster in Hamburg stellten ein für uns neues Thema dar, nämlich den hochwertigen Wohnungsbau, der die gründerzeitlichen Altbauten in einem Teil ihres Formenkanons neu interpretiert, teils direkt kopiert.

In einem international eingeladenen Wettbewerb wurden 1997 für das interessante Grundstück folgende Vorgaben gemacht: Vorne, an der Promenade nach Südwesten, durfte, gemäß der Hamburger Außenalsterverordnung, der in hellen Farben zu gestaltende Baukörper die Länge von 15 m nicht überschreiten. In der Mitte des Grundstücks galt es, einen großen Baum zu schützen. Nach Osten hin bot der Feenteich eine zweite Orientierung für die rückwärtige Bebauung.

So entstanden zwei dreigeschossige Häuser mit einem Staffelgeschoß mit insgesamt 15 Wohnungen, zwischen 140 m² und 260 m² groß. Ein Haus wendet sich zur Außenalster, das andere zum Feenteich. Die beiden Eingangssituatio-

Two residential buildings on the Außenalster, Hamburg, 1998/99

These two residential buildings on the Außenalster in Hamburg presented us with a new subject matter, namely high-quality apartment building that reinterprets and sometimes directly copies, in part, the formal canon of building in the late 19th century.

An international, invited competition in 1997 for this interesting site, specified that in accordance with the planning regulations for the Außenalster, at the front, on the southwest promenade, lightly coloured building forms should not exceed 15 m in length. A large tree in the middle of the site had to be protected. Towards the east a small pond provided a second orientation for the building at the rear.

Two three-storey buildings with a setback on the fourth floor were erected. They have a total of 15 apartments, between 140 m² and 260 m² in size. One building faces the Außenalster, the other faces the small pond. Each of the

1. Ansicht der Gebäude vom Garten. (Photo: Stefan Müller.)
2. Detailansicht der Fassade.
3. Lageplan.

1. View of the buildings from the garden. (Photo: Stefan Müller.)
2. Detailed elevation of the façade.
3. Site plan.

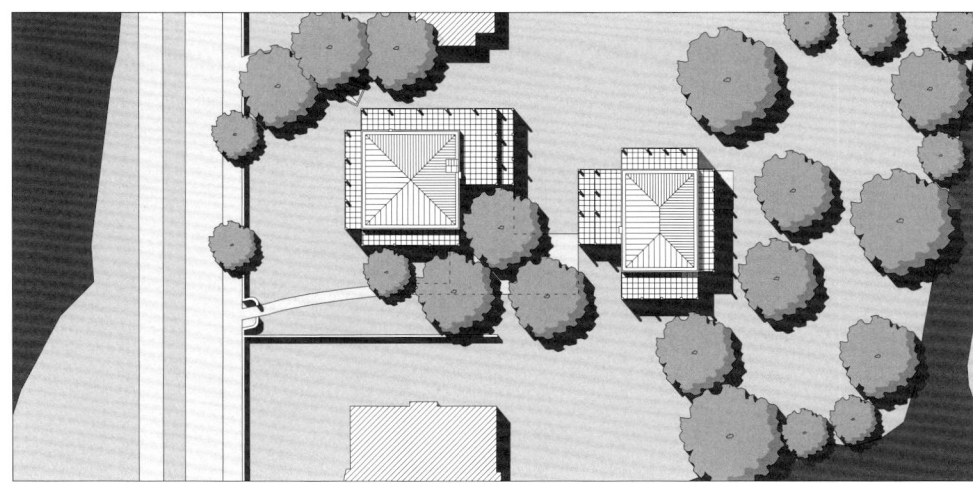

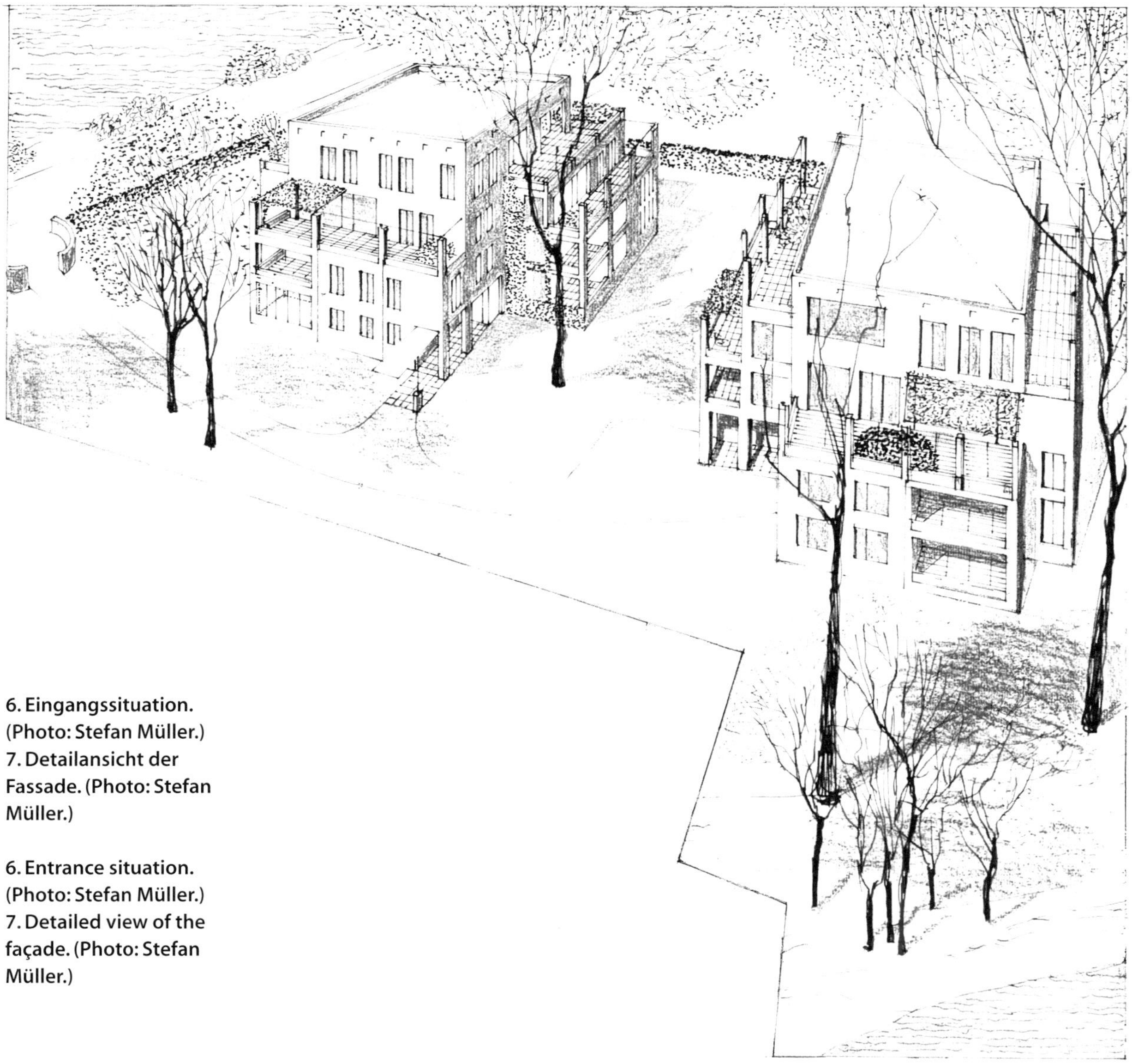

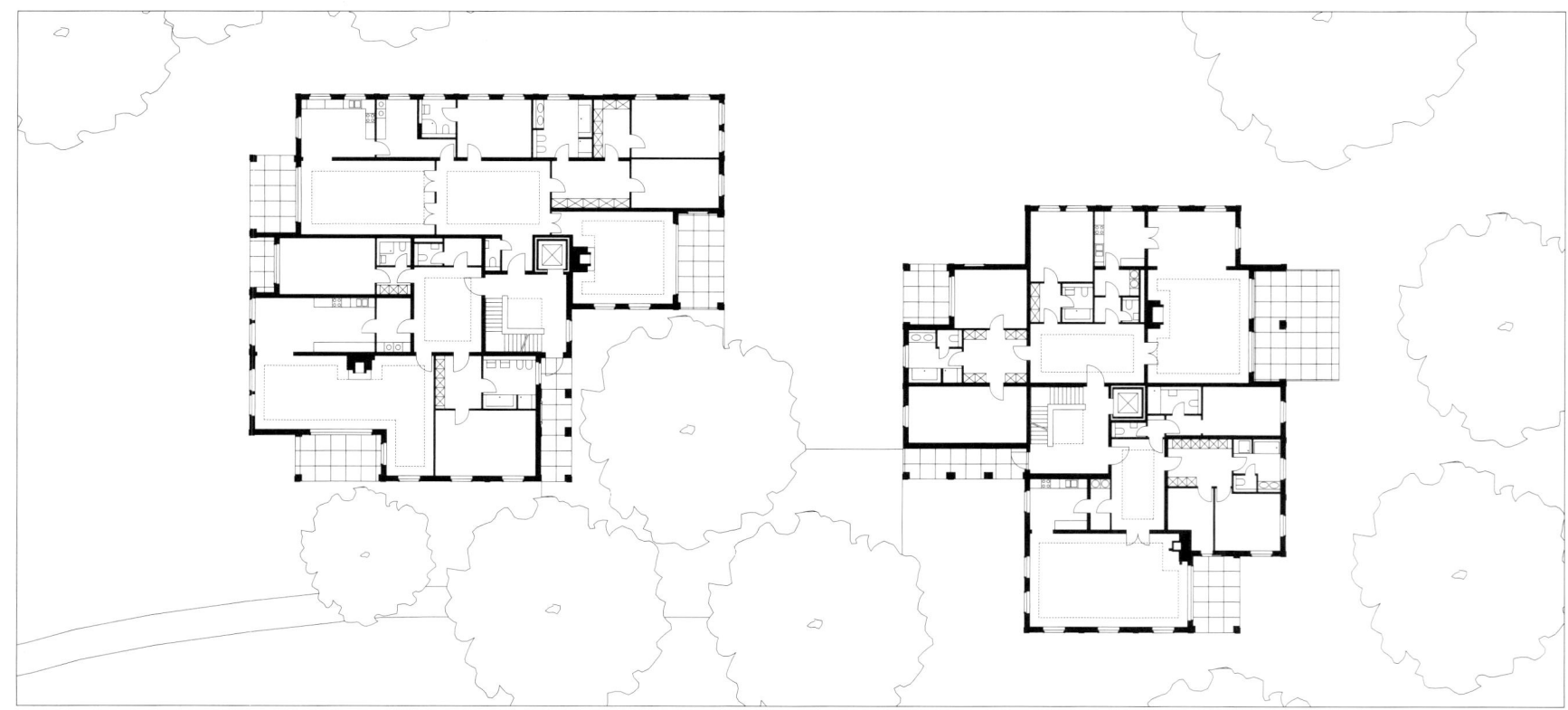

4. Vogelperspektive.
5. Grundriß (Erdge-
schoß).

4. Bird´s-eye view.
5. Floor plan (ground
floor).

6. Eingangssituation.
(Photo: Stefan Müller.)
7. Detailansicht der
Fassade. (Photo: Stefan
Müller.)

6. Entrance situation.
(Photo: Stefan Müller.)
7. Detailed view of the
façade. (Photo: Stefan
Müller.)

entrance areas is orientated towards the large beech tree between the two buildings.

The two stairwells have generous proportions. Walls clad in natural stone surround an oversized stairwell. A skylight measuring almost 3 m^2 is the source for dramatic lighting. There are one or two apartments on each storey.

The characteristic feature of each apartment is a large, unlit entrance, the foyer, measuring between 15 m^2 and 30 m^2. It is from this point that the floor

nen orientieren sich jeweils an der großen Buche zwischen den Häusern.

Die beiden Treppenhäuser sind großzügig gestaltet: natursteinverkleidete Wände umgeben ein übergroßes Treppenauge, ein Oberlicht von fast 3 m^2 sorgt für dramatische Belichtung. Pro Geschoß lagern sich ein oder zwei Wohnungen an.

Das Charakteristikum jeder Wohnung ist ein großzügiges, unbelichtetes Eingangszimmer, das Foyer, zwischen 15 m^2 und 30 m^2 groß. Von hier aus entwickeln sich die Grundrisse weiter, ähnlich wie bei gründerzeitlichen Konzepten: Eine Doppeltür öffnet sich zum Wohnzimmer, der Blick geht weiter auf die Terrasse und von dort auf das Wasser.

Ein offener Kamin, eine lichte Raumhöhe von 3 m und zwei Bäder sind weitere Merkmale. Zur Terrasse kommt meist noch ein überdachter Freisitz hinzu.

Da die Baukörper in jeder Etage etwas zurückspringen, sich also betont unregelmäßig und asymmetrisch gliedern, gleicht keine Wohnung im Grundriß der anderen.

Zwei Wohnhäuser an der Außenalster, Hamburg,
1998–99

Die Putzfassaden haben ein tektonisches Ordnungsprinzip: Senkrechte Pilaster enden oben an der Fassade in Pfeilern, welche die Terrassen umsäumen und zusammen mit den französischen Fenstern, mit ihren dunkelgrünen Leibungen aus Naturstein, der Fassade ihr charakteristisches Aussehen geben. Zum räumlichen Abschluß spannen sich zwischen den Pfeilerköpfen schlanke, mehrfach geknickte Stahlprofile. Sie stellen ein modernes Element dar, welches sich prägnant gegen den Himmel abzeichnet.

Projektleiter: Peter Westermann, Herman Duquesnoy
Mitarbeiter: Kirsten Händel, Nina Otto, Jan Pautzke

Two residential buildings on the Außenalster, Hamburg, 1998/99

8, 9. Treppenraum. (Photos: Stefan Müller.)

8, 9. Staircase. (Photos: Stefan Müller.)

10. Blick von einer Terrasse. (Photo: Stefan Müller.)

11. Blick in einen Wohnraum. (Photo: Stefan Müller.)

10. View from a terrace. (Photo: Stefan Müller.)

11. View into a living room. (Photo: Stefan Müller.)

plans evolve, similar to the concepts of the late 19th century. A double door opens to the living-room from where one can look out onto the terrace and from there onto the water.

Further features are an open fire-place, ceiling heights of 3 m and two bathrooms. Most terraces have a covered area.

Because the buildings are partially set back at every storey and thereby deliberately irregular and asymmetrical in their structure, no apartment is similar in ground plan.

The plaster façades are structured tectonically. Vertical pilasters end at the top of the façades in piers that border the terraces and together with the French windows with their dark green reveals of natural stone lend the façades their distinctive appearance. Slender, bent steel profiles spanning between the column heads form a spatial conclusion. They are a modern element and make a concise statement against the backdrop of the sky.

Project architects: Peter Westermann, Herman Duquesnoy
Collaborators: Kirsten Händel, Nina Otto, Jan Pautzke

Stadtbibliothek und Jugendmusikschule, Pforzheim, 1999–2002

im Jahr 1988 gewannen wir einen städtebaulichen Wettbewerb, in dem wir in der Innenstadt Pforzheims ein herkömmliches Stadtsystem mit Block, Straße, Gasse und einer einheitlichen Traufhöhe definierten, um dem sehr unruhigen Zentrum wieder eine Normalität zu geben und die undefinierten begrünten Resträume zwischen den Solitären zu schließen.

Die Städteplaner Leon und Rob Krier hatten im Jahr 1986 bereits mit einem ähnlichen Ansatz versucht, die Stadt an ihre baulichen und historischen Ursprünge zu erinnern, indem sie ein besonders im Mittelalter beliebtes traditionelles Architekturelement auf der Enzbrücke realisierten, nämlich eine Brückenskulptur – *Flößer* – auf einem säulenumstandenen Sockel.

Elf Jahre später erhielten wir den Auftrag zur Realisierung eines Gebäudes, der Stadtbibliothek.

Die Hauptfassade des Hauses orientiert sich nach Süden zu dem neu definierten Boulevard und bildet eine Blickbeziehung zur Enzbrücke. Gemäß den städtebaulichen Vorgaben ist die Südfassade im Radius von 70 m leicht gerundet. Die beiden südlichen Gebäudeecken sind als Rundung im Radius von 2,5 m ausgebildet.

Das hauptsächliche Fassadenmaterial des Hauses ist ein hellbeiger Sandstein aus Spanien, Bateig bianca, der uns wegen seines an die menschliche Haut erinnernden Farbtons begeistert. Dieser in nur einer Ebene verlegte Stein von

City library and youth music school, Pforzheim, 1999–2002

In 1988 we won an urban design competition for the inner city of Pforzheim in which we laid out a conventional urban network of blocks, streets, passageways and a uniform eaves' height. We aimed to restore some normality to the erratic centre and to close the undefined, green, rest areas between the solitary buildings.

In 1986 the town planners Leon and Rob Krier had already had the similar idea of reminding the city of its architectural and historical origins. They placed an architectural element that was very popular in the Middle Ages, namely the bridge sculpture – theirs' is known as *Flößer* (raftsman) – on a pedestal surrounded by columns on the bridge over the Enz river.

Eleven years later we were given the task of designing the city library.

The building's main façade is orientated towards the south, towards the newly defined boulevard, creating a visual relationship to the Enz bridge. In accordance with the urban development stipu-

1. Ansicht des Gebäudes von Süden. (Photo: Stefan Müller.)

1. View of the building from the south. (Photo: Stefan Müller.)

2. Lageplan.
3. Rob Krier, Brückenskulptur auf einem Sockel von Léon Krier. (Photo: Archiv Krier-Kohl.)

2. Site plan.
3. Rob Krier, sculpture on a bridge with a pedestal by Leon Krier. (Photo: Archiv Krier-Kohl.)

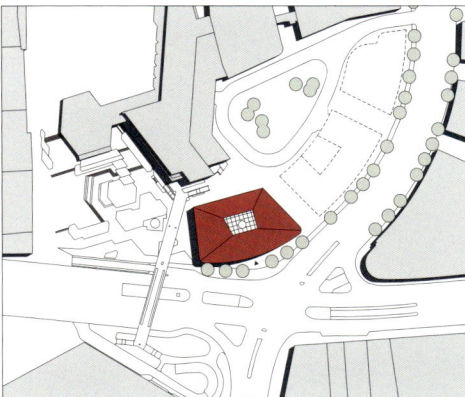

Stadtbibliothek und Jugendmusikschule,
Pforzheim, 1999–2002

4. Detailansicht der
Fassade. (Photo: Ste-
fan Müller.)
5. Ansicht des Gebäu-
des von Südwesten.
(Photo: Stefan Müller.)

4. Detailed view of the
façade. (Photo: Stefan
Müller.)
5. View of the building
from the southwest.
(Photo: Stefan Müller.)

6. Ansicht der südöst-
lichen Gebäudeecke.
(Photo: Stefan Müller.)

6. View of the south-
east corner. (Photo:
Stefan Müller.)

Stadtbibliothek und Jugendmusikschule,
Pforzheim, 1999–2002

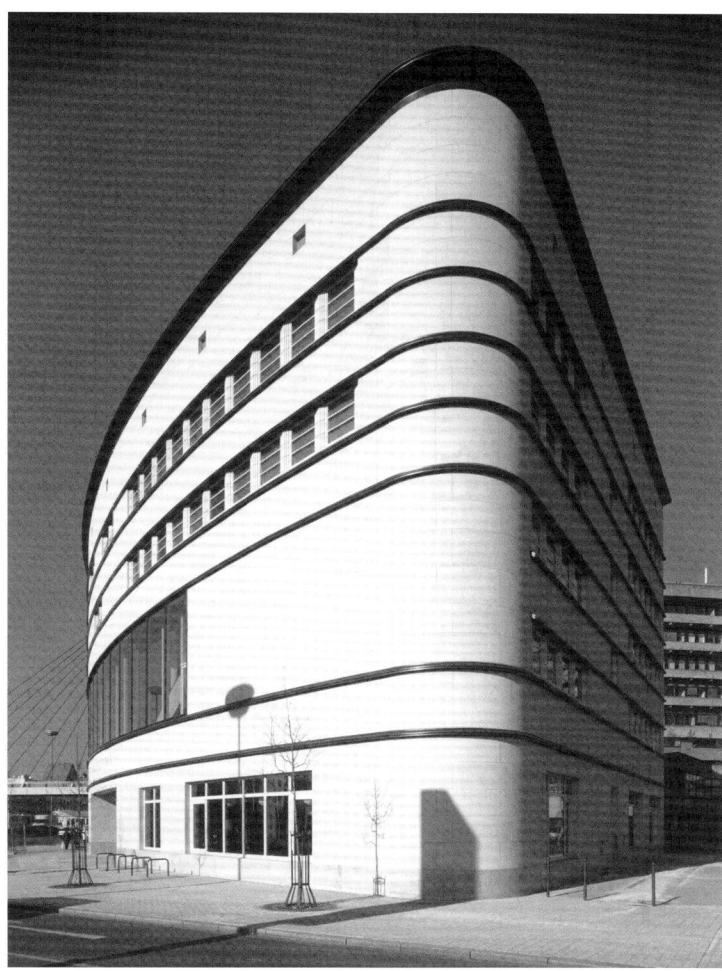

5 cm bis 7 cm Stärke wird kontrastiert durch dunkelrote, stark plastische, horizontal verlaufende Aluminiumprofile, die jeweils den unteren und oberen Abschluß der Fensterbänder bilden. Diese bestehen aus einer Reihung von mehreren Einzelflügeln nebeneinander, die durch zwei horizontale Fenstersprossen geteilt sind. Zwischen den einzelnen Fensterflügeln befinden sich die detailmäßigen Kulminationspunkte der Fassade: Als Gegenrichtung zur dominierenden Horizontalität bildet sich der senkrechte Pfosten mit zehn dicht nebeneinanderliegenden vertikalen Vor- und Rücksprüngen aus. Um dieses Motiv nochmals zu überhöhen, ziehen sich die Horizontalen der Fenstersprossen plastisch über diese Ebenenversprünge und ähneln damit den Rutenbündeln, den Amtszeichen der römischen Liktoren, Sinnbild für Macht und Gerechtigkeit.

Über dem Haupteingang ist der Schriftzug »Stadtbibliothek« als permanenter Bestandteil der Fassade in großen Lettern in Stein gemeißelt.

lations, the south-facing façade is slightly rounded at a radius of 70 m. Both of the southern corners of the building form curves at a radius of 2,5 m.

The main material used on the building's façade is a light, beige sandstone from Spain, Bateig bianca, that won our enthusiasm because its different hues of colour remind one of human skin. There is only one layer of this stone with a thickness of 5 cm to 7 cm and it contrasts with the dark-red, strongly moulded, horizontal, aluminium profiles at the top and bottom ends of the strip windows. These consist of a row of several casements beside each other that are divided by two horizontal glazing bars. Between the individual casements are the most detailed points of the façade and in this sense its culmination. The vertical mullions, with ten closely spaced salients and returns, run in a direction different to the dominating horizontal direction. This motif finds further emphasis in the way that the horizontal direction of the glazing bars is contin-

109

7. Schriftzug über dem
Haupteingang. (Photo:
Stefan Müller.)

8, 9. Treppenaufgang
in der Bibliothek. (Photos: Stefan Müller.)

7. The inscription over
the main entrance.
(Photo: Stefan Müller.)

8, 9. Staircase in the
library. (Photos: Stefan Müller.)

Die Fassade des Hauses ist klassisch in drei Zonen aufgebaut:

– Die Sockelzone des Erdgeschosses mit großflächigen, horizontalen Fensterformaten und einem kniehohen Spritzschutz aus Granit.

– Die Hauptfunktion des Gebäudes, der große, zweigeschossige Bibliotheksraum im ersten Obergeschoß mit einer Grundfläche von 1000 m^2, drückt sich in einem riesigen, 125 m^2 großen Fenster aus. Darüber liegen die beiden Geschosse mit den beschriebenen Fensterbändern.

– Das Dachgeschoß zeigt nur winzige, rechteckige Luken, ein 50 cm auskragendes Metallprofil bildet den Abschluß nach oben.

Das Gebäude beherbergt zwei Nutzer: die Stadtbibliothek und die Jugendmusikschule. Als weiteres Angebot ist an die Bücherei im Erdgeschoß ein Café angegliedert, das unabhängig von den Öffnungszeiten betrieben werden kann.

Zentrales architektonisches Element im öffentlichen Bibliotheksbereich ist

ued on the salients at the different levels, thereby resembling a fasces, a sign of office for the Romans that was a symbol of justice and power.

Above the main entrance »Stadtbibliothek« (city library) has been chiselled permanently into the façade.

The building's façade has been given the classic division of three zones.

– The ground floor has a large expanse of horizontal windows and a knee-high, granite splash-guard.

– The building's main function, fulfilled by the large two-storey room for the library, is to be found on the first storey. With a base of 1000 m^2 this room finds expression in a huge window of 125 m^2. Above lie the two storeys with the strip windows described above.

– The attic storey has only small, rectangular openings as windows. An endpoint is formed by a metal profile that projects upwards for 50 cm.

The building houses both the city library and the music school for young people. A café is attached to the library

City library and youth music school, Pforzheim, 1999–2002

Stadtbibliothek und Jugendmusikschule,
Pforzheim, 1999–2002

10–13. Grundrisse (Erd-
geschoß, 1. Oberge-
schoß, 2. Obergeschoß)
und Schnitt.

10–13. Floor plans
(ground floor, 1st floor,
2nd floor) and section.

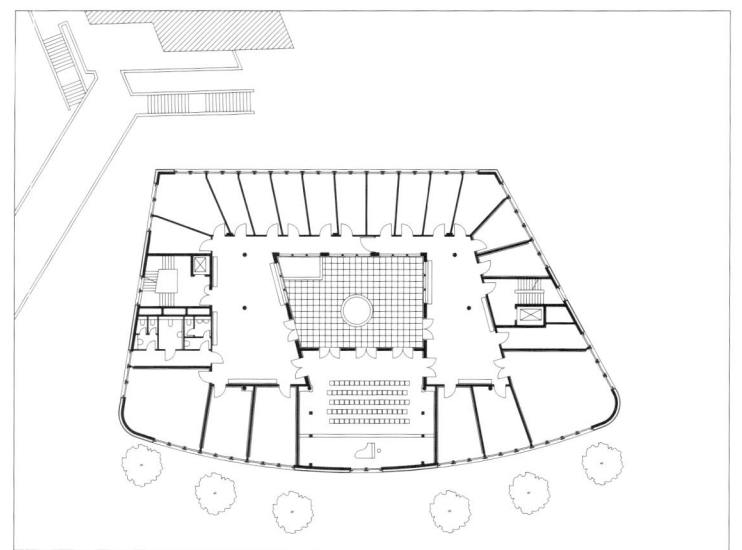

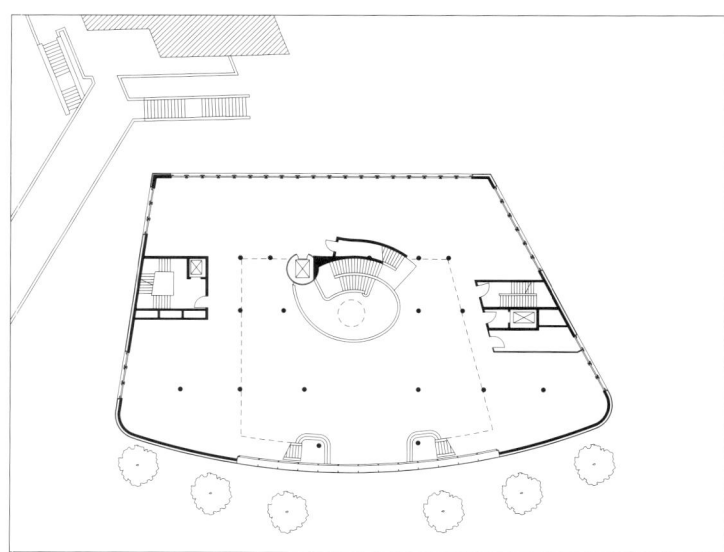

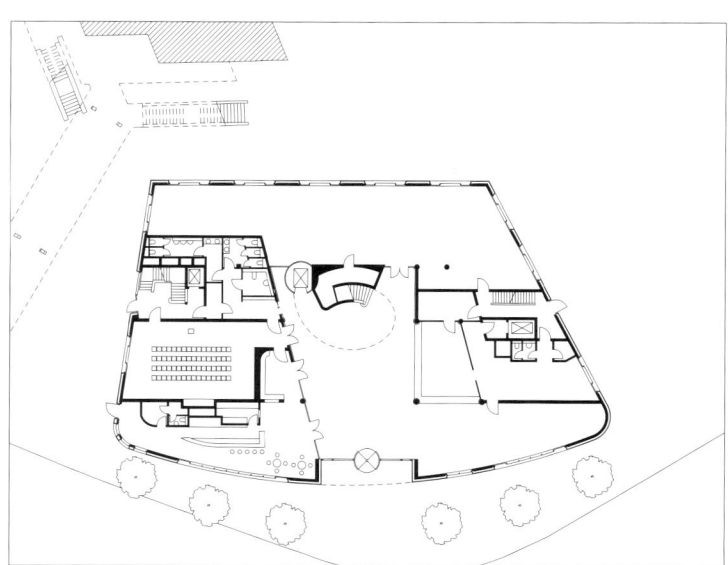

die geschwungene Treppenanlage, die
vom 4,5 m hohen Foyer in den großen
Bibliotheksraum und von dort weiter auf
die Galerie führt. Die räumliche Insze-
nierung wird durch die Lichtführung
noch gesteigert, Tageslicht fällt drama-
tisch durch ein Oberlichtauge bis ins
Erdgeschoß. Der Besucher wird gleichsam zum Licht hin nach oben geleitet.
Als Kontrapunkt ist seitlich an die Treppenanlage ein gläserner Aufzug ange-
fügt.

Der eigentliche Bibliotheksbereich
nimmt dann die gesamte Fläche des
ersten Obergeschosses mit dem zuge-
hörigen Galeriegeschoß ein.

Das große Kastenfenster prägt die
Wirkung des Innenraumes, der sich mit
seiner Galerie und dem großen Volumen von 6500 m^3 an barocken Vorbil-
dern orientiert. Trotz der großen Tiefe
des Baukörpers ist die Bibliothek hell
mit Tageslicht belichtet. Von den Leseplätzen aus bietet sich ein weiter Aus-
blick nach Süden.

Die Jugendmusikschule hat ihren
eigenen Haupteingang an der Westseite
des Hauses. Eine breit angelegte Treppe führt den Besucher hoch ins zweite
Obergeschoß. Hier gibt es einen Vor-
spielsaal mit 100 Plätzen, die Decke mit
ihrem flachen, abgehängten Tonnenge-
wölbe ist gegenüber den anderen Räumen des Geschosses um einen halben
Meter angehoben.

Von außen nicht erkennbar um-
schließen die Räume der Jugendmusikschule einen innenliegenden Lichthof.
Er steht Lehrern und Schülern in den
Pausen als Terrasse zur Verfügung, dient
aber auch bei Veranstaltungen als Erweiterung des Vorspielsaals ins Freie.

Die gesamte Möblierung des Biblio-
theksraumes wurde in einem dunklen
Rot gehalten, um die unruhige Farbigkeit der Bücherrücken zu fassen. Gleichzeitig strahlt jenes Korallenrot ein Ge-

on the ground storey and can be operat-
ed independently of the library's opening hours.

The central architectonic element
in the public area of the library is the
curved staircase that rises from the
4,5 m high foyer to the large library
space and from there to the gallery.
The effect made by this space is further
heightened by the way in which the light
is used. A skylight allows for the dramatic
entrance of daylight all the way to the
ground storey. It could also be said that
the light leads the visitor upwards. A
glass elevator to the side of the staircase
is a counterpoint.

The actual library area occupies the
entire first storey and its accompanying
gallery storey.

The large double-skin glazing element
determines the effect of the interior
space whose gallery and large volume of
6500 m^3 is influenced by Baroque prece-
dents . Despite the great depth of the
building, the library is brightly illuminated by daylight. From the reading desks
there is a good view towards the south.

The youth music school has its own
main entrance on the western side of
the building. The visitor ascends along a
generously proportioned staircase to the
second floor. This is the location of the
concert hall that seats 100. The structural ceiling with its flat, suspended barrel
vault is raised half a metre higher than
the ceilings of the other rooms in the
same storey.

The music school's rooms enclose an
inner air-well that cannot be seen from
the outside. It can be used as a terrace
by teachers and students during their
breaks and also serves as an outside extension of the concert hall during performances.

All of the furniture in the library is in
dark red and has a calming influence on
the effect made by the many different

14–16. Innenraum der
Bibliothek. (Photos:
Stefan Müller.)

14–16. Interior of the
library. (Photos: Stefan
Müller.)

fühl von Ruhe und Würde aus. Die grünen Leuchten an den Leseplätzen assoziieren bewußt die traditionellen Bibliotheksräume, so daß der Leser abends – wie Faust in seiner Studierstube – nur sich selbst und seine Lampe im großen, leeren Raum wahrnimmt.

Projektleiter: Alexander Waimer
Mitarbeiter: Ulrike Feucht, Peter O'Callaghan, Veronika Praxmarer-Breuer, Peter Westermann

colours of the books. At the same time this coral red emanates a sense of repose and dignity. The green lamps on the reading desks are a conscious reference to traditional rooms for libraries, so that in the evening the reader – like Faust in his study – is only aware of himself and his lamp in the large, empty room.

Project architect: Alexander Waimer
Collaborators: Ulrike Feucht, Peter O'Callaghan, Veronika Praxmarer-Breuer, Peter Westermann

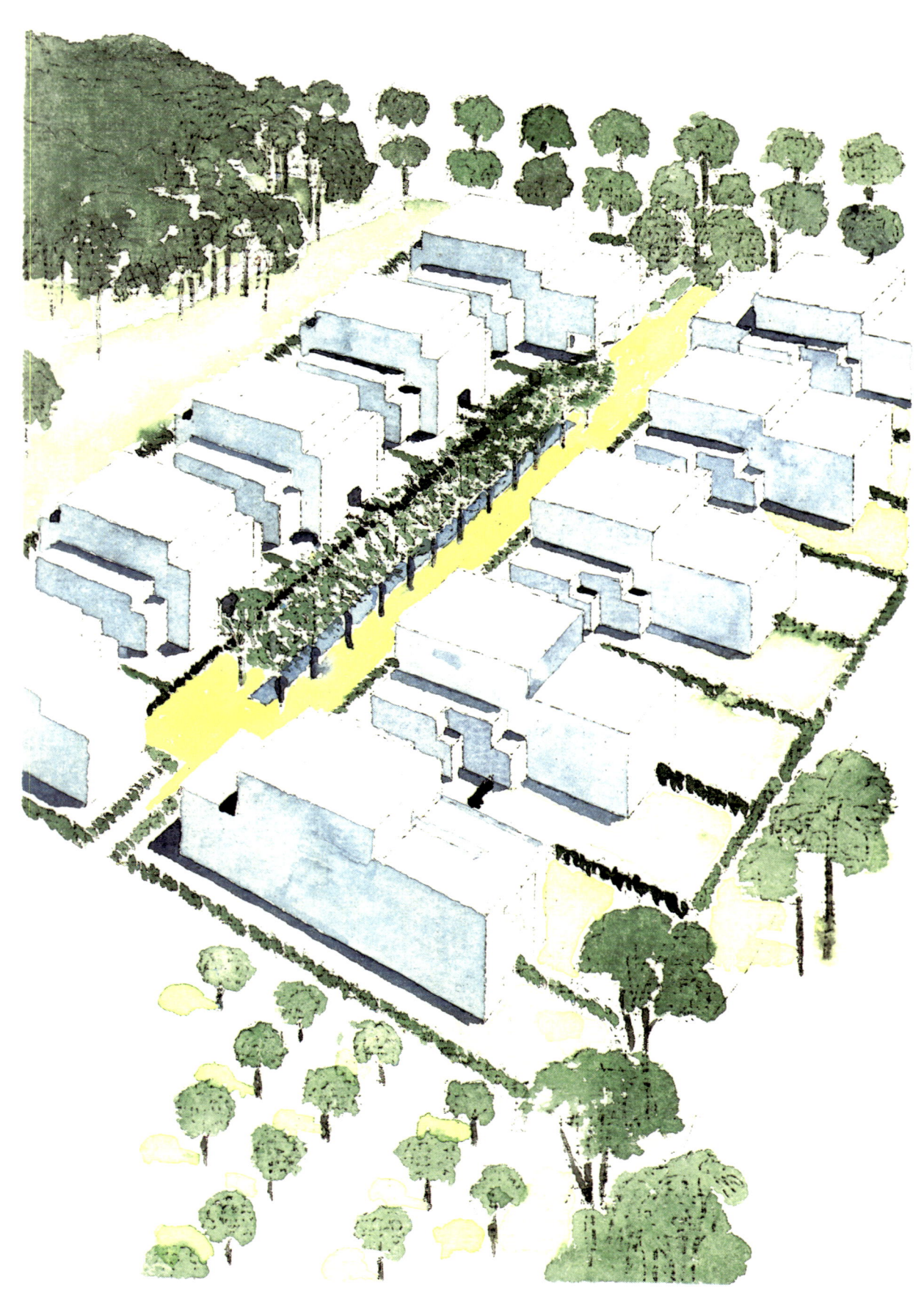

Wohnbebauung am Olympiaberg, München, 1999–2002

Der Wettbewerb im Jahr 1995/96 stellte die Aufgabe, auf einem unbebauten Grundstück am Münchner Olympiagelände ein hochwertiges Wohngebiet zu kreieren.

Zehn freistehende Häuser bilden einen strengen städtischen Raum, der allein den Fußgängern vorbehalten bleibt. Sein Zentrum bildet ein flaches Wasserbecken, das von Bäumen eingerahmt wird. Dieses Motiv geht zurück auf das Bild von einem kleinen Ort in der Provence.

Alle Häuser sind unterirdisch durch eine zweigeschossige Tiefgarage miteinander verbunden, die mit zwei Rampen von der östlich gelegenen Winzererstraße angefahren wird. Dieses Erschließungskonzept, das eine Trennung zwischen Fußgänger- und PKW-Verkehr vorsieht, erinnert eher an die 60er Jahre des 20. Jahrhunderts, bringt jedoch große Vorteile für das Außenraumkonzept.

Die einzelnen Häuser sind alle fünfgeschossig, wobei sich die beiden obersten Ebenen unregelmäßig zurückstaffeln – ähnlich wie bei den gleichzeitig entstandenen Häusern in Hamburg (siehe S. 100–105). Um die Orientierung der Wohnungen zu optimieren, sind die fünf südlichen Häuser tiefer ausgeführt und enthalten bis zu sechs Wohnungen pro Geschoß, während die fünf nördlichen nur bis zu vier Wohnungen enthalten. So wird die auf den ersten Blick erscheinende Symmetrie bei genauerer Betrachtung wieder aufgehoben.

Residential development, Olympiaberg, Munich, 1999–2002

The competition in 1995/96 set the task of creating a high-quality residential area on an undeveloped site on the grounds of the Munich Olympics.

Ten freestanding houses form a rigorous urban space, reserved only for pedestrians. At its centre is a flat pond, framed by trees. This image is based on that of a small town in Provence.

An underground, two-storey garage connects all houses to each other. Two ramps at the east, on Winzerstraße, provide access to this garage. While the separation of pedestrian and automobile traffic is somewhat of a throwback to the 1960s, it has big advantages in the planning of the exterior space.

The individual houses all have five storeys with the uppermost levels set back irregularly, similar to the residential buildings in Hamburg (see p. 100–105) that were constructed at the same time. In order to ensure the best possible orientation of the individual apartments, the five buildings to the south are deeper in plan and have up to six apartments on each storey, while the five buildings to the north only have up to four apartments. The symmetry that seems appar-

1. Vogelperspektive.

1. Bird's-eye view.

2. Schnitt.
3. Ort in der Provence. (Photo: Katharina Sattler.)

2. Section.
3. A scene from Provence. (Photo: Katharina Sattler.)

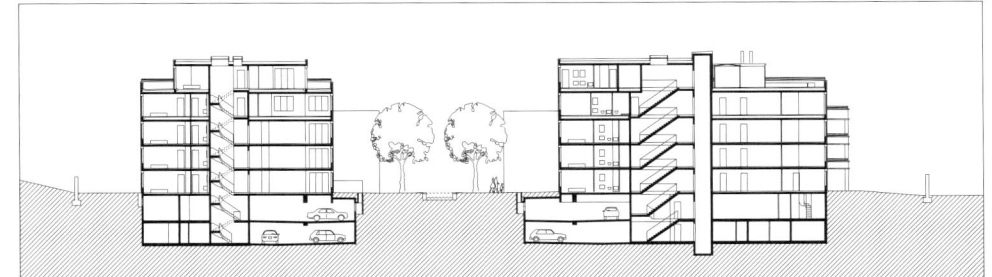

Wohnbebauung am Olympiaberg, München, 1999–2002

ent at first sight does not hold up to closer viewing.

All of the stairwells and almost all of the bathrooms are in the inner reaches of the buildings. This means that the buildings are relatively deep and that there is a good relationship between the surface area and volume. Most of the balconies are located at the corners of the buildings, which means that they are orientated in two directions.

The principle underlying the appearance of the façades is consciously based on an ambivalence between traditional architecture and modernity. On the ground floor the horizontal profiles in the plaster façades suggest a rustication and in the same way the white, wooden frames of the windows can be placed within a traditional canon of forms. On the other hand, this characteristic is

4, 5. Ansicht der Gebäude entlang des zentralen Wasserbeckens. (Photos: Stefan Müller.)

4, 5. View of the buildings along the water basin. (Photos: Stefan Müller.)

6. Grundriß (Erdgeschoß).
7. Luftbild. (Photo: Stefan Müller.)

6. Floor plan (ground floor).
7. Aerial view. (Photo: Stefan Müller.)

Sämtliche Treppenhäuser und fast alle Bäder sind im Hausinneren angeordnet, was die Häuser verhältnismäßig tief werden läßt und zu einer günstigen Relation zwischen Hüllfläche und Volumen führt. Die meisten Balkone liegen an den Hausecken, um sich dadurch nach zwei Seiten zu orientieren.

Das Gestaltungsprinzip der Fassaden will eine Ambivalenz zwischen traditioneller Architektur und Moderne bewußt aufbauen: Im Erdgeschoß sind die Putzfassaden als Andeutung einer Rustika horizontal profiliert, ebenso tragen die weißgestrichenen Holzfenster zu einem eher traditionellen Gestaltungskanon bei. Andererseits wird dieser Charakter durch die helle, fast südlich anmutende Fassadenfarbe und die konsequente Verwendung von Flachdächern wieder konterkariert.

Alle Rückstaffelungen der Geschosse dienen als Terrassen, deren gemauerte Brüstungen durch profilierte horizontale Bänder abgeschlossen werden – eben-

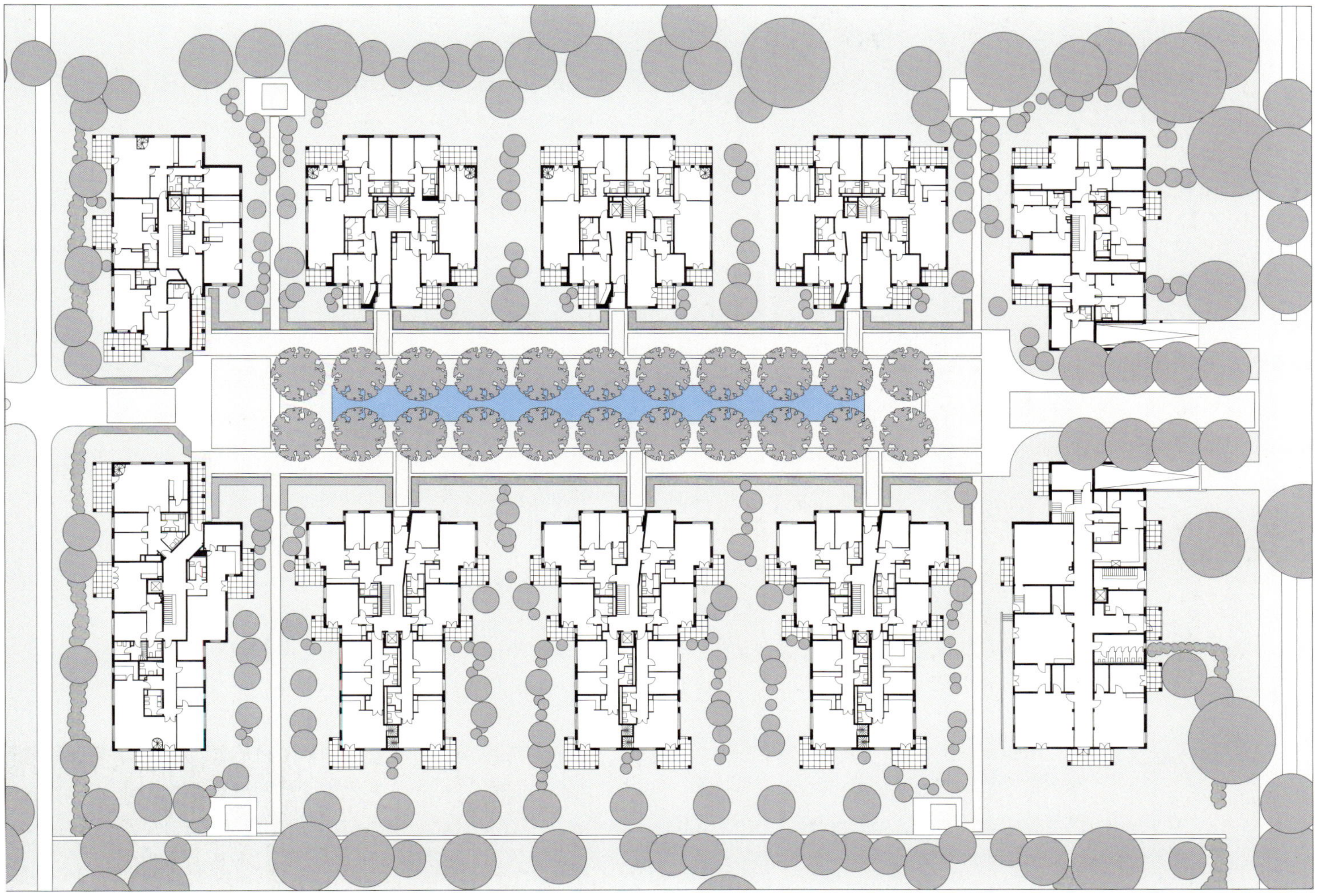

8. Ansicht der Anlage von Nordwesten. (Photo: Stefan Müller.)

8. View of the complex from the northwest. (Photo: Stefan Müller.)

9. Blick zwischen die Gebäude Richtung Norden. (Photo: Stefan Müller.)
10. Ansicht der Anlage von Süden. (Photo: Stefan Müller.)

9. View northwards between the buildings. (Photo: Stefan Müller.)
10. View of the complex from the south. (Photo: Stefan Müller.)

so wie der oberste Dachrand. Oberhalb der Brüstungen lassen gemauerte Pfeiler die Putzfassaden quasi in den Himmel auslaufen und erzeugen – trotz der großzügigen Befensterung – den eher massiven Charakter der Wohnanlage. Dies wird durch eine bewußte Vermeidung von filigranen Metallgeländern unterstützt und erinnert an frühe Arbeiten von Le Corbusier und Mallet-Stevens.

Fünf Jahre nach dem Wettbewerb mit eher städtebaulichem Schwerpunkt konnte der Entwurf architektonisch umgesetzt werden.

Projektleiter: Ulrich Greiler
Mitarbeiter: Daniel Türcke
Ausführungsplanung: Architekturbüro
Bernd Obersteiner

counteracted by the bright, almost southern-like colour of the façade and the consistent use of flat roofs.

All setbacks in the storeys serve as terraces. Profiled horizontal bands top off the masonry parapets on the terraces, in the same way as at the top edge of the roof. Above the masonry parapets the plaster façade is continued on with masonry columns and reaches, so to speak, into the sky. Despite the generous fenestration, this engenders the more massive character of the development. To support this impression, filigree metal railings have been deliberately avoided. The complex recalls the early work of Le Corbusier and Mallet-Stevens.

Five years after the competition, with its emphasis on town planning, the design found architectonic realization.

Project architect: Ulrich Greiler
Collaborator: Daniel Türcke
Working drawings: Architekturbüro Bernd Obersteiner

1. Blick auf Haus 5 und Haus 6 vom Hans-Dürr-meier-Weg. (Photo: Stefan Müller.)

1. View of house 5 and house 6 from Hans-Dürrmeier-Weg. (Photo: Stefan Müller.)

Drei Wohnhäuser auf der Theresienhöhe, München, 1999–2002

Der Masterplan von Otto Steidle sieht für das ehemalige Messegelände auf der Theresienhöhe rund um den Bavariapark für die Wohnbaugrundstücke freistehende, schachbrettartig gegeneinander versetzte, punktförmige Einzelgebäude vor.

Das Freistellen der Gebäude ermöglicht im Gegensatz zum geschlossenen Zeilenbau eine Rundumbefensterung nach allen Himmelsrichtungen mit optimalen Belichtungsmöglichkeiten. Auch der Grundrißgestaltung sind größere Freiräume gegeben.

Durch diese Vorgaben des Bebauungsplans wird die architektonische Gestalt der Wohnhäuser in Grund- und Aufriß deutlich mitgeprägt.

Haus 1 (Ben-Chorin-Straße 1): Das Normalgeschoß besteht aus vier Zweizimmerwohnungen, die sich jeweils an den Hausecken zu einem Balkon öffnen. Somit orientieren sich sowohl die Wohnungen als auch deren Balkone nach zwei Himmelsrichtungen. Ein minimiertes Treppenhaus mit Aufzug erschließt das Haus. Über den sieben gleichen Geschossen liegt das zurückgestaffelte Dachgeschoß mit einer großen Wohnung, die das Thema Terrasse in verschiedenen Varianten durchspielt: Eine schmale Terrasse ist zum Himmel offen, eine andere ist überdacht, geht aber in eine offene über, während die sie umschließende Wand mit ihren großen Öffnungen weiterläuft.

Alle Fassadendetails sind rechtwinklig und scharfkantig ausgebildet, die Hori-

Three residential buildings on the Theresienhöhe, Munich, 1999–2002

Otto Steidle's master plan for the former exhibition centre on the Theresienhöhe surrounding the Bavariapark envisages single, freestanding, detached houses laid out in a chequered pattern for the residential building sites.

As the buildings are freestanding, an all-round fenestration in all directions as well as excellent lighting could be realized. This would not be possible with terraced housing. There is also more leeway in the design of the floor plans.

2. Lageplan. 1, 5, 6 Hilmer & Sattler und Albrecht; 2, 4, 7, 8 Ortner & Ortner; 3, 9 Esplanade Süd, Mitte, Nord Steidle + Partner; 10 Krischanitz.

2. Site plan. 1, 5, 6 Hilmer & Sattler und Albrecht; 2, 4, 7, 8 Ortner & Ortner; 3, 9 Esplanade Süd, Mitte, Nord Steidle + Partner; 10 Krischanitz.

zontale ist das dominierende Element.

In den beiden untersten Geschossen weist die Fassade eine Putzstruktur auf, das erhöhte Erdgeschoß wird zusätzlich durch ein Gesimsband von den darüberliegenden Geschossen abgesetzt. Darüber sind die Fenster durch horizontale Brüstungs- und Sturzbänder miteinander verwoben.

Da die Fassade durch die beschriebenen Elemente eine starke plastische Differenzierung aufweist, wurde eine zurückhaltende Farbgebung gewählt.

Haus 5 (Ganghoferstraße 35): Inmitten von Gebäuden mit scharfkantigen, rechtwinkligen Konturen bildet dieses Haus mit seiner organisch geschwungenen Körperhaftigkeit einen bewußten Kontrast zu seinen Nachbarn ringsum. Während bei diesem Haus alle Horizontalen

3, 4. Ansicht Haus 1 von der Ben-Chorin-Straße. (Photos: Stefan Müller.)

3, 4. View of house 1 from Ben-Chorin-Straße. (Photos: Stefan Müller.)

5–7. Grundrisse Haus 1 (Erdgeschoß, Normalgeschoß, Dachgeschoß).
8. Blick auf Haus 1 vom Hans-Dürrmeier-Weg. (Photo: Stefan Müller.)

5–7. Floor plans house 1 (ground floor, typical floor, top floor).
8. View of house 1 from Hans-Dürrmeier-Weg. (Photo: Stefan Müller.)

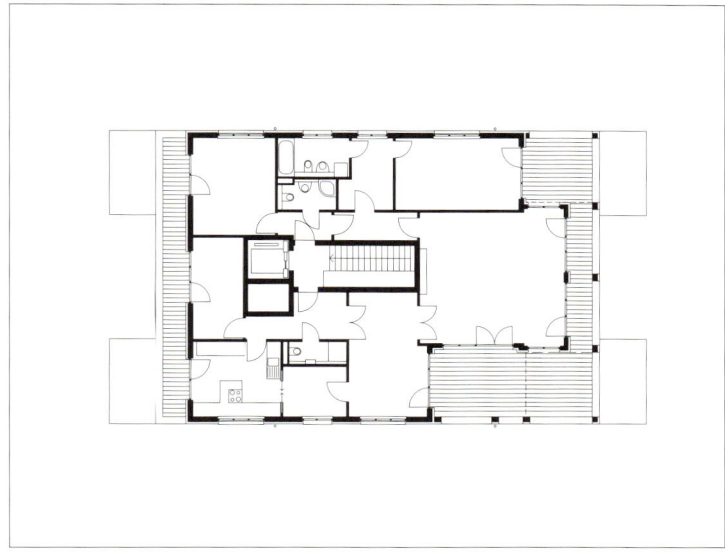

The architectural form of the residential buildings is clearly influenced by the requirements of the development plan both in plan and elevation.

House 1 (Ben-Chorin-Straße 1): The typical floor plan is made up of four two-room apartments each opening to balconies at the corners of the building. The apartments and their balconies are thereby orientated towards two directions. A minimized stairwell with an elevator provides internal access. Above the seven typical storeys the attic storey is set back with one large apartment, which plays with the theme of terrace in several variations. A small terrace is open to the sky; another is roofed over but merges into an uncovered terrace, while the surrounding wall with its large openings continues on its course.

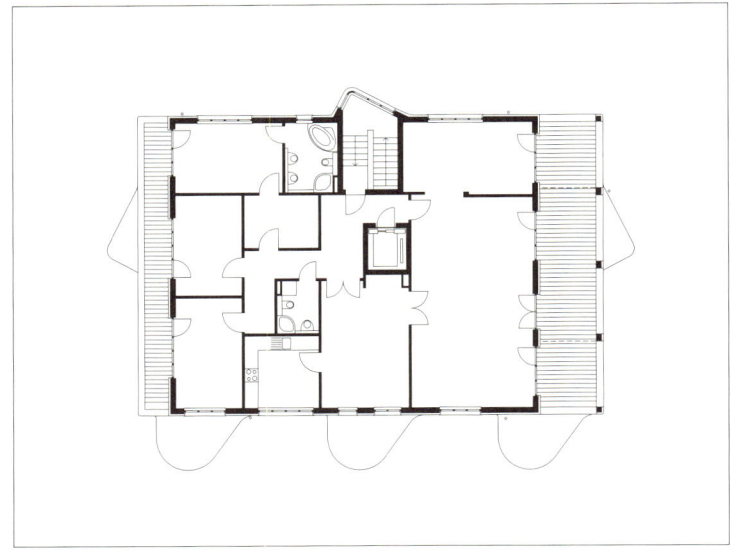

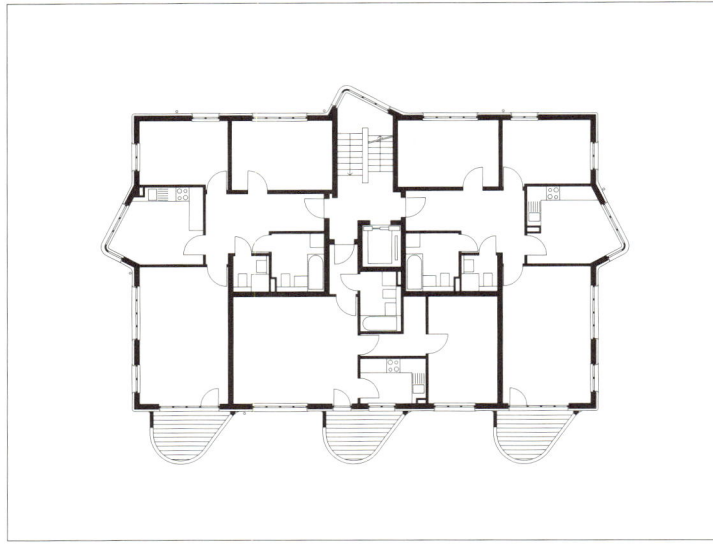

(Stürze und Fensterbänke) scharfkantig ausgebildet sind, sind die Vertikalen gerundet. Diese Ausrundung wird sichtbar erfahren durch den Schatten, den der Sturz auf die Leibung wirft. Die ansonsten unbeliebte »Thermohaut« hat diese plastische Fassadengestaltung ermöglicht.

Je Geschoß sind drei Wohnungen angeordnet. Den südorientierten Wohnräumen sind weit ausladende Balkone vorgelagert. Eine große Terrassenwohnung bildet den oberen Abschluß des Hauses.

Haus 6 (Hans-Dürrmeier-Weg 10): Die Mitte des Hauses bildet ein innenliegendes Treppenhaus mit oberer Belichtung. Von hier aus sind je Geschoß vier Wohnungen erschlossen, die sich übereck zu jeweils zwei Himmelsrichtungen orientieren. Auch hier bildet eine große Terrassenwohnung den oberen Abschluß des Hauses.

Horizontale Gesimse und vertikale Lisenen, deren Geometrie den inneren

9–11. Grundrisse Haus 5 (Erdgeschoß, Normalgeschoß, Dachgeschoß).
12. Ansicht Haus 5 vom Hans-Dürrmeier-Weg. (Photo: Stefan Müller.)

9–11. Floor plans house 5 (ground floor, typical floor, top floor).
12. View of house 5 from Hans-Dürrmeier-Weg. (Photo: Stefan Müller.)

13. Detailansicht der Fassade von Haus 5. (Photo: Stefan Müller.)

13. Detailed view of the façade of house 5. (Photo: Stefan Müller.)

All of the façade's details are right-angled with sharp edges. The horizontal line is the dominating element.

The façades of the two lower stories have a textured plaster finish. The raised ground floor is further set apart from the other storeys by a moulding. The windows above are interwoven by means of horizontal bands at sill and lintel level.

Because the described elements make strong plastic differentiations in the façade, a restrained colour was chosen.

House 5 (Ganghoferstraße 35): In the midst of buildings with sharp-edged and right angle contours, this building with its organic, curved corporeality forms a deliberate contrast to its surrounding neighbours. While all of the horizontal lines (lintels and window sills) on this building have sharp edges, the vertical lines have been rounded. This roundness can be seen in the shadow made by the lintel on the reveal. The otherwise unpopular rendered external insulation has made the plasticity of this façade possible.

On every storey there are three apartments. The rooms that face south have large, projecting balconies. A large apartment with terrace forms the top end of the building.

House 6 (Hans-Dürrmeier-Weg 10): An inner stairwell lit from above forms the centre of the building. From here, there is access at each storey to four apartments that are orientated in two directions around the corner of the building. Here too a large apartment with terrace forms the top end of the building. Depending on the time of day, the horizontal and vertical mouldings – whose geometry reflects the building's inner construction – create different effects of light and shadow on the façade and make this building utterly unique and distinctive. This subdivision is further

14. Ansicht Haus 6 von Süden. (Photo: Stefan Müller.)
15. Ansicht Haus 6 von Westen. (Photo: Stefan Müller.)

16–18. Grundrisse (Erdgeschoß, Normalgeschoß, Dachgeschoß).
19. Ansicht Haus 6 vom Hans-Dürrmeier-Weg. (Photo: Stefan Müller.)

14. View of house 6 from the south. (Photo: Stefan Müller.)
15. View of house 6 from the west. (Photo: Stefan Müller.)

16–18. Floor plans (ground floor, typical floor, top floor).
19. View of house 6 from Hans-Dürrmeier-Weg. (Photo: Stefan Müller.)

Aufbau des Hauses widerspiegelt, erzeugen je nach Sonnenstand wechselnde Licht- und Schattenwirkungen auf der Fassade und geben dem Haus eine unverwechselbare spezifische Eigenart. Diese Gliederung wird noch verstärkt durch die Farbgebung, welche die einzelnen Elemente voreinander absetzt.

Projektleiter: Daniel Türcke
Mitarbeiter: Daniel Kahala, Barbara Schindhelm
Ausführungsplanung: Architekturbüro Bernd Obersteiner

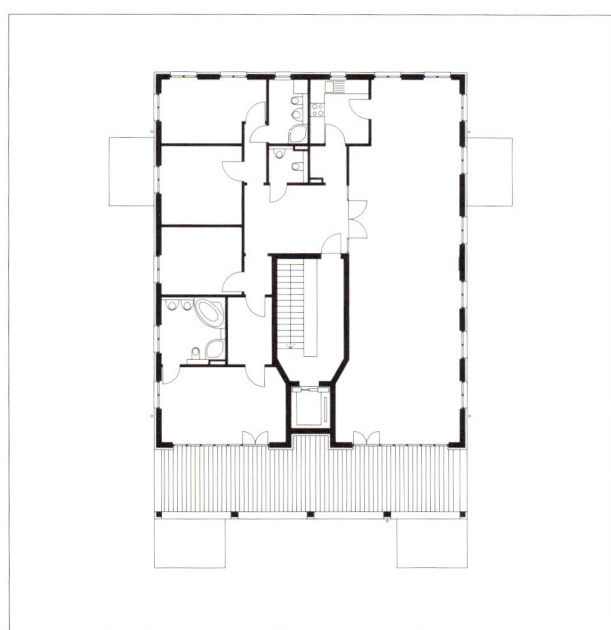

emphasized by the colour concept that separates the individual elements from each other.

Project architect: Daniel Türcke
Collaborators: Daniel Kahala, Barbara Schindhelm
Working drawings: Bernd Obersteiner Architects

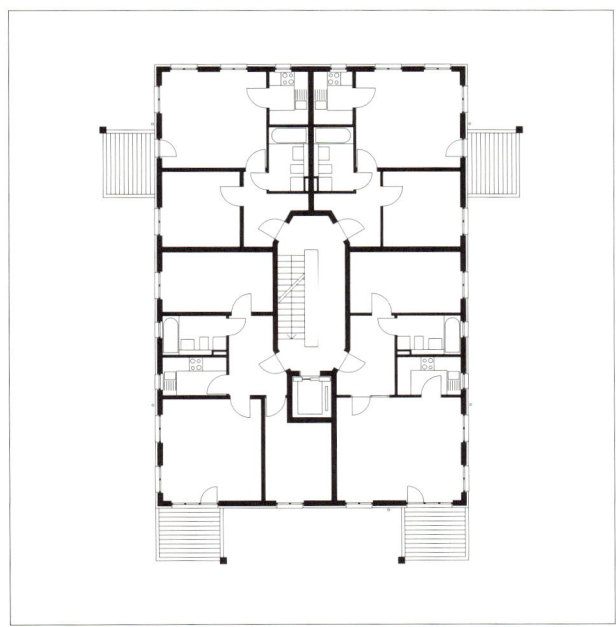

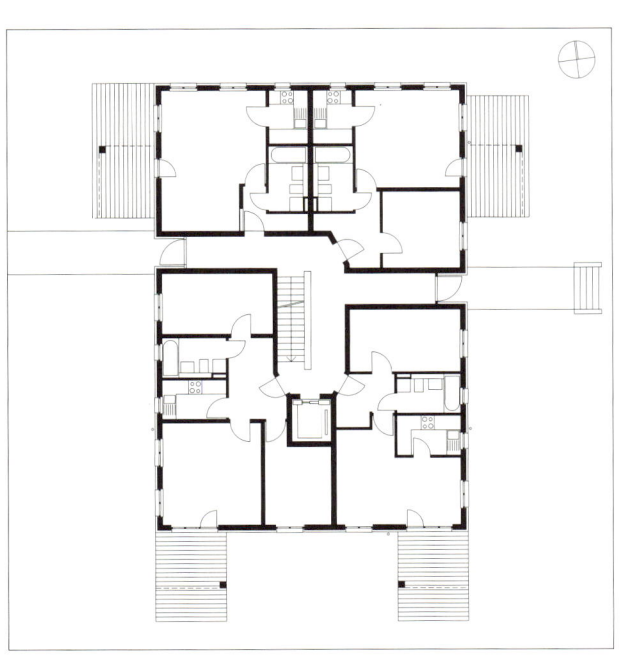

Wohn- und Geschäftshaus Salvatorstraße, Fünf Höfe, München, 1999–2003

Ein Architektenwettbewerb hatte im Jahr 1994 dieses vier Hektar große Grundstück in bester Lage der Münchner Innenstadt zum Thema. Dieses hochwertige und intensiv genutzte Quartier direkt an der Fußgängerzone war mit Nachkriegsbauten verdichtet, die nicht mehr den heutigen Sicherheitsbestimmungen entsprachen, so daß sich die Eigentümerin, die damalige Bayerische Hypotheken- und Wechsel-Bank, entschloß, unter Erhalt der historischen Bausubstanz das Ensemble neu fassen zu lassen.

Das Schweizer Büro Herzog & de Meuron erhielt den ersten Preis und wurde mit der Erstellung des sogenannten Masterplans beauftragt. Dessen städtebauliches Konzept orientierte sich an der nur dreihundert Meter östlich gelegenen Münchner Residenz, die ebenfalls eine spannungsreiche Abfolge von räumlich unterschiedlichen Höfen besitzt. Im Laufe der weiteren Bearbeitung veränderte sich das architektonische Konzept aber immer mehr zu einem kommerziellen Ansatz, der in der endgültigen Fassung hauptsächlich überdachte Passagen und kaum noch offene Höfe in den direkten Verkehrswegen der Fußgänger aufweist. Der attraktivste Bezugspunkt des Quartiers ist die 1985 eröffnete Hypo-Kunsthalle. Um sie herum bilden die Passagen und Höfe ein erlebnisreiches Ensemble mit verschiedensten Nutzungen: Läden, Cafés, Restaurants, Büros und auch Wohnungen. In ihrer belebten Dichte erinnern

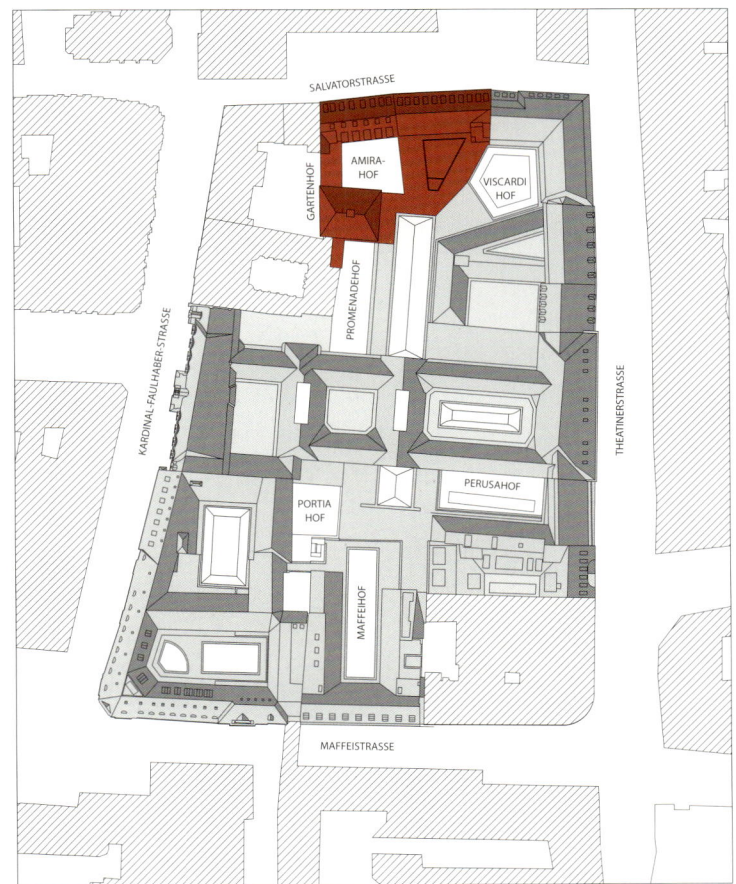

Residential and commercial building, Salvatorstraße, Fünf Höfe (Five Courtyards), Munich, 1999–2003

2. Lageplan.

2. Site plan.

In 1994 there was an architectural competition for this site with an area of approximately four hectares in a choice location in Munich's inner city. This high-quality quarter, in direct proximity to the pedestrian zone, is used intensively. After the War it had been heavily developed with buildings that no longer conformed to contemporary regulations and its owner at the time, the Bayerische Hypotheken- und Wechsel-Bank, decided that while the historic building sub-

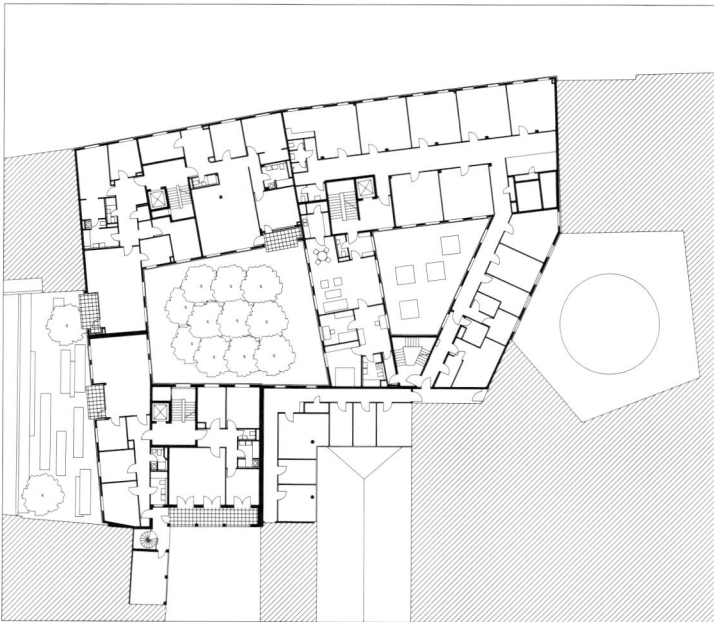

3, 4. Grundrisse (Erd-
geschoß, Normalge-
schoß).

3, 4. Floor plans
(ground floor, typical
floor).

sie an die Innenstadt von Verona, auch
wenn die Flucht vor der Sonne hierzu-
lande durch die vor Dauerregen ersetzt
wird.

Drei Architekturbüros haben die einzelnen Flächen in diesem Quartier realisiert: die Wettbewerbssieger Herzog &
de Meuron, der Tessiner Architekt Ivano
Gianola und wir. Unsere Aufgabe war
das Haus zur Salvatorstraße, bestehend
aus einem Bauteil mit Wohn- und einem

stance should be retained, the ensemble
should be renewed.

The Swiss firm Herzog & de Meuron
received first prize and was commissioned to draw up the so-called master
plan. Their urban concept orientated
itself towards Munich's former royal
residence. Lying only three hundred
metres to the east, it also has an interesting sequence of spatially differing courtyards. In the course of further work,

Residential and commercial building Salvatorstraße, Fünf Höfe, Munich, 1999–2003

5, 6. Detailansichten
der Fassade des Büro-
und des Wohnhauses.
(Photos: Stefan Müller.)

5, 6. Detailed views of
the façade of the office
and residential build-
ing. (Photos: Stefan
Müller.)

however, commercial interests took precedence over the architectonic concept. This is clearly evident in the final version with its covered arcades and almost no open courtyards for pedestrians. The most attractive reference point in the quarter is the Hypo-Kunsthalle (art museum) that opened in 1985. The arcades and courtyards that surround this museum make up a lively ensemble that serves different purposes – cafés, restaurants, offices as well as apartments. Its animated, compact atmosphere reminds one of Verona, even if in this country one flees from the rain and not from the sun.

Three architectural firms were responsible for individual areas in this quarter; the winners of the competition, Herzog & de Meuron, the Tessin architect Ivano Gianola and ourselves. Our commission was the building facing Salvatorstraße, consisting of a part for residential use and a part for office use in the upper storeys, with light finely profiled plaster façades, as well as the Amirahof. In a time of ventilated façades we were happy to be involved in this, a theme typical to Munich. On the other side of the street is the powerful building for the cloister of St Kajetan with the Theatinerkirche. Its strongly structured plaster façade is an almost Eichendorffian reference to a yearning for Italy, a land not so far away.

Project architect: Fritz Treugut
Collaborators: Peter Adrian, Gerhard Bolkart, Ulrich Greiler, Ulrik Hinze, Christian Winter

mit Büronutzung in den Obergeschossen, mit hellen, fein profilierten Putzfassaden, sowie der Amirahof. In einer Zeit der hinterlüfteten Fassaden waren wir froh, uns mit diesem typisch Münchner Thema beschäftigen zu können. Auf der gegenüberliegenden Straßenseite befindet sich der mächtige Klosterbau St. Kajetan mit der Theatinerkirche, deren reich gegliederte Putzfassade einen geradezu Eichendorffschen Bezug auf das nicht ferne Sehnsuchtsland Italien bildet.

Projektleiter: Fritz Treugut
Mitarbeiter: Peter Adrian, Gerhard Bolkart, Ulrich Greiler, Ulrik Hinze, Christian Winter

7. Der Passagenein-
gang. (Photo: Stefan
Müller.)

7. The entrance to the
arcade. (Photo: Stefan
Müller.)

8. Ansicht des Gebäu-
des vom Promenade-
hof. (Photo: Stefan
Müller.)
9. Ansicht des Gebäu-
des vom Amirahof.
(Photo: Stefan Müller.)

8. View of the building
from the Promenade-
hof. (Photo: Stefan
Müller.)
9. View of the building
from the Amirahof.
(Photo: Stefan Müller.)

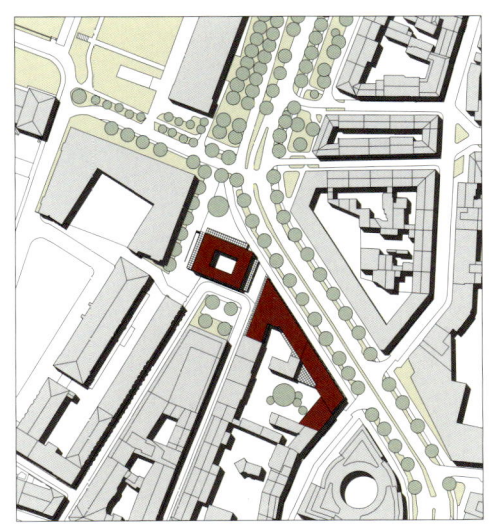

Bürohäuser am Karl-Scharnagl-Ring, München, 1999–2003

Die platzartige Aufweitung des Karl-Scharnagl-Rings vor der Bayerischen Staatskanzlei erhält einen südlichen Abschluß durch einen achtgeschossigen Turm. Die Fortsetzung des Altstadtrings in südlicher Richtung wird durch ein zweites Bürogebäude als Straßenraum gefaßt. Das Ensemble ist somit ein Beitrag zum Thema »Stadtarchitektur«.

Das achtgeschossige Turmgebäude weist einen Rücksprung der Fassaden über dem fünften Obergeschoß auf. An allen vier Gebäudeseiten entstehen dort unterschiedlich tiefe Terrassenflächen. Zur Steigerung seiner Prägnanz hat es nach Norden einen zweigeschossigen Eingang, der in den überdachten, acht Geschosse hohen Innenhof führt. Dieser läßt alle Nutzer des Hauses an seiner räumlichen Wirkung teilhaben.

Das ca. 100 m lange, sechsgeschossige Gebäude staffelt sich in der angrenzenden Nebenstraße gemäß den baulichen

Office buildings, Karl-Scharnagl-Ring, Munich, 1999–2003

The expansion of the Karl-Scharnagl-Ring in front of the Bavarian State Chancellery, square-like in character, recieves a southern boundary through an eight-storey tower. A second office building borders the street space that continues the ring road around the old part of the city in a southern direction. The ensemble can thereby be understood as making a contribution to the theme of »urban architecture«.

The eight-storey tower building has a setback on the façades above the fifth storey. All four sides of the building will have terraced surfaces of varying depths. The building's succinctness is heightened by its northern, two-storey en-

1. Perspektive der beiden Gebäude vom Karl-Scharnagl-Ring.

1. Perspective of both buildings from Karl-Scharnagl-Ring.

2. Lageplan.
3. Ansicht der beiden Gebäude vom Karl-Scharnagl-Ring. (Photo: Stefan Müller.)

2. Site plan.
3. View of both buildings from Karl-Scharnagl-Ring. (Photo: Stefan Müller.)

4. Ansicht des sechs-
geschossigen Gebäu-
des an der Einmün-
dung der Herzog-Ru-
dolf-Straße in den Karl-
Scharnagl-Ring. (Pho-
to: Stefan Müller.)
5. Ansicht des sechs-
geschossigen Gebäu-
des vom Karl-Schar-
nagl-Ring. (Photo: Ste-
fan Müller.)

4. View of the six-sto-
rey building at the
junction of Herzog-
Rudolf-Straße and
Karl-Scharnagl-Ring.
(Photo: Stefan Müller.)
5. View of the six-sto-
rey building from Karl-
Scharnagl-Ring. (Pho-
to: Stefan Müller.)

6. Ansicht des Turm-
gebäudes vom Karl-
Scharnagl-Ring. (Pho-
to: Stefan Müller.)
7. Grundriß (Erdge-
schoß).

6. View of the tower
building from Karl-
Scharnagl-Ring. (Pho-
to: Stefan Müller.)
7. Floor plan (ground
floor).

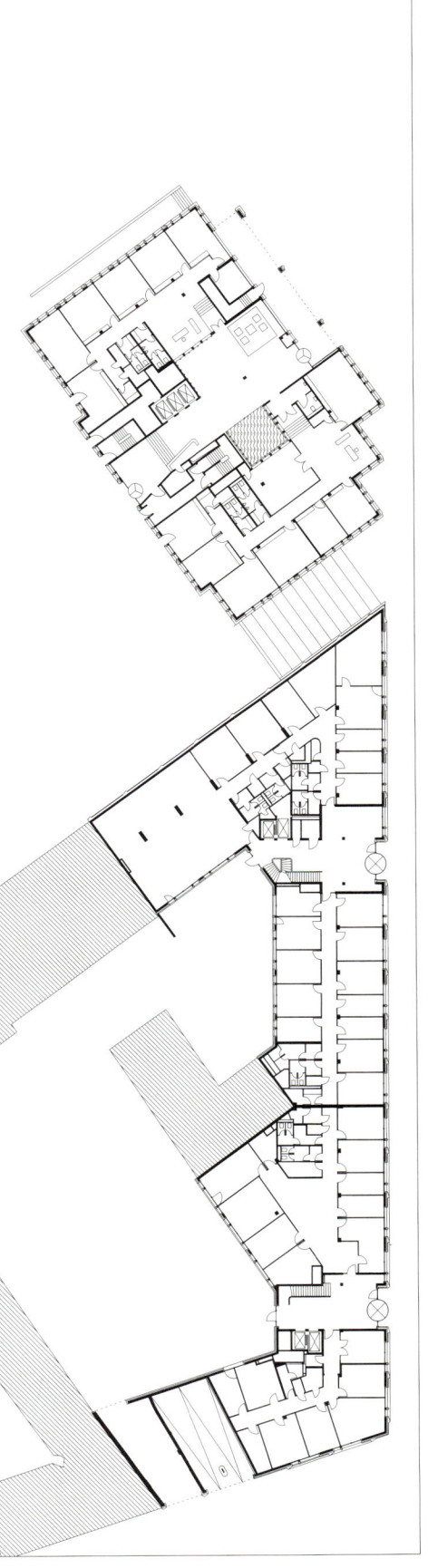

Gegebenheiten auf fünf Geschosse ab, wobei zwei separate Eingangssituationen dem Haus die notwendige Flexibilität verleihen.

Beide Gebäude sind mit Terrakottasteinen verkleidet, wie das bis in die angrenzende Maximilianstraße wirkende Gebäude des Bayerischen Landtags, das Maximilianeum. Die beiden Häuser zeigen, trotz hohem Glasanteil, architektonische Masse und stehen im bewußten Gegensatz zur benachbarten Glas- und Blecharchitektur. Die Stützen des niedrigeren Gebäudes sind ungewöhnlicherweise asymmetrisch profiliert. Im Turmhaus dominieren weiche, gerundete Ecken, während das flachere Haus scharfkantige Profile zeigt, so daß sich ein feiner Strukturunterschied herausbildet.

trance that leads into the covered inner courtyard of eight storeys. This courtyard allows everyone who makes use of the building to participate in the spatial impression that it makes.

The other six-storey building, c. 100 m in length, is staggered over five storeys according to the existing structural conditions in the adjoining side street. Two separate entrances give the building the necessary flexibility.

Both of the buildings are clad in terracotta facing, as is the case with the Maximilianeum, the Bayerische Landtag (Bavarian state parliament), that still has an effect on the bordering Maximilianstraße. Despite their high proportion of glass, both buildings exhibit architectonic mass and are in conscious contrast to the neighbouring glass and metal

8. Ansicht des sechs-
geschossigen Gebäu-
des von der Herzog-
Rudolf-Straße. (Photo:
Stefan Müller.)

8. View of the six-sto-
rey building from Her-
zog-Rudolf-Straße.
(Photo: Stefan Müller.)

9. Ansicht des Turmgebäudes vom Karl-Scharnagl-Ring. (Photo: Stefan Müller.)

9. View of the tower building from Karl-Scharnagl-Ring. (Photo: Stefan Müller.)

Durch Kastenfenster – außen Metall, innen Holz – wird sowohl der Lärmschutz gewährleistet als auch der Energiehaushalt des Gebäudes optimiert. Ein transluzenter Sonnenschutz liegt im Zwischenraum des Kastenfensters.

Projektleiter: Christian Winter
Mitarbeiter: Veronika Barth, Jan Faller, Natalie Friedrich, Janka-Karita Guhl, Sabine Krause, Nina Otto, Jan Pautzke, Barbara Schindhelm, Volker Schmid, Alexandra Stepanienko, Martin Waldorf

cladding architecture. The supports of the lower building are unusual in the asymmetry of their profiles. In the tower building soft, rounded corners dominate, while the flatter building has profiles with sharp angles. The two buildings exhibit refined structural differences.

Double-layer windows, metal on the outside and wooden on the inside, ensure noise reduction as well as allowing for the optimum use of energy. A translucent sun screen lies in the space between the two layers.

Project architect: Christian Winter
Collaborators: Veronika Barth, Jan Faller, Natalie Friedrich, Janka-Karita Guhl, Sabine Krause, Nina Otto, Jan Pautzke, Barbara Schindhelm, Volker Schmid, Alexandra Stepanienko, Martin Waldorf

10. Detailansicht der Fassade des Turmgebäudes. (Photo: Stefan Müller.)

10. Detailed view of the façade of the tower building. (Photo: Stefan Müller.)

11. Ansicht des sechsgeschossigen Gebäudes vom Karl-Scharnagl-Ring. (Photo: Stefan Müller.)

12. Detailansicht der Fassade des sechsgeschossigen Gebäudes. (Photo: Stefan Müller.)

11. View of the six-storey building from Karl-Scharnagl-Ring. (Photo: Stefan Müller.)

12. Detailed view of the façade of the six-storey building. (Photo: Stefan Müller.)

143

13. Blick in den Durch-
gang zwischen den
Gebäuden. (Photo:
Stefan Müller.)
14. Ansicht der beiden
Gebäude von der Mar-
stallstraße. (Photo: Ste-
fan Müller.)

13. View into the pas-
sageway between the
buildings. (Photo:
Stefan Müller.)
14. View of both build-
ings from Marstall-
straße. (Photo: Stefan
Müller.)

15. Blick aus einem
Büroraum in das Atri-
um. (Photo: Stefan
Müller.)
16. Das Atrium. (Pho-
to: Stefan Müller.)

15. View from an office
into the atrium. (Pho-
to: Stefan Müller.)
16. The atrium. (Photo:
Stefan Müller.)

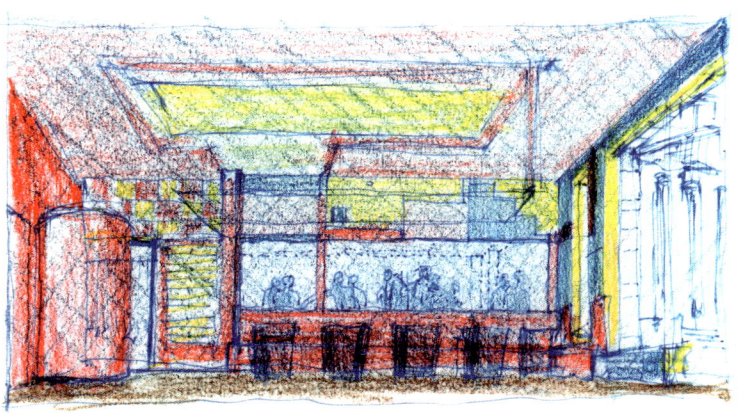

925 Lounge Bar, Berlin-Mitte, 2000

Die Aufgabe bestand darin, eine ausgesprochene Nachtbar zu entwerfen, die eine starke Außenwirkung hat und sozusagen ihre Fenster als Werbeträger benutzt.

Der Innenraum befindet sich an einer Blockecke mit drei 6,2 m breiten Fenstern und öffnet sich zum Gendarmenmarkt.

Die Bar selbst muß im Inneren so dunkel sein, daß neben dem beleuchteten Tresen nur das draußen auf dem Gendarmenmarkt stehende, nachts immer hell angestrahlte Schauspielhaus von Karl Friedrich Schinkel optisch eine Rolle spielt.

Ein der Theaterarchitektur entlehntes Dach schwebt über dem Tresen in der Mitte des Raumes. Es erinnert an den französischen Architekten Mallet-Stevens. Die Tresenoberfläche ist mit 925 Sterling Silber belegt.

Die Wand- und Deckenoberflächen sind als unregelmäßig versetzte Ebenen gestaltet, alles ist im korallenroten Farbton gehalten.

Wenige, unauffällige Lichtakzente hinter dunkelblauen Tafeln halten das Auge im fast düsteren Licht bei 35 Lux in Bewegung, so daß sich die Aufmerksamkeit des Gastes auf die silberne Tresenoberfläche und die Silhouetten der anderen Barbesucher vor der beleuchteten Kulisse der beiden Gontardschen Dome und des Schinkelschen Schauspielhauses richtet.

Projektleiter: Sigurd Hauer
Mitarbeiter: Ruth Schroers

925 Lounge Bar, Berlin-Mitte, 2000

The task was to design a real bar that made a strong impression on the world outside and so to speak used its windows to advertise itself.

The interior is located at the corner of a block opening to the Gendarmenmarkt. It has three windows, each 6,2 m wide.

The interior has to be so dark that apart from its lit counter, the only visual role is played by Karl Friedrich Schinkel's Schauspielhaus. Located on the Gendarmenmarkt, it is always illuminated at night.

A roof indebted to stage architecture hangs above the bar in the middle of the room. It calls the French architect Mallet-Stevens to mind. The counter's surface has been covered with 925 sterling silver.

The surfaces of the walls and ceilings are in irregularly staggered levels. Everything is in coral red.

A few, unobtrusive lighting accents behind dark-blue panels keep the eye moving in the interior's almost gloomy light of 35 lux. The guest's attention is thereby drawn towards the silver surface of the counter and the silhouettes of the other visitors to the bar in front of the illuminated backdrop of Gontard's cathedrals and Schinkel's Schauspielhaus.

Project architect: Sigurd Hauer
Collaborator: Ruth Schroers

Wohn- und Geschäftshaus Leipziger Platz 8, Berlin-Mitte, 2000–03

Mit diesem Gebäude hatten wir die Möglichkeit, die Intentionen unseres eigenen städtebaulichen Masterplans für den Leipziger Platz von 1991 in ei-nem Gebäude nun auch architektonisch aus-zudrücken. Durch die eng gefaßten Vor-gaben ist das kleinste Haus am Platz räumlich fast vollständig vorgegeben.

Alle Geschosse unterhalb der histori-schen Traufhöhe von 22 m werden ge-werblich genutzt. An dieser Stelle springt die Fassade um 2 m zurück und verdeut-

Residential and commercial building Leipziger Platz 8, Berlin-Mitte, 2000–03

With this building we had the chance to give architectural expression to the intentions behind our own urban devel-opment master plan of 1991 for Leipzi-ger Platz. Because of the rigorous guide-lines the smallest building on the square was spatially almost completely pre-de-termined.

All of the storeys under the historic eaves' height of 22 m are for commercial purposes. After this point the façade is set back 2 m, thereby not only clearly indicating the discontinuity between the historic eaves' height and the modern one of 35 m, but also that the upper four storeys are used for residential purposes.

A light sandstone has been used for all of the buildings on the square and we have used a Spanish Bateig. Because of the stipulated uniformity of the build-ings, the architects were given the won-derful chance to express themselves sole-ly in the variations and refinements on the façades. For our theme we chose an inwardly curving façade.

With its flat moulding, the two sto-reys of the base form a zone that recedes inwards. In the right-hand area is a two-storey foyer whose full height can be viewed from outside through an exten-sive bronze window. A deliberate proxim-ity to models from the late 19th century (Gründerjahre) is evident in the wall covering of natural stone and in the stairway to the upper storey that is func-tionally actually not necessary. Above the foyer lie five storeys of offices with tall French windows. Each storey has been

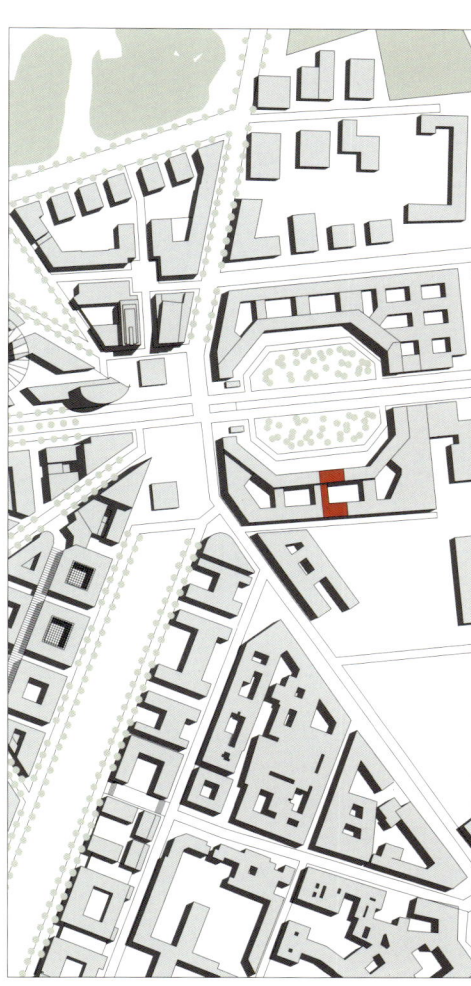

1. Perspektive der Fas-sade vom Leipziger Platz.

2. Fassadenausschnitt. (Photo: Stefan Müller.)
3. Lageplan.

1. Perspective view of the façade from Leip-ziger Platz.

2. Part elevation. (Pho-to: Stefan Müller.)
3. Site plan.

Wohn- und Geschäftshaus Leipziger Platz 8,
Berlin-Mitte, 2000–03

4. Ansicht des Gebäudes vom Leipziger Platz. (Photo: Stefan Müller.)

4. View of the building from Leipziger Platz. (Photo: Stefan Müller.)

licht so nicht nur den Bruch zwischen
der historischen und modernen Traufhöhe von 35 m, sondern auch den der
Nutzung, die in den obersten vier Geschossen dem Wohnen vorbehalten
ist.

Sämtliche Gebäude am Platz sind in
einem hellen Sandstein gehalten, in
unserem Falle in spanischem Bateig.
Durch die vorgegebene Gleichheit aller
Häuser haben die Architekten die wunderbare Chance, sich lediglich in den
Variationen und Verfeinerungen des Fassadenreliefs auszudrücken – wir wählten
als Thema die nach innen geschwungene Fassade.

Der zweigeschossige Sockel wird als
flach profilierte, lediglich nach innen
zurückspringende Zone ausgebildet. Im
rechten Feld ist ein zweigeschossiges
Foyer angeordnet, das in seiner ganzen
Höhe durch großflächige Bronzefenster
von außen eingesehen werden kann. Mit
seiner Wandverkleidung aus Naturstein
und der funktional nicht wirklich notwendigen Treppe ins Obergeschoß sucht
es die Nähe zu gründerzeitlichen Vorbil-
dern. Die fünf darüber liegenden Bürogeschosse mit hohen französischen Fenstern gliedern sich pro Geschoß in vier
leicht nach innen gewölbte Felder. Jedes
dieser konkaven Felder ist wiederum
durch zwei 20 cm schmale, gerundete
Sandsteinstützen dreigeteilt. Der Übergang zwischen den vierachsigen Obergeschossen und der darunter liegenden
dreiachsigen Sockelzone ist ein bewuß-
ter Bruch der Tektonik.

Hier befindet sich auch der formal
anspruchsvollste Punkt der Fassade:
durch eine komplexe Geometrie der
Steinoberfläche wird ein weicher Übergang von der geraden Wand zu den vier
konkaven Fassadenfeldern erreicht.

Zur deutlichen Unterscheidung
haben die Wohnetagen zwar dieselbe
steinerne, konkave Fassadenstruktur wie

divided into four areas that project
slightly inwards. Each of these concave
areas has been in turn divided into three
parts by two narrow, rounded sandstone
supports of 20 cm. The transition between the four axes of the upper storeys
and the three axes of the socle zone that
lies beneath them is a deliberate break
in the tectonic.

In formal terms this is the most ambitious part of the façade. A soft transition
from the straight wall to the four concave façade areas is achieved through the
complex geometry of the stone surfaces.

A clear distinction has been made in
the façades of the residential storeys, for
although these have the same stone concave structure as the office storeys, their
different purpose is made clear by the
slight outward projection of the narrow,
bronze balconies. In the uppermost resi-

5. Fassadenausschnitt.
(Photo: Stefan Müller.)

5. Part elevation. (Pho-
to: Stefan Müller.)

151

Wohn- und Geschäftshaus Leipziger Platz 8,
Berlin-Mitte, 2000–03

6. Detailansicht der Fassade. (Photo: Stefan Müller.)

6. Detailed view of the façade. (Photo: Stefan Müller.)

7–9. Grundrisse (Erdgeschoß, Normalgeschoß) und Schnitt. 10. Fassadenausschnitt. (Photo: Stefan Müller.)

7–9. Floor plans (ground floor, typical floor) and section. 10. Part elevation. (Photo: Stefan Müller.)

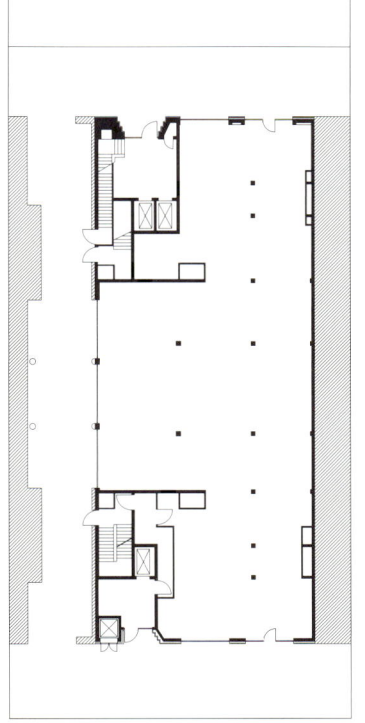
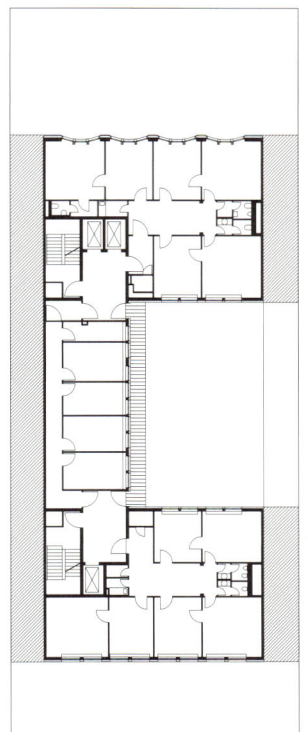

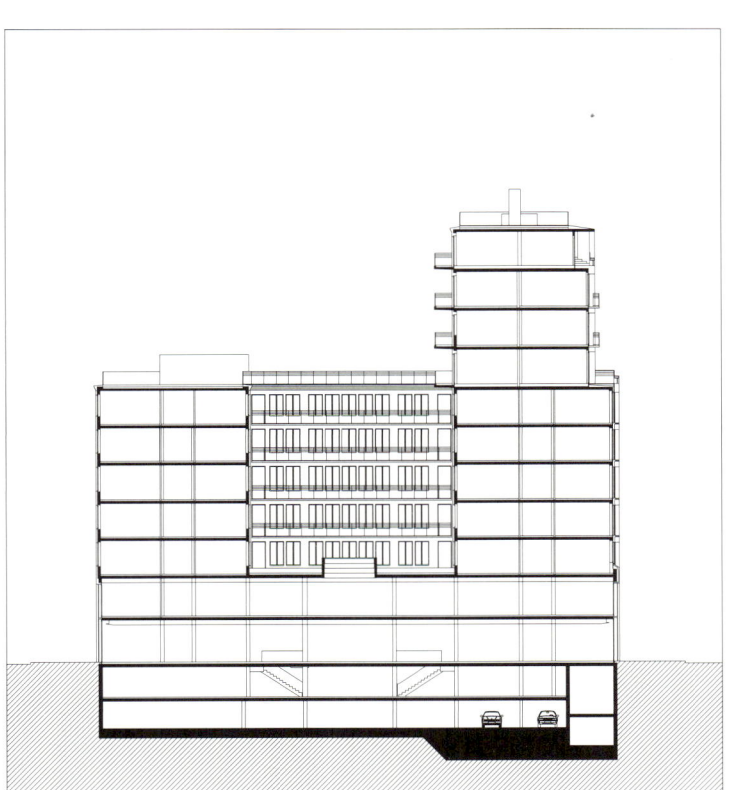

die Bürogeschosse, die andere Nutzung wird jedoch verdeutlicht durch die leicht nach außen gewölbten, schmalen bronzenen Austritte. In der obersten Wohnetage löst sich die Wand in fünf Stützen und einen horizontalen Balken auf. Dahinter ist eine in die Tiefe gestaffelte Loggia ausgebildet. Der lineare Balken, der als Motiv auch beim Rücksprung drei Etagen tiefer vorhanden ist, besteht aus massiv erscheinenden Steinquadern und steht in einem räumlichen Spannungsverhältnis zu den konkaven Fassadenfeldern.

Projektleiter: Peter Westermann
Mitarbeiter: Frauke Blasy, Sigurd Hauer,
Peter O'Callaghan, Peter Solhdju, Frigga
Uhlisch, Nadine Zietlow
Ausführungsplanung: Architekturbüro
Volkhausen + Lubkoll

dential storey the wall disperses into five supports and a horizontal beam. Behind this is a loggia with a staggered depth. The linear beam, already present as a motif in the set-back three storeys below and made apparently of solid stone blocks, maintains a spatially tense relationship to the concave façade areas.

Project architect: Peter Westermann
Collaborators: Frauke Blasy, Sigurd Hauer,
Peter O'Callaghan, Peter Solhdju, Frigga
Uhlisch, Nadine Zietlow
Working drawings: Volkhausen + Lubkoll
Architects

11–13. Die Lobby. (Photos: Stefan Müller.)

11–13. The lobby. (Photos: Stefan Müller.)

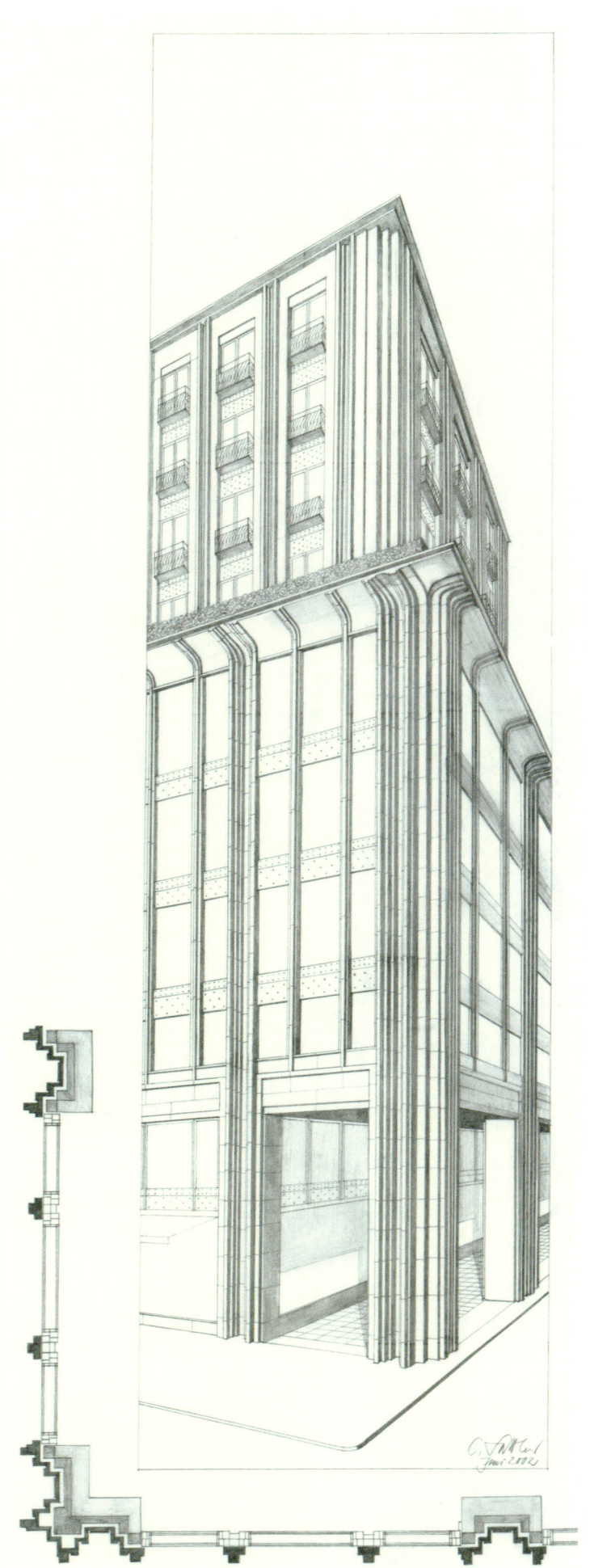

Leipziger Platz Carrée, Berlin-Mitte, 2002–05

Das Kaufhaus Wertheim des großen Berliner Architekten Alfred Messel von 1904 gehörte zu den wichtigsten Berliner Gebäuden vor 1945. Der ehemalige Anbau und Abschluß des Kaufhauskomplexes an der Ecke Leipziger Platz und Leipziger Straße hatte gemäß dem Zeitgeschmack stark gotisierende Züge.

Im Jahr 2001 wurde ein Wettbewerb für einen Neubau an dieser Stelle ausgeschrieben. Wir schlugen eine Neuinterpretation vor, die einerseits den Messelschen Geist wiederaufleben läßt, andererseits aber den Richtlinien unseres eigenen Masterplans folgt, der einen zweiten, höher gelegenen Bauteil von vier Wohngeschossen oberhalb der historischen Blockstruktur fordert.

Der heutige Neubau ist in seiner räumlichen und funktionalen Disposition komplett festgelegt: Im Erdgeschoß

Leipziger Platz Carrée, Berlin-Mitte, 2002–05

The Wertheim department store designed by the great Berlin architect Alfred Messel in 1904 belonged to the most important of Berlin's buildings before 1945. In accordance with the taste of the times, the former department store complex on the corner of Leipziger Platz and Leipziger Straße had marked, Gothic-like features.

In 2001 a competition for a new building at this location was held. We proposed a new interpretation that would on the one hand revive the spirit of Messel but on the other hand would also follow the guidelines of our own master plan, which called for the second part of a building of four residential storeys to be placed above the historic block structure.

The spatial and functional disposition of the new building has been precisely stipulated. On the ground floor and the mezzanine there are stores and a two-storey loggia onto Leipziger street, then four storeys of offices to the set-back that is 22 m high. On top of this are four residential storeys. The primary colour for all of the buildings on Leipziger Platz – a light, beige natural stone – was also pre-determined. The only opportunity for architectonic creativity – an opportunity that thereby becomes all the more interesting – lies in the formation of the façade details.

Gothic-like piers with stark vertical profiles, stepped backwards, create an interplay of light and shadow. The cornice's profile projects upwards to a

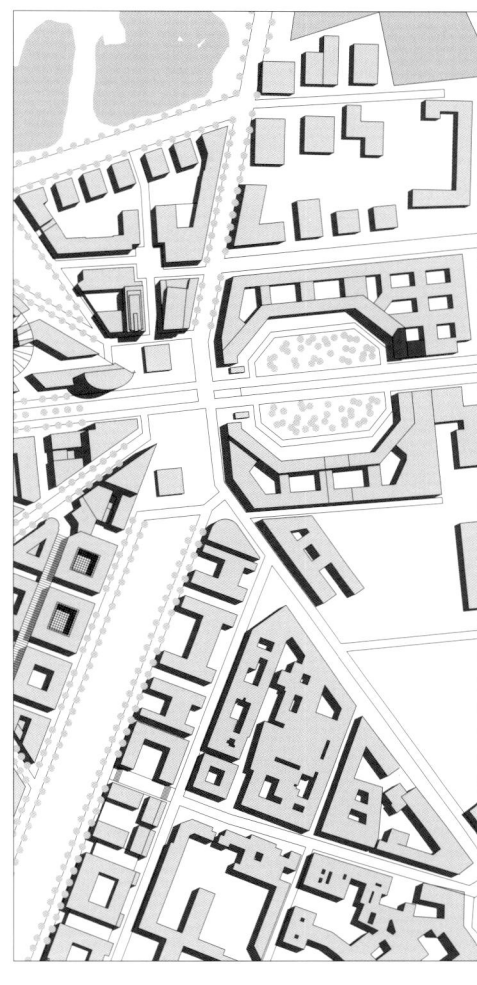

1. Perspektive der Gebäudeecke Leipziger Platz / Leipziger Straße.

1. Perspective view of the corner at Leipziger Platz / Leipziger Straße.

2. Alfred Messel, Kaufhaus Wertheim, Berlin-Mitte, 1904.
3. Lageplan.

2. Alfred Messel, Wertheim department store, Berlin-Mitte, 1904.
3. Site plan.

4. Detailschnitt durch die Gebäudeecke.
5. Grundriß (Erdge-schoß).

6. Muster eines Brüs-tungspaneels aus Guß-aluminium. (Photo: Stefan Müller.)

4. Detailed section of the corner.
5. Floor plan (ground floor).

6. Sample for a panel of cast aluminium. (Photo: Stefan Müller.)

und Mezzanin Ladennutzung und eine zweigeschossige Loggia zur Leipziger Straße, vier Bürogeschosse bis zum Rück-sprung in 22 m Höhe, darüber vier Wohngeschosse. Auch die Grundfarbe aller Gebäude am Leipziger Platz ist vor-gegeben: Ein leicht beiger Naturstein, so daß als einzige – aber dafür um so inter-essantere – architektonische Gestaltungs-möglichkeit die Detaillierung der Fassa-de bleibt:

Stark senkrecht profilierte, sich nach innen zurückstaffelnde, gotisierende Pfeiler entfalten eine starke Licht- und Schattenwirkung. Das einen Meter weit auskragende Gesimsprofil in 22 m Hö-he – der historischen Traufhöhe des Leipziger Platzes – teilt das Haus sicht-bar in Büro- und Wohnnutzung.

Die von unten kommenden Pfeiler-profile werden hier in einer Rundung um 90° nach außen gebogen und zeigen ihren Querschnitt an der Unterseite der Traufe in reduzierter Form.

Zur Steigerung der vertikalen Fassa-denwirkung sind die zwischen den Pfei-lern liegenden Fensterflächen lediglich vertikal gegliedert und plan in eine Ebene mit den Brüstungspaneelen aus Gußaluminium gelegt. Diese Paneele drücken sichtbar aus, daß sie in einem Stück gegossen sind und keine ver-schraubte Konstruktion darstellen: Ein umlaufender Rahmen faßt die zurück-

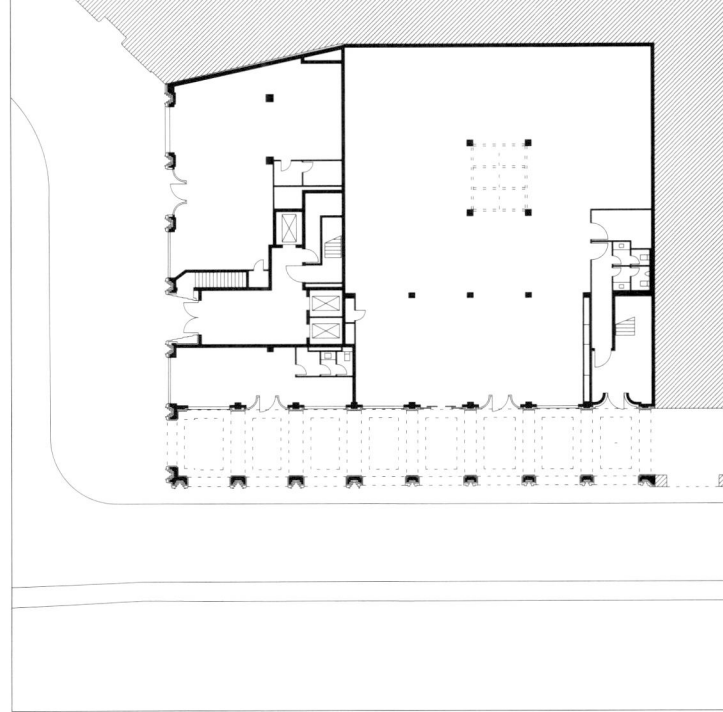

height of 22 m – the historic eaves' height on Leipziger Platz – and thereby visibly divides the building's office and residential uses.

The profiles of the piers from below bend outwards here in a curve of 90° and on the underside of the eaves a re-duced form of their cross section can be seen.

The vertical effect made by the façade is further heightened by the window areas between the piers that are vertical-ly structured and placed on the same level as the panels of cast aluminium. It is obvious that these panels have been cast in once piece and are not part of a construction that has been bolted together. A frame encloses the levels that have been stepped backwards with swel-ling, round breast motifs.

The façade above for the apartments is simpler in its structure and has a lar-ger proportion of wall. Narrow, tall French windows with flat metal balconies or loggias onto Leipziger Platz are clear indications of residential use. Above the

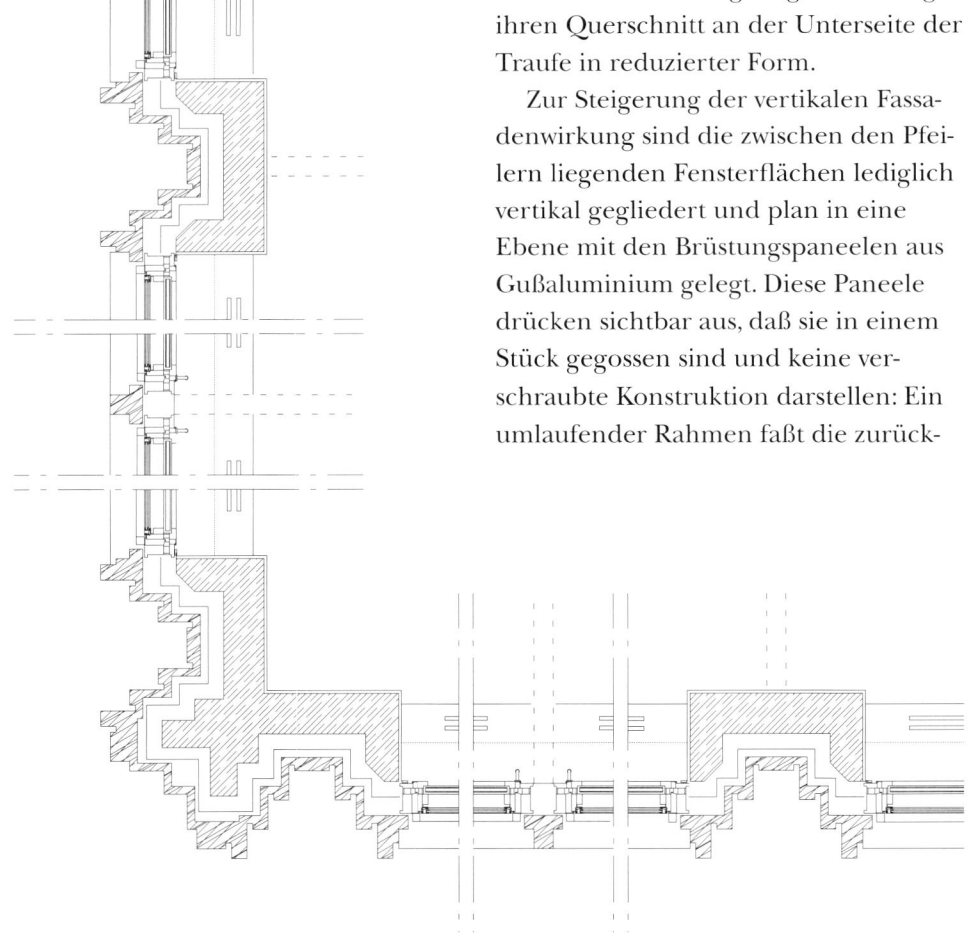

gestaffelten Ebenen zusammen, aus der sich runde Brustmotive herauswölben.

Die darüber liegende Fassade der Wohnungen ist einfacher gegliedert und hat einen größeren Wandanteil: Schmale hohe französische Fenster mit flachen metallenen Austritten bzw. Loggien zum Leipziger Platz weisen klar auf eine Wohnnutzung hin. Oberhalb des auskragenden Gesimsprofils an der oberen Traufkante zeichnet sich über die gesamte Länge des Gebäudes die Silhouette einer geschnittenen Hecke ab.

Der Gebäudeteil zum Leipziger Platz, der sich übereck noch über die ersten drei Achsen an der Leipziger Straße erstreckt, ist zehn Geschosse hoch. Daran schließt sich in östlicher Richtung der sieben Geschosse hohe Bauteil entlang der Leipziger Straße an. Die Schnittstelle wird durch einen Rücksprung im Grundriß akzentuiert.

Projektleiter: Peter Westermann
Mitarbeiter: Dietmar Husmann, Peter O'Callaghan, Frigga Uhlisch, Evelyn Galsdorf

cornice's projecting profile, at the upper edge of the eaves the silhouette of a trimmed hedge, that covers the entire length of the building, can be seen.

The part of the building facing Leipziger Platz is ten storeys high and extends at a right angle to stretch over the first three axes on Leipziger Straße. It is joined on this eastern side by the seven-storey building along Leipziger Straße. The intersection is accented by a set-back in the floor plan.

Project architect: Peter Westermann
Collaborators: Dietmar Husmann, Peter O'Callaghan, Frigga Uhlisch, Evelyn Galsdorf

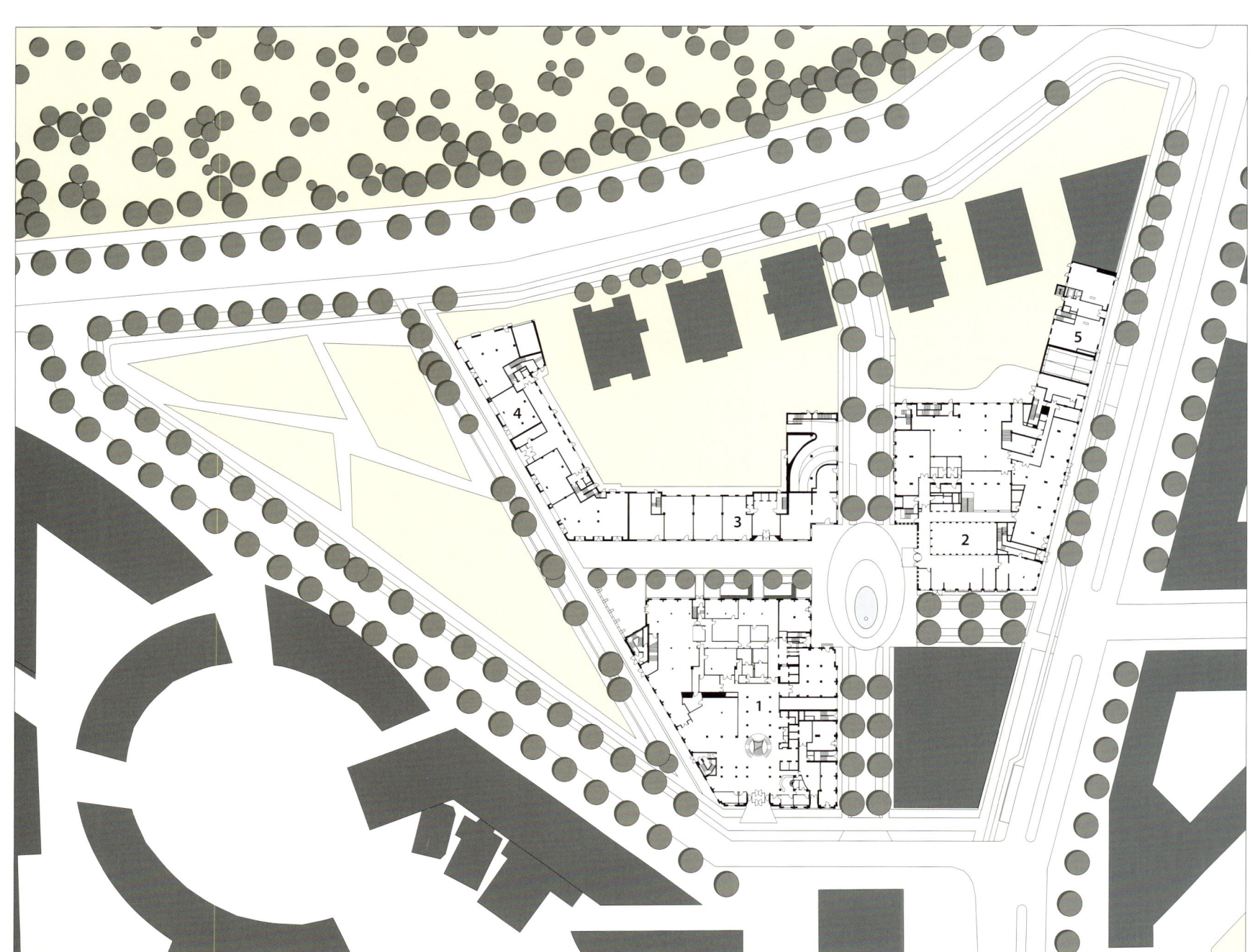

Beisheim-Center – städtebauliche Konkretisierung, Berlin-Tiergarten, 2000–03

Der städtebauliche Wettbewerb definierte 1991 am Potsdamer und Leipziger Platz Grundprinzipien wie Traufhöhen, Lage der fünf Hochhäuser, Straßenführung, Blockbildung und Straßenbreite, die dann bis 1994 in den Bebauungsplan einflossen. Die einzelnen Teilgebiete der Investoren wurden aber im folgenden noch ein zweitesmal genauer durch einzelne Wettbewerbe weiter definiert (siehe Seite 236–243).

Es war für uns eine besondere Freude, im letzten Teilstück, im früheren Hertie-, jetzt Beisheim-Areal nicht nur zwei Häuser realisieren zu können, sondern auch vorher die städtebauliche Gestaltung bestimmen zu können.

Der im Sommer 2000 ausgelobte Wettbewerb stellte die Aufgabe, das 41 000 m² Bruttogeschoßfläche große Raumprogramm des Ritz-Carlton Hotels in dem Block E 1 direkt am Potsdamer Platz unterzubringen, was nur zu lösen war, indem dieser Block um exakt 15 m nach Norden vergrößert wurde, so daß die bis zu diesem Zeitpunkt im vorliegenden Bebauungsplan noch gerade, bis zum Henriette-Hertz-Park durchgezogene Hans-von-Bülow-Straße jetzt an einem kleinen, fast intimen Platz endet.

Dieser Platz wurde als Würfel definiert, seine Grundfläche – durch die ausgenommenen Ecken der drei neu zu planenden Gebäude vergrößert – beträgt jetzt 32 m mal 37 m, seine Höhe entspricht der vorgegebenen Blockhöhe, nämlich 35 m.

Genau im Kreuzungspunkt der Achsen der Hans-von-Bülow-Straße und der Auguste-Hauschner-Straße – also weithin sichtbar in drei Himmelsrichtungen – wurde eine Skulptur vorgeschlagen, die diesem Platz und damit diesem kleinen Quartier eine eigene Identität verleiht.

Beisheim-Center – development of the urban form, Berlin-Tiergarten, 2000 to 2003

The competition for the design of Potsdamer Platz and Leipziger Platz in 1991 defined fundamental principles such as the height of the eaves, location of the five skyscrapers, the routes followed by the streets as well as their width and block formation. These were taken into the development plan until 1994. The investors' individual areas were, however, defined a second time in more detail in separate competitions (see page 236–243).

It was a special pleasure for us that, in the end, we not only constructed two buildings in the area formerly occupied

by the Hertie department store, now the Beisheim-Center, but that prior to this we were able to determine the area's urban structure.

The competition in the summer of 2002 set the task of placing the gross floor area of 41,000 m² of the development programme of the Ritz-Carlton Hotel in Block E 1 directly onto Potsdamer Platz. This was only possible if this block were expanded 15 m to the north. The existing development plan had foreseen Hans-von-Bülow-Straße ending straight in Henriette-Herz-Park but it would now end in a small, almost intimate square.

1. Lageplan.

1. Site plan.

2. Place Fürstenberg, Paris.

3. Place de la Sainte-Catherine, Paris.

4, 5. Modell. (Photos:
Stefan Müller.)

4, 5. Model. (Photos:
Stefan Müller.)

Die formale Anlehnung an den Place
Fürstenberg oder an den Place de la
Sainte-Catherine, beide in Paris, ist
durchaus beabsichtigt.

Im Laufe der Weiterbearbeitung
wurde dieser doch nicht unerhebliche
Eingriff in den vorliegenden, rechtsgül-
tigen Bebauungsplan sowohl vom Investor als auch vom Land Berlin positiv
aufgenommen; der Investor fügte zur
Idee der Skulptur noch die Idee des
Brunnens hinzu und ließ beides aus-
führen – was durchaus nicht selbstverständlich ist. Die Senatsverwaltung

akzeptierte die Verschiebung der Hans-
von Bülow-Straße ohne formelle Ände-
rung der Rechtsgrundlage, was ein lan-
ges, kompliziertes Verfahren bedeutet
hätte. Der Bezirk verzichtete auf die
sonst üblichen Fußgänger- und Radwege
am Platz, indem dieser als Fußgängerzone ausgewiesen wurde.

Die beiden angrenzenden Areale von
Debis und Sony am Potsdamer Platz sind
in ihrer städtebaulichen Konkretisierung
von einem völlig anderen Konzept geprägt, nämlich der introvertierten Ein-
kaufspassage.

Das direkt angewandte Modell unseres Masterplans von 1991 mit Block,
Gasse und Quartiersplatz bildet einen
Höhepunkt unserer Tätigkeit als Stadt-
planer.

Projektleiter: Ursula Gonsior

This square was laid out as a cube. Its base, enlarged through the excluded corners of the three new buildings that had to be planned, now measures 32 m by 37 m. Its height corresponds to the prescribed block height, i. e. 35 m.

A proposal was made for a sculpture at the exact point where the axes of Hans-von-Bülow Straße and Auguste-Hauschner-Straße meet. It was thought that a sculpture, visible from three directions, would impart this square and this small quarter with its own identity. This formal dependence on the Place Fürstenberg or the Place de la Sainte-Catherine, both in Paris, is deliberate.

This not insignificant intervention in the existing, legally valid development plan eventually found acceptance both on the part of the investor and the city of Berlin. The investor even had the idea of adding a fountain to the sculpture and the two were built. This sort of action should not be taken for granted. The civic administration accepted the repositioning of Hans-von-Bülow-Straße without a formal, legal change. This would have entailed a long and complicated procedure. The district agreed to do without the usual paths for pedestrians and cyclists on squares by making the square itself into a pedestrian zone.

The two bordering areas belonging to Debis and Sony on Potsdamer Platz are defined by a completely different concept in urban development, namely that of the introverted shopping arcade.

The direct application of our master plan of 1991 with block, alley and square, forms one of the highpoints in our work as urban developers.

Project architect: Ursula Gonsior

6. Perspektive.

6. Perspective view.

Ritz-Carlton Hotel und Apartment-Tower, Beisheim-Center, Berlin-Tiergarten, 2000–03

Die Gestalt dieses letzten der fünf markanten Hochhäuser am Potsdamer Platz orientiert sich formal an der großen Zeit des Art Déco der Hochhäuser in New York und Chicago. Einerseits markieren diese Bauten einen Aufbruch zur Moderne, andererseits sind sie der klassischen europäischen Baukunst verpflichtet.

Das hauptsächlich sichtbare Baumaterial des Hauses ist ein heller, beiger Kalkstein aus Portugal, der uns wegen seiner optimistischen Leichtigkeit begeistert.

Das Haus ist klassisch in drei Zonen gegliedert: Über einer kräftig ausgeprägten zweigeschossigen Sockelzone mit reichem Steindekor und bronzenen Fenstern entwickelt sich der Schaft

1. Perspektive des Gebäudes vom Potsdamer Platz.

1. Perspective view of the building from Potsdamer Platz.

2. Ansicht des Gebäudes vom Potsdamer Platz. (Photo: Stefan Müller.)
3. Eliel Saarinen, Chicago Tribune Tower, Wettbewerbsprojekt, 1922.

2. View of the building from Potsdamer Platz. (Photo: Stefan Müller.)
3. Eliel Saarinen, Chicago Tribune Tower, competition project, 1922.

Ritz-Carlton Hotel and apartment tower, Beisheim-Center, Berlin-Tiergarten, 2000 to 2003

In formal terms the last of the five prominent skyscrapers on Potsdamer Platz is oriented to the great age of the Art Déco skyscrapers in New York and Chicago. While these buildings represent the emergence of the modern age, they are also indebted to classic European architecture.

The main visible building material is a light, beige limestone from Portugal, that appealed to us because of its optimistic facility.

The building has a classic division of three zones. A shaft rises above a distinctive two-storey socle zone with profuse stone ornamentation and bronze windows to come finally to an expressive end at the top, where it can be seen from a great distance. This powerful soaring

Ritz Carlton Hotel und Apartment-Tower,
Beisheim-Center, Berlin-Tiergarten, 2000–03

166

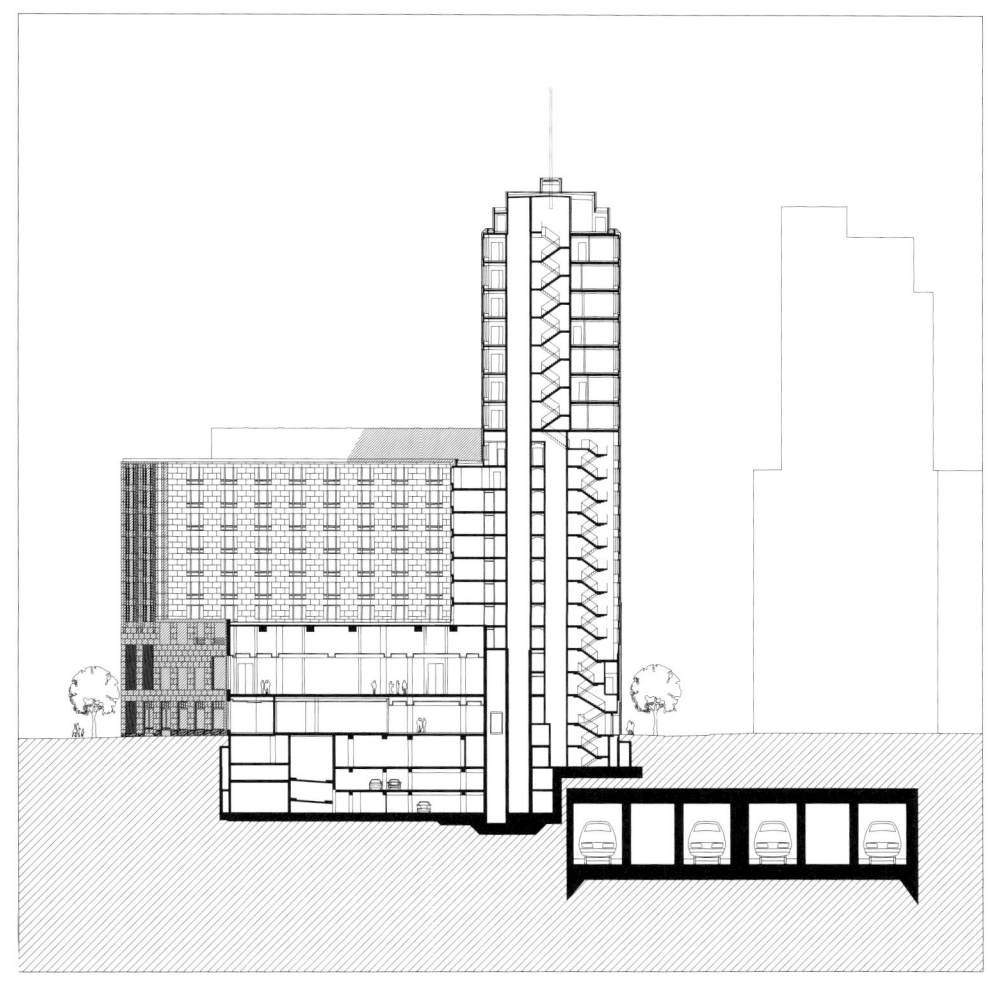

4. Ansicht des Gebäu-
des vom Potsdamer
Platz. (Photo: Stefan
Müller.)

4. View of the building
from Potsdamer Platz.
(Photo: Stefan Müller.)

5, 6. Schnitt und
Grundriß (Erdge-
schoß).

5, 6. Section and floor
plan (ground floor).

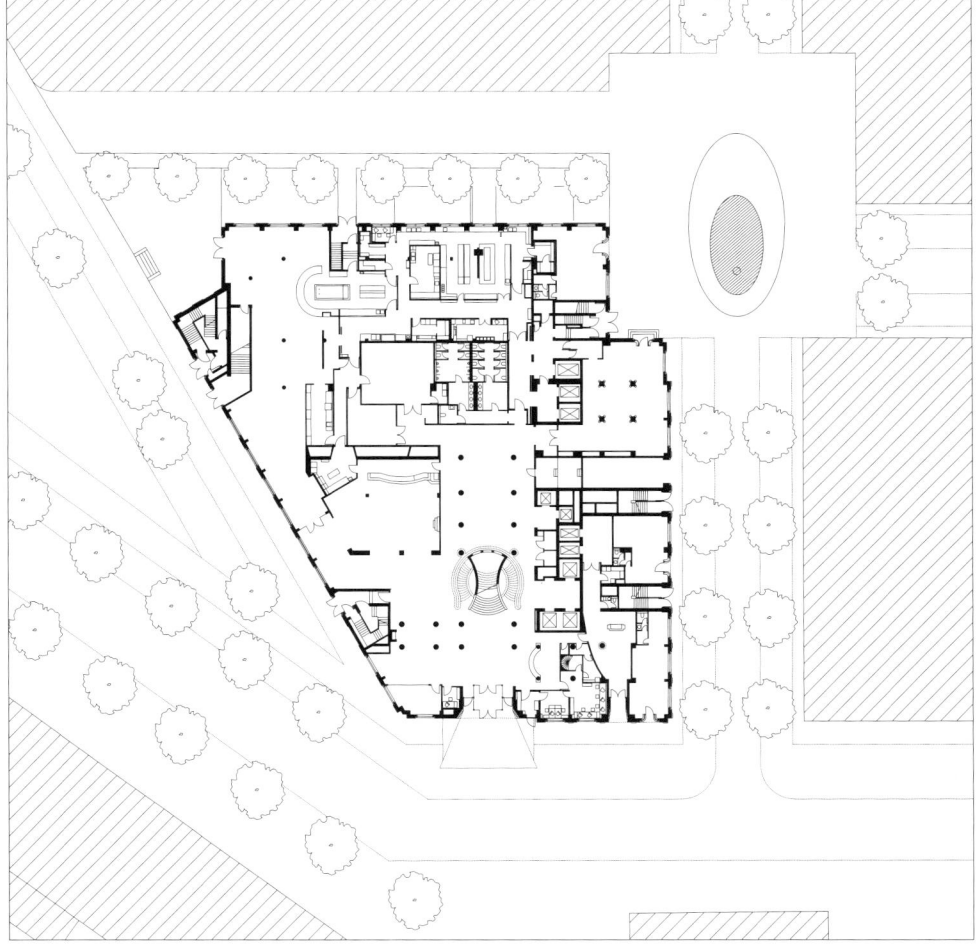

167

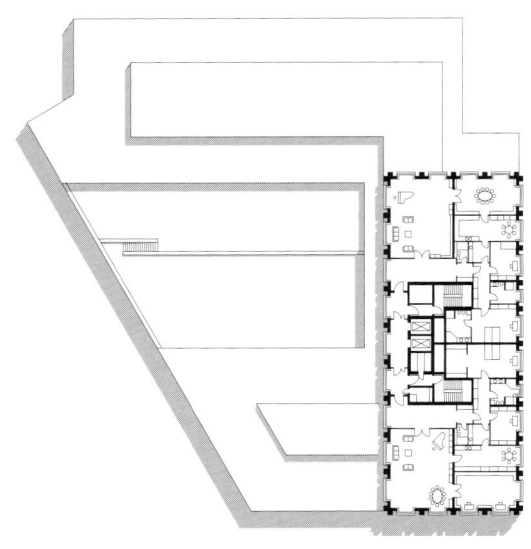

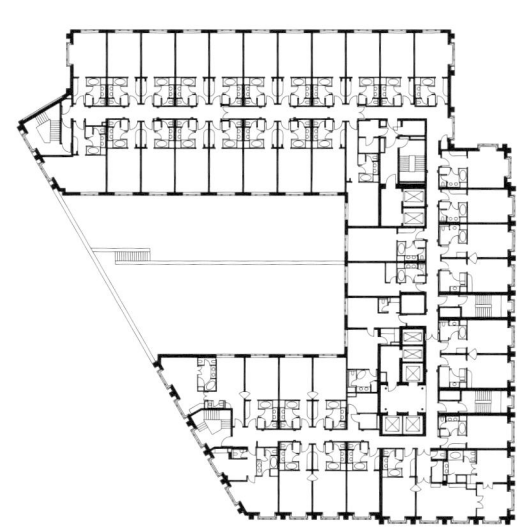

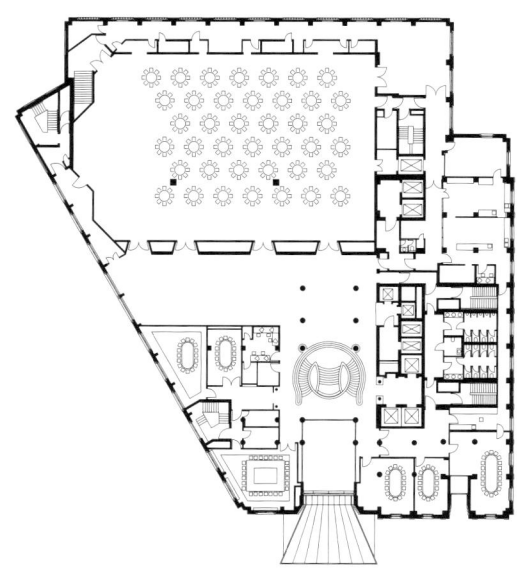

7–9. Grundrisse (1. Ober-
geschoß, Normalge-
schoß Hotel, Normal-
geschoß Apartments).

7–9. Floor plans (1st
floor, typical floor of the
hotel, typical floor of
the apartments).

10. Blick in Richtung
Potsdamer Platz. (Pho-
to: Stefan Müller.)

10. View towards Pots-
damer Platz. (Photo:
Stefan Müller.)

vertikal nach oben und endet schließlich
in einem weithin sichtbaren, ausdrucks-
vollen oberen Abschluß. Das mächtige
Aufstreben wird überhöht durch die vertikalen Vertiefungen, welche die Fassade
in Pfeiler und erkerartige Fenster gliedern. Zum Motiv des oberen Abschlusses
gehört unbedingt die gleißenden Metallspitze, auf der in 82 m Höhe eine Kugel
balanciert.

Neben diesem 72 m hohen Turm
besteht das Gebäude, wie alle anderen
am Potsdamer und Leipziger Platz, aus

action is banked by the vertical depres-
sions that divide the façade into piers
and bow-like windows. The motif of the
upper zone is expressed in its glistening
metal point that balances a sphere at a
height of 82 m.

Apart from this tower with its height
of 72 m, the building – as is the case with
all of the buildings on Potsdamer and
Leipziger Platz – is a block, 35 m in
height. On the tower the silhouette of
the façade's relief is sketched against the
sky, while in the case of the block this

169

Ritz-Carlton Hotel und Apartment-Tower,
Beisheim-Center, Berlin-Tiergarten, 2000–03

11–13. Fassadenaus-
schnitte. (Photos:
Stefan Müller.)

11–13. Part elevations.
(Photos: Stefan Müller.)

einem 35 m hohen Block. Beim Turm
zeichnet sich die Silhouette des Fassadenreliefs gegen den Himmel ab, während sie beim Block durch eine Attika
eingefaßt wird. Ebenso gibt es eine Differenzierung zwischen Turm und Block
bei den Ornamenten im Sockelbereich.
Während die an Kanneluren erinnernden Zylindersegmente im Blockbereich
horizontal verlaufen, streben sie im
Turmbereich senkrecht nach oben.

Der Hoteleingang im Block mit
einem weit auskragenden Vordach ist

relief is encircled by an attic storey.

There is also a difference made in
the ornamentation on the tower and
the block in the socle area. While the
cylindrical segments reminiscent of fluting follow a horizontal direction on
the block, on the tower they aspire upwards.

The entrance to the hotel in the block
has a huge canopy and at two storeys is
almost oversized. Access to the luxury
apartments is in the tower. This entrance
is just as high as the entrance to the ho-

14. Detailansicht der
Fassade des Turms.
(Photo: Stefan Müller.)
15. Detailansicht der
Fassade des Blocks.
(Photo: Stefan Müller.)

16. Fassadenausschnitt
des Blocks. (Photo: Ste-
fan Müller.)
17. Fassadenausschnitt
des Turms. (Photo: Ste-
fan Müller.)

14. Detailed view of
the tower's façade.
(Photo: Stefan Müller.)
15. Detail view of the
blocks façade. (Photo:
Stefan Müller.)

16. Part elevation of
the block. (Photo: Ste-
fan Müller.)
17. Part elevation of
the tower. (Photo: Ste-
fan Müller.)

zweigeschossig fast übergroß ausgebildet. Im Turmbereich befindet sich der
Zugang zu den Luxuswohnungen, der
genauso hoch, aber schmaler ist. Durch
die beiden verschiedenen Eingänge
zeigt die Fassade die zwei unterschiedlichen Nutzungen.

In die steinerne Turmspitze sind in
2 m hohen Buchstaben die Initialen
des Bauherrn eingemeißelt und werden
damit zum permanenten Bestandteil
der Architektur.

Im Grundriß springt der Turm an
der Süd- und Ostseite um 50 cm vor die
Blockkante und erhält dadurch mehr
Eigenständigkeit.

Der Block enthält ein Fünf-Sterne-Ho-
tel mit 300 Zimmern, vier Restaurants, Ta-
gungsräumen und einem 900 m² großen
Ballsaal. Die drei Untergeschosse beinhal-
ten unter anderem einen Fitneßbereich,
ein Schwimmbad, eine Tiefgarage und
eine unterirdische LKW-Anlieferrampe.

tel but narrower. Through these two different entrances, the façade indicates
the two different uses.

At the stone top of the tower, the initials of the building's owner have been
chiselled in 2 m high letters. These initials have thereby become a permanent
component of the architecture.

The ground plan foresees the tower
jutting out around 50 cm in front of the
block boundary on the southern and
eastern sides. The tower thereby attains
more independence.

The block contains a five-star hotel with 300 rooms, four restaurants,
conference rooms and a ballroom
measuring 900 m². Amongst other
things, the three basement levels boast
a fitness area, a pool, a car park and
an underground delivery ramp for
trucks.

In the tower seven residential storeys
lie above the hotel. On each floor there

Ritz Carlton und Apartment Tower, Beisheim-
Center, Berlin-Tiergarten, 2000–03

18. Der Hoteleingang.
(Photo: Stefan Müller.)

18. Hotel entrance.
(Photo: Stefan Müller.)

19, 20. Der Eingang zu
den Apartments. (Pho-
tos: Stefan Müller.)

19, 20. Entrance to the
apartments. (Photos:
Stefan Müller.)

21. Fassadenausschnitt der Nordfassade. (Photo: Stefan Müller.)

22. Oberer Gebäudeabschluß. (Photo: Stefan Müller.)

21. Detailed view of the north façade. (Photo: Stefan Müller.)

22. Top of the building. (Photo: Stefan Müller.)

Im Hochhaus befinden sich über dem Hotel sieben Wohngeschosse. Pro Etage sind entweder eine Wohnung mit 580 m^2 oder zwei Wohnungen mit 290 m^2 angeordnet.

Wie im Hotelbau üblich, waren wir als Architekten nur für den Hochbau und die Fassade, nicht für den Innenausbau verantwortlich.

Projektleiter: Herman Duquesnoy
Mitarbeiter: Carsten Baur, Frauke Blasy,
Peter Dörrie, Christiane Gabler, Sigurd
Hauer, Stefano Magistretti, Wolfgang Met-
schan, Christian von Oppen, Till Roggel,
Peter Solhdju, Myriam Wiedemann, Frigga
Uhlisch, Nadine Zietlow

is either one apartment measuring 580 m^2 or two apartments, each measuring 290 m^2.

As is common with hotel building, we as architects were only responsible for the construction and the façade, not for the interior fit-out.

Project architect: Herman Duquesnoy
Collaborators: Carsten Baur, Frauke Blasy,
Peter Dörrie, Christiane Gabler, Sigurd
Hauer, Stefano Magistretti, Wolfgang Met-
schan, Christian von Oppen, Till Roggel,
Peter Solhdju, Myriam Wiedemann, Frigga
Uhlisch, Nadine Zietlow

177

Bürogebäude, Beisheim-Center, Berlin-Tiergarten, 2000-03

Das an der Nordwestecke des kleinen Platzes, hinter dem Hotel gelegene zehngeschossige Bürogebäude lehnt sich formal stark an die frühen Hochhäuser von William Le Baron Jenney an, speziell an das First Leiter Building in Chicago aus dem Jahr 1879. Le Baron Jenney verstand diesen Bautypus als direkte Weiterführung des Klassizismus mit sichtbaren Wandpfeilern, Kapitellen und profilierten Brüstungen.

Unser Ehrgeiz bestand darin, die Lebhaftigkeit dieser früheren Fassaden zu erreichen, ohne dabei die einzelnen Elemente mit ihren Verzierungen direkt zu kopieren. Vielmehr wollten wir einen ähnlichen Effekt mit den Mitteln der heutigen Bautechnik erzielen.

Entsprechend den Gesetzen der Tektonik verjüngen sich die Pfeiler nach oben und springen gestaffelt hinter die Baulinie zurück, je weiter sie zum Himmel schießen. Ein zweigeschossiger Sockel, sechs Normalgeschosse und zwei Laternengeschosse machen eine deutliche Dreiteilung ablesbar. Ein 1 m auskragendes Gesimsprofil als Betonfertigteil mit stark profilierter Untersicht schließt das Haus nach oben ab.

Das ungewöhnlich breite Ausbauraster von 1,5 m und ein zweigeschossiger Eingangsbereich erlauben eine großzügige Fassadengliederung.

Ein wichtiges Motiv ist der Farbunterschied zwischen den Pfeilern und Brüstungen aus gelbem Sandstein und den grauen Kapitellen aus Betonfertigteilen. Da die Fassade durch die Lage des Hau-

Office building, Beisheim-Center, Berlin-Tiergarten 2000-03

The ten-storey office building located behind the hotel on the northwestern corner of the small square is indebted to the early skyscrapers of William Le Baron Jenney, especially to the First Leiter Building from the year 1879. Le Baron Jenney saw this type of building as a direct continuation of Classicism with visible pilasters, capitals and moulded spandrel panels.

We hoped to achieve the vividness of these earlier façades but did not want to make direct copies of the individual elements with their ornamentation. We were far more interested in obtaining a similar effect using the means offered by contemporary building technology.

In accordance with the laws of tectonics, the pillars become narrower towards the top and the higher they become the more they recede in staggered formation behind the building line. The two-storey base, six normal storeys and two lantern storeys make the tripartite division clearly evident. The building is finished off at the top with a pre-fabricated concrete cornice projecting 1 m and strongly profiled on the underside.

An unusually broad grid of 1.5 m and a two-storey entrance area allow for an exuberant structuring of the façade.

An important motif is the difference in colour between the pillars and spandrel panels of yellow sandstone and the grey capitals out of pre-fabricated concrete parts. Since the location of the building in the narrow street means that the façade can only be viewed from an

1. Ansicht des Gebäudes vom Inge-Beisheim-Platz. (Photo: Stefan Müller.)

2. William Le Baron Jenney, First Leiter Building, Chicago, 1879.

1. View of the building from Inge-Beisheim-Platz. (Photo: Stefan Müller.)

3. Detailansicht des
Gesimsprofils. (Photo:
Stefan Müller.)
4. Detailansicht der
Fassade. (Photo: Ste-
fan Müller.)

3. Detail view of the
cornice. (Photo: Stefan
Müller.)
4. Detail view of the
facade. (Photo: Stefan
Müller.)

5, 6. Schnitt und
Grundriß (Normal-
geschoß).

5, 6. Section and floor
plan (typical floor).

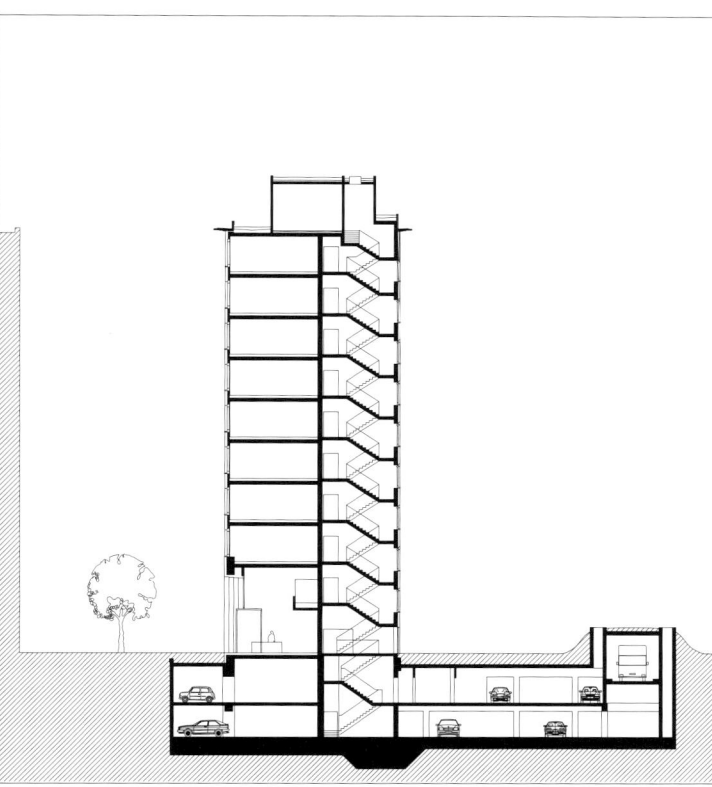

extremely distorted perspective, its plastic elements also had to be formed with this special effect in mind. The curvature in the capital, measuring merely a few millimetres, can only be observed after closer inspection and even then, the flatter the angle of vision, the better it can be seen.

The strongly profiled panel elements carry on a lively dialogue with the moulded metal window profiles. In the two lower storeys these profiles are in bronze, in all other storeys they are coated in grey aluminium.

The large entrance area is two storeys high – almost 7 m – with an internal balcony at the level of the first floor. The elevators, with their framed with natural-stone portals, lie across from the entrance doors in such a way that they are visible from as far away as the street. As a supplement to the two colours of the exterior many colours are used here. The three different types of marble wall cladding, vertically structured, in white, red and green create a cheerful atmosphere. As a conclusion the walls above have a bright ochre plaster finish. All of the metal elements in this room are in

ses in der engen Straße immer nur aus einer extrem verzerrten Perspektive wahrgenommen werden kann, mußten auch die plastischen Elemente für diese spezielle Wirkung gestaltet werden: Die nur wenige Millimeter flache Wölbung im Kapitell gibt sich erst beim näheren Hinsehen zu erkennen, und zwar um so besser, je flacher der Blickwinkel ist.

Die stark profilierten Brüstungselemente führen einen lebendigen Dialog mit den plastisch ausgeformten, metallenen Fensterprofilen, die in den unteren beiden Geschossen in Bronze, darüber in grau beschichtetem Aluminium ausgeführt sind.

Der großzügige Eingangsbereich ist zweigeschossig – fast 7 m hoch – mit einem inneren Balkon auf der Ebene des ersten Obergeschosses. Die Aufzüge liegen dem Windfang direkt gegenüber, so daß sie mit ihren mit Naturstein umrahmten Portalen bis auf die Straße hin sichtbar sind. Als Steigerung zu der Zweifarbigkeit außen treten hier mehrere Farben auf: Die drei verschiedenen Marmorsorten an den Wänden, vertikal gegliedert, in Weiß, Rosé und Grün verbreiten eine heitere Stimmung. Darüber schließt ein hell-ockerfarbener Putz die Wände nach oben ab. Alle Metallteile in

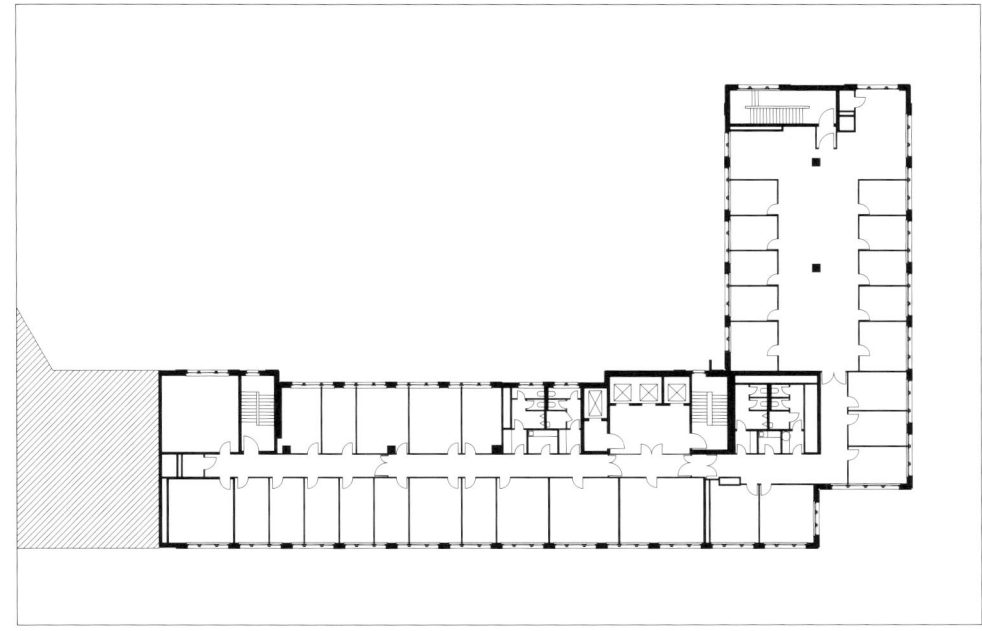

diesem Raum sind – wie auch außen die Fassade – in Bronze ausgebildet, so auch das mäandrierende Geländer am Erschließungsbalkon. Die direkte Anregung für diese Wandgestaltung kam von der Medrese-Moschee in Kairo aus dem Jahr 1386.

Im Nordflügel ist die Erschließung für die gemeinsame, dreigeschossige Tiefgarage des Beisheim-Centers angeordnet. Wird also im Ballsaal des Ritz-Carlton Hotels weit nach Mitternacht die Bühne abgebaut, um den Raum um

bronze, including the meandering balustrade on the access balcony, as is the case on the façade outside. The stimulus for this wall composition was directly prompted by the Medrese Mosque in Cairo from the year 1386.

The three-storey, shared car park for the Beisheim-Center is in the north wing. This means that if, for example the stage in the ballroom of the Ritz-Carlton Hotel is being dismantled long after midnight, to prepare the room for a press-conference the next day at 8:00

7. Fassadenausschnitt. (Photo: Stefan Müller.)

7. Part elevation. (Photo: Stefan Müller.)

8. Ansicht der Gebäudeecke vom Inge-Beisheim-Platz. (Photo: Stefan Müller.)

8. View of the corner of the building from Inge-Beisheim-Platz. (Photo: Stefan Müller.)

Bürogebäude, Beisheim-Center, Berlin-Tiergarten, 2000–03

9. Detailansicht des
Geländers. (Photo: Ste-
fan Müller.)

9. Detailed view of the
handrail. (Photo: Ste-
fan Müller.)

10, 11. Die Lobby. (Pho-
tos: Stefan Müller.)

10, 11. The lobby. (Pho-
tos: Stefan Müller.)

acht Uhr morgens für eine Pressekonferenz völlig umgestaltet zu haben, so fahren die Lastwagen mit den Dekorationselementen an der abgelegensten Stelle des Komplexes heraus, um eine Belästigung der Hotelgäste zu vermeiden.

*Projektleiter: Ursula Gonsior, Till Roggel
Mitarbeiter: Frauke Blasy, Henrik Eichler, Jens Förster, Thomas Katzke, Mehra Mehrdadi, Sven Meller, Peter O'Callaghan*

a. m., the trucks transporting the decorative furnishings use the most remote point of the complex and thereby avoid disturbing the hotel's guests.

*Project architects: Ursula Gonsior, Till Roggel
Collaborators: Frauke Blasy, Henrik Eichler, Jens Förster, Thomas Katzke, Mehra Mehrdadi, Sven Meller, Peter O'Callaghan*

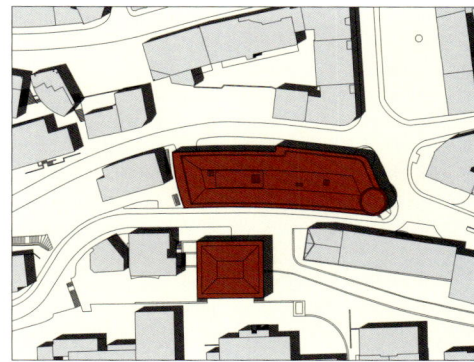

Einstein-Kongress, St. Gallen, Schweiz, 2001–06

In engem räumlichen und funktionalen Zusammenhang mit dem noblen Hotel Einstein des Bauherrn entsteht ein Kongreßgebäude in der St. Gallener Altstadt, dicht bei der berühmten Stiftskathedrale. Der neue Baukörper gliedert sich in zwei Bauteile, deren Fassaden aus beigefarbenem Kalksandstein sich in einem differenziert gestaffeltem Reliefduktus unterschiedlich gliedern.

Der Kongreßteil mit seinen offenen Foyerzonen orientiert sich zum Hotelvorplatz und besitzt eine turmartige Treppenverbindung zwischen den Kongreßbereichen. Die gerundete Turmform am Gebäudekopf neben dem Hotel reflektiert vergleichbare Eckausbildungen in der St. Gallener Innenstadt. Sie erzeugt eine charakteristische Figur für die neue Nutzung vor allem aus dem Blickwinkel des Oberen Grabens, von dem die meisten Gäste sowohl zu Fuß als auch mit dem Auto ankommen. Vom Inneren des Foyers ermöglicht sie einen Blick in diesen wunderbaren, leicht gekrümmten Stadtraum, in dem sich ungewöhnlicherweise auch Gärten befinden.

Der Büroteil auf der Westseite setzt sich vom Kongreßteil ab und definiert räumlich den kleinen Platz an der Wassergasse. Er enthält die für Innenstädte klassisch gestaffelten Nutzungen: Läden im Erdgeschoß, Büros, Praxen und Serviceeinrichtungen des Kongreßteils im ersten bis vierten Obergeschoß und Wohnungen in dem zurückversetzten Dachgeschoß mit Terrassen.

Einstein-Kongress, St. Gallen, Switzerland, 2001–06

A convention centre is under construction in St. Gallen's old quarter, close to the famous cathedral, and will be spatially and functionally closely connected to the client's illustrious Hotel Einstein. The new building is in two parts. The façades of beige limestone differ from each other in the structure of their reliefs.

The convention part of the building has an open foyer zone and is orientated towards the hotel's forecourt. It has a tower-like staircase providing access to the different areas. The rounded tower form at the head of the building beside the hotel recalls similar rounded corners in St. Gallen's inner city. It engenders for the new use a characteristic form particularly when viewed from the Oberer Graben, from which most of the guests arrive both as pedestrians and by car. From the foyer it allows for a view of this wonderful, slightly curved urban space with gardens, in which as is unusal gardens are situated.

The office part of the building on the western side is separate from the convention centre and gives spatial definition to the small square on the Wassergasse. It contains the classic uses of the inner city. On the ground-floor there are stores, between the first and fourth storeys are offices, practices, and premises for services needed by the convention centre and the top storey has been set back with terraces for apartments.

The aim is to achieve a completely new building through a further develop-

1. Aufriß des Gebäudes von Norden.
2, 3. Aufrisse des Gebäudes von Osten und von Westen.

4. Lageplan.

1. Elevation of the building from the north.
2, 3. Elevations of the building from the east and from the west.

4. Site plan.

187

5–7. Schnitt und
Grundrisse (Erdge-
schoß, Normalge-
schoß).

5–7. Section and floor
plans (ground floor,
typical floor).

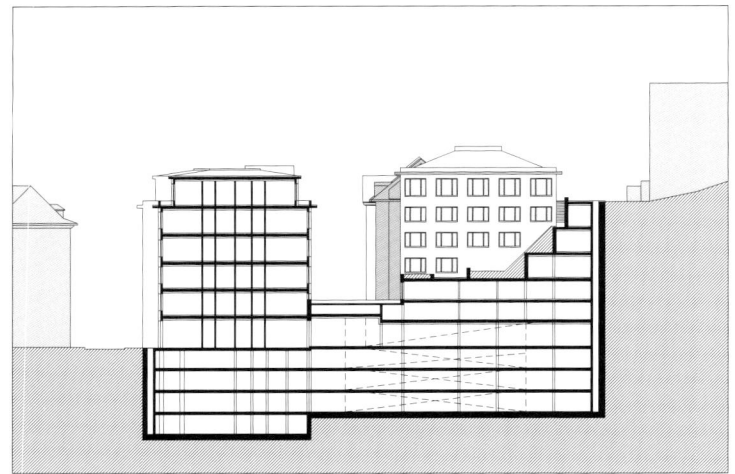

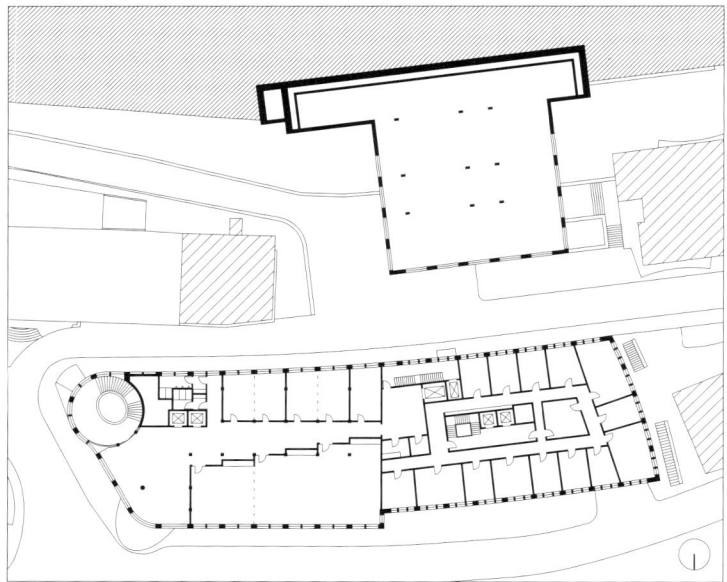

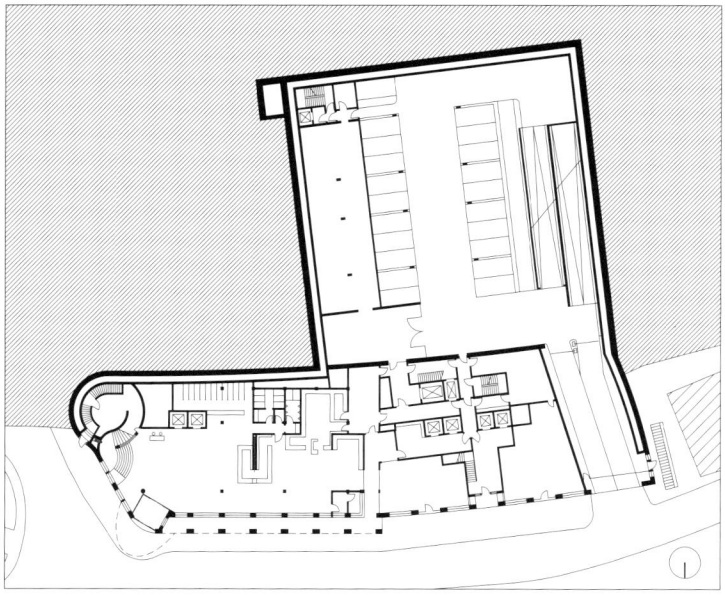

Ziel ist es, nicht durch kontrastierende Architekturelemente und Materialien, sondern durch die Weiterentwicklung der örtlichen Ansätze ein gänzlich neues Gebäude zu entwickeln, das sich erst auf den zweiten Blick als ein solches zu erkennen gibt.

Projektleiter: Rita Ahlers
Mitarbeiter: Jan Faller, Jan Pautzke

ment of the local character, that is not recognizable at first glance, and not by means of contrasting architectural elements and materials.

Project architect: Rita Ahlers
Collaborators: Jan Faller, Jan Pautzke

8. Perspektive der Gebäudeecke vom Oberen Graben.

8. Perspective view of the corner of the building from Oberer Graben.

189

Wohnhaus in den Bergen, 2000–03

Zwei tektonische Grundideen bilden die Basis für den Entwurf.

Zum einen: Auf dem steil abfallenden Grundstück wird eine hohe Steinmauer errichtet, um eine neue Ebene für Haus und Gärten zu erzeugen.

Und zweitens: Die leicht gekrümmte Struktur des Hauses basiert auf quadratischen Grundrißfeldern von ca. 4,5 m x 4,5 m, die von flachen Kappengewölben überdeckt sind. Dieses fast industriebaumäßige Rasterfeld wird durch Einbauelemente und gliedernde Wände soweit verfremdet, daß die einzelnen Funktionsbereiche wie Wohnen, Essen, Arbeiten, Schlafen definiert sind und dennoch fließende Raumzusammenhänge entstehen, die beim Durchschreiten des Hauses etwa vom Eingang bis in den Schlafteil alle fast gleichzeitig erlebbar sind. Das Durchgängige der Rastergliederung ist unterschwellig spürbar, der individuelle Ausdruck der einzelnen Räume wird jedoch dominant wirksam.

Weiterer Grundsätze des Gebäudes sind große Fensteröffnungen in Süd-

Residence in the mountains, 2000–03

This design is based on two tectonic ideas.

First, in order to create a new level for the house and gardens a high stone wall was built on the steeply dropping site.

Secondly, the slightly curved structure of the house is based on square fields in the floor plan of c. 4,5 m by 4,5 m, covered by a very flat cove dome. Fitted ele-

ments and structuring walls have a distancing effect upon this almost industrial grid. While the functional areas for living, eating, working, and sleeping are defined, the rooms are smoothly connected to each other and can be experienced almost simultaneously when one goes through the house from entrance to sleeping area.

1. Ansicht des Gebäudes von Süden. (Photo: Stefan Müller.)

1. View of the building from the south. (Photo: Stefan Müller.)

2. Lageplan.
3. Ansicht des Gebäudes von Westen. (Photo: Stefan Müller.)

2. Site plan.
3. View of the building from the west. (Photo: Stefan Müller.)

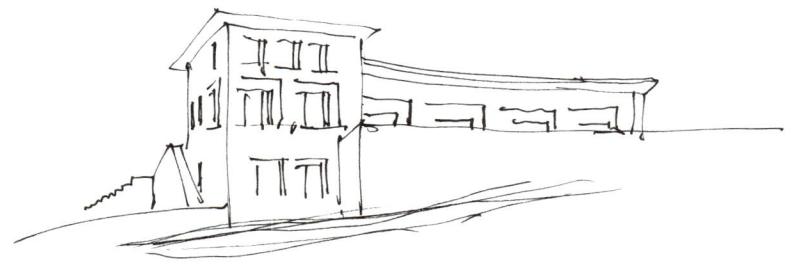

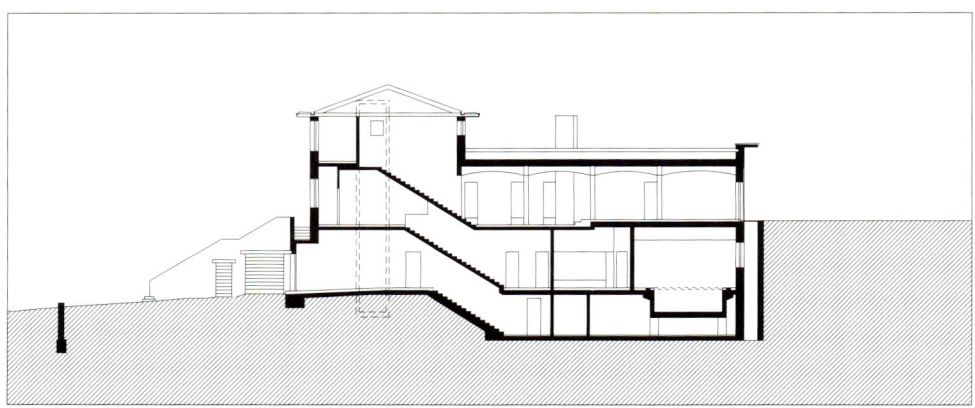

4. Ideenskizze.
5–7. Schnitt und Aufrisse des Gebäudes von Westen und von Norden.

4. Concept sketch.
5–7. Section and elevations of the building from the west and from the north.

8. Ansicht des Gebäudes von Norden. (Photo: Stefan Müller.)
9. Detailansicht der Fassade. (Photo: Stefan Müller.)

8. View of the building from the north. (Photo: Stefan Müller.)
9. Detailed view of the façade. (Photo: Stefan Müller.)

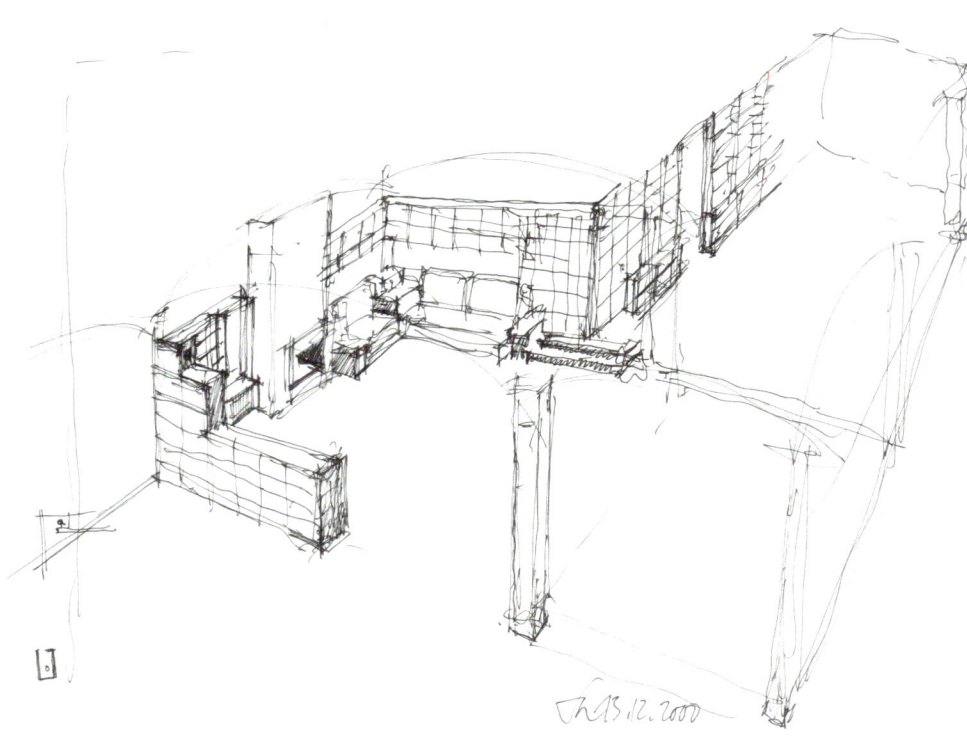

10. Blick in den Wohn-
raum. (Photo: Stefan
Müller.)
11. Das Arbeitszimmer.
(Photo: Stefan Müller.)
12. Ideenskizze.

10. View into the living
room. (Photo: Stefan
Müller.)
11. The study. (Photo:
Stefan Müller.)
12. Concept sketch.

13. Der Wohnraum.
(Photo: Stefan Müller.)

13. The living room.
(Photo: Stefan Müller.)

und Westrichtung aufgrund des über-
ragenden Blickes in die Landschaft und
intimere Wohnzonen für Bücher und
Kunstwerke in den zurückliegenden
Raumzonen.

Projektleiter: Rita Ahlers
Mitarbeiter: Ursula Gonsior

Although the constant presence of
the structuring grid is felt subliminally,
what dominates is the individual expression of each of the room sections.

The outstanding view of the landscape means that a further principle underlying the building is large openings
for windows in southern and western
directions. More intimate living zones
for books and art works are in the room
zones lying more to the back.

Project architect: Rita Ahlers
Collaborator: Ursula Gonsior

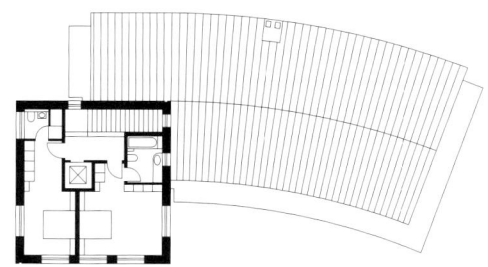

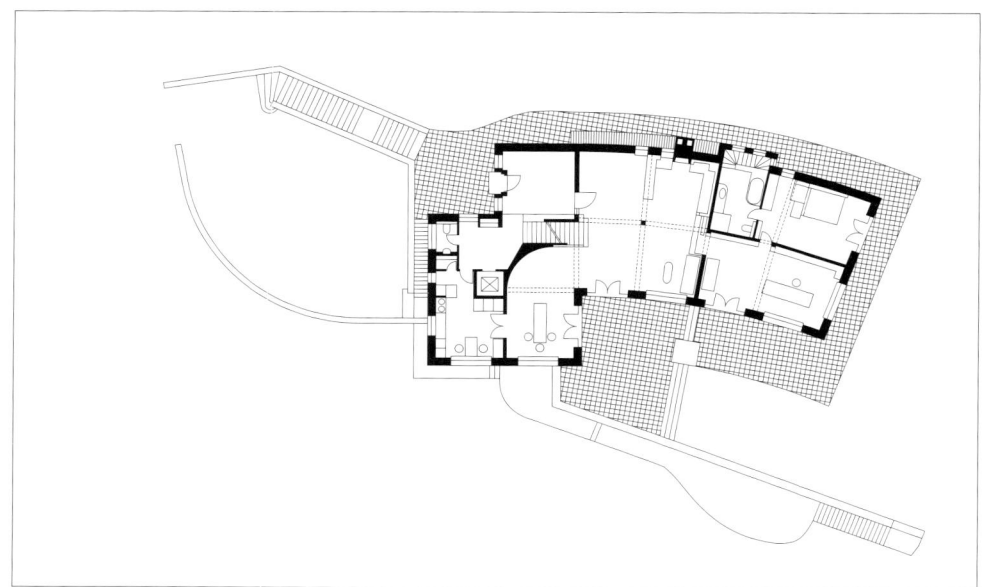

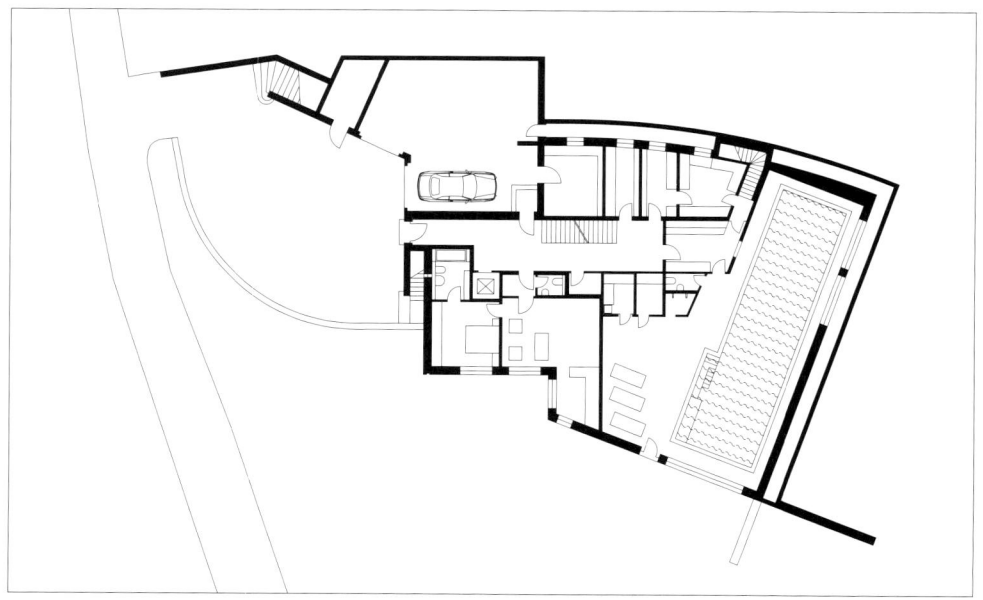

14–16. Grundrisse
(Untergeschoß, Erdge-
schoß, 1. Oberge-
schoß).

17, 18. Der Eßplatz.
(Photos: Stefan Müller.)

14–16. Floor plans
(lower level, ground
floor, 1st floor).

17, 18. The dining area.
(Photos: Stefan Müller.)

Wohnhaus in den Bergen, 2000–03

19. Die Treppe ins 1.
Obergeschoß. (Photo:
Stefan Müller.)
20. Die Eingangshalle.
(Photo: Stefan Müller.)

21. Die Schwimmhalle.
(Photo: Stefan Müller.)
22. Das Fenster der
Schwimmhalle. (Photo:
Stefan Müller.)

19. Stairway to the 1st
floor. (Photo: Stefan
Müller.)
20. The entrance hall.
(Photo: Stefan Müller.)

21. The indoor pool.
(Photo: Stefan Müller.)
22. The window to the
indoor pool. (Photo:
Stefan Müller.)

T. Albert 7/03

1. Vogelperspektive.

1. Bird's-eye view.

Das neue Globushaus, Schloß Gottorf, Schleswig, 2001–03

Die Bauaufgabe für das Schleswiger Globushaus könnte nicht ungewöhnlicher sein: Ab dem Jahr 1637 ließ der schleswigsche Herzog Friedrich III, ein begeisterter Astronom, neben seiner Residenz einen terrassierten, frühbarocken Garten anlegen. In dessen Mittelpunkt befand sich ein Lusthaus mit dem eigentlichen Höhepunkt der Anlage: dem sogenannten Gottorfer Globus – damals nicht nur in Norddeutschland, sondern auch weltweit bekannt – mit einem Durchmesser von 3,10 m.

Dieser Globus war drehbar gelagert und zeigte von außen die Erde in der damaligen Vorstellung, die Meere mit Fischen und Seeungeheuern prächtig bemalt. Ins Innere konnte man durch eine kleine Luke gelangen. Dort bot eine umlaufende Bank Platz für zehn Personen, die nur beim Schein einer Kerze die Erde, den Mond und die Sonne als Modelle simuliert bekamen. Auch die innere Oberfläche des Globusses war ausgemalt. Sie stellte das Firmament dar, indem die Sternbilder gemäß ihrer Symbolik phantasievoll dargestellt wurden. Vergoldete Plättchen formten die Sterne nach. Während der Globus sich drehte, verharrte die Bank in der festen Position. Man konnte so den Wechsel der Jahreszeiten und die Bewegung der Sternbilder simulieren. Es handelte sich um die frühe Form eines modernen Planetariums.

Zar Peter der Große bekam den Globus im Sommer 1713 als »Geschenk« übereignet – vorausgegangen waren

The new Globushaus (house for a globe), Schloß Gottorf, Schleswig, 2001–03

The construction of the new Globushaus (house for a globe) in Schleswig could not be preceded by a more unusual history. In 1637 the Duke of Schleswig, Frederick III, an enthusiastic astronomer, started work on a terraced, early Baroque garden beside his palace. Its focal point was a building containing the garden's actual highlight – the so-called Gottorfer Globe, with a diameter measuring 3,10 m. At the time it was well known not just in northern Germany but all over the world.

The outside of this revolving globe depicted contemporary ideas of what the earth looked like. Its seas had splendidly painted fish and sea monsters. The globe could be entered through a small hatch. A bench, encircling the interior, had space for ten people. By candlelight, they could view simulations of the earth, the moon and the sun. Paintings could also be found on the globe's inner surface. The heavens were shown, while the symbols for the constellations were imaginatively presented. Small, gilded tiles were used to portray stars. When the globe revolved, the bench remained immobile. In this way the changing seasons and the movements of the constellations could also be simulated. All in all, this was an early form of the modern planetarium.

Tsar Peter the Great acquired the globe as a »gift« in the summer of 1713 – this was preceded by military clashes in the German-Danish war from which he emerged as the victor. The long transport to St. Petersburg was not without

Das neue Globushaus, Schloß Gottorf, Schleswig, 2001–03

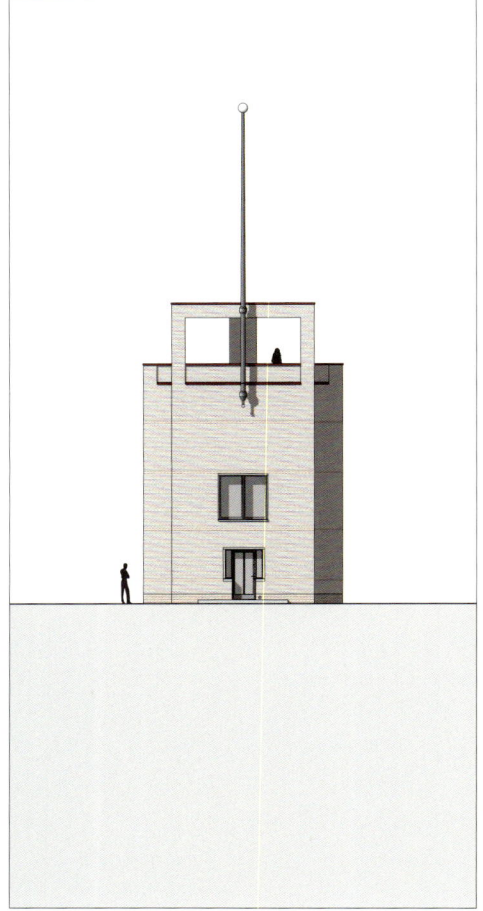 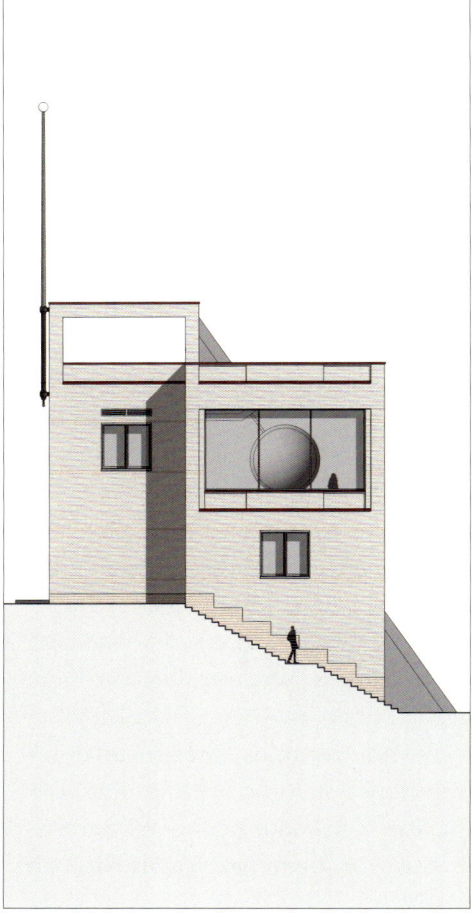 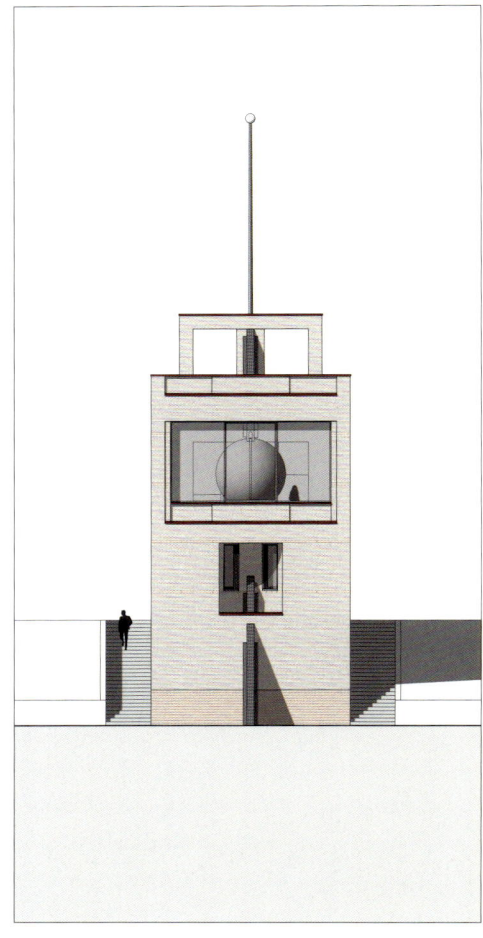

2–4. Aufrisse der Fassaden von Norden, von Westen und von Süden.

5, 6. Modell. (Photos: Stefan Müller.)

2–4. Elevations of the façades from the north, the west and the south.

5, 6. Model. (Photos: Stefan Müller.)

kriegerische Auseinandersetzungen während des Deutsch-Dänischen Krieges, aus denen Peter der Große als Sieger hervorgegangen war. Der lange Transport nach Sankt Petersburg war nicht unproblematisch: Der über vier Tonnen schwere Globus mußte wegen des anhaltenden Nordischen Krieges mehrfach umgeladen werden, vom Schiff auf Schlitten und umgekehrt, und gelangte schließlich im März 1717 nach St. Petersburg. Während dieser fast vierjährigen Reise mußten selbst Alleen einseitig gerodet werden, damit die Schlitten mit ihrer ungewöhnlich breiten Fracht passieren konnten.

Ein Brand zerstörte 1747 den Globus fast vollständig, doch wurde er bis 1750 erstmals nach historischen Quellen rekonstruiert, weshalb man dieses Kuriosum – trotz verschiedener Veränderun-

its problems. Because of the continuing Nordic War, the globe, weighing over four tons, had to be reloaded a few times. It finally arrived in St. Petersburg by ship and sled in March 1717. During this trip, that lasted almost four years, avenues had to be cleared on one side so that the sleds with their unusually broad cargo could pass through.

The globe was almost completely destroyed by fire in 1747, but by 1750 it had been reconstructed on the basis of historical sources. That is why one can still view this curiosity today, despite some changes, in the Lomonossow Museum in St. Petersburg.

When the globe was taken out of its building in 1713 its southern façade was deliberately broken off. This effectively destroyed the building's purpose and its charming disposition.

Because of the lack of historical documents, a reconstruction of the building surrounding the globe is not planned.

The terraced park north of the regional museum (Landesmuseum) Gottorf has been undergoing stages of restoration since 1994. The globe building is to be completed by the end of 2003 and will house a reconstruction of the globe.

Our task was to build a very small museum with an exhibition area of only 60 m² and to present the globe itself. As the building is the focal point of the park that measures almost six hectares, on three sides it is opened up by huge modern windows and like a modern museum displays its valuable contents to the outside world. A small terrace that functions as an observation platform allows the visitor to view the surrounding park, but is also a reminder of the Persian observatories, that served as models for the building constructed in 1637.

gen – noch heute in Sankt Petersburg im Lomonossow Museum besichtigen kann.

Als man 1713 den Globus aus dem Lusthaus herausholte, wurde dessen Südfassade dafür abgebrochen, ein Eingriff, der – abgesehen von der Sinnentleerung durch den Verlust des Globusses – den Untergang der reizvollen Situation einleitete, so daß heute mangels Quellen eine Rekonstruktion des Lusthauses nicht vorgenommen wird.

Seit 1994 wird der terrassierte Park nördlich des Landesmuseums Gottorf in verschiedenen Etappen wiederhergestellt. Bis Ende 2003 soll das Globushaus fertiggestellt sein, eine Rekonstruktion des Globusses wird dann dort aufgestellt.

Dementsprechend stellte sich uns die Bauaufgabe eines sehr kleinen Museums mit einer Ausstellungsfläche von nur

In keeping with tradition the globe
will be placed – i. e. hung in the room –
in such a way that its axis will be parallel
to the actual axis of the earth. In our
design this parallel to the earth's axis is
continued throughout the entire building. It extends outside to the building
in the park and rises out of the terrace.
It has been carried out in a finely structured, cast aluminium that has been
staggered at a number of different levels.

Two buildings with a relationship to
the stars clearly used the earth's axis in
their construction and served as an inspiration to us. The Jantar Mantar in
India, built in approximately 1730, is
also a solar and stellar observatory. The
other building is the Kitt Peak Solar
Observatory in Arizona, USA. A research
centre, this solar observatory was built in
1962 by Myron Goldsmith, a student of
Mies. (Myron Goldsmith taught architecture at the ITT in Chicago and Christoph Sattler and Thomas Albrecht were
his students.)

The building in this corner qualifies
both the meaning of location and of
time, for as with sacred buildings it
points to a much larger cosmic order.

60 m² und der Präsentation des Globusses selbst. Da das Haus den Mittelpunkt
des fast sechs Hektar großen Parks bildet, wird es nach drei Seiten durch über-
große moderne Fenster geöffnet und
zeigt seinen wertvollen Inhalt nach außen wie ein modernes Museum. Eine
kleine Terrasse als Aussichtsplattform
läßt den Besucher den Park von seiner
Mitte aus überblicken; sie erinnert aber
auch an die persischen Observatorien,
die dem Vorgängerbau von 1637 als Vorbild dienten.

Traditionsgemäß wird jeder Globus
so aufgestellt bzw. in den Raum gehängt,
daß seine Achse parallel zur wirklichen
Erdachse geführt wird. In unserem Entwurf wurde die somit entstehende Paral-
lele zur Erdachse durch das ganze Haus
geführt, sie erstreckt sich auch vor das
Gebäude in den Park und ragt oben aus
der Terrasse heraus. Sie ist als mehrfach
gestaffeltes, fein gestaltetes Gußalumini-
umprofil ausgeführt.

Zwei Gebäude mit Bezug zu den Ge-
stirnen haben diese Erdachse ebenfalls
sichtbar nachgebaut und uns inspiriert:
das Jantar Mantar in Indien, auch eine
Sternen- und Sonnenbeobachtungsstation, etwa aus dem Jahr 1730. Weiter das

Kitt Peak Solar Observatory in Arizona,
USA, eine wissenschaftliche Sonnenbeobachtungsstation aus dem Jahr 1962
des Mies-Schülers Myron Goldsmith.
(Myron Goldsmith lehrte Architektur
am IIT in Chicago, und Christoph Sattler und Thomas Albrecht studierten
bei ihm.)

Der gebaute Winkel relativiert die
Bedeutung des Ortes und der Zeit, indem er – ähnlich sakralen Gebäuden –
auf die wesentlich größere kosmische
Ordnung hinweist.

Unser Entwurf hat einerseits traditionelle und regionale Elemente – wie ein
rustiziertes Sockelgeschoß, Ebenenversprünge in der Außenwand, profilierte
Fenstergesimse und gemauerte Brüstungen – nicht durchsichtige Stahlgeländer –, andererseits weisen die großflächige Verglasung, die exakten kubischen
Formen und die rötlich durchschim-
mernde Farbe der gestrichenen Verklin-
kerung auf die Moderne hin.

Ein Blitzableiter trägt eine polierte
Edelstahlkugel als Symbol der Erde hoch
über dem Park. Sie befindet sich exakt
in der linearen Verlängerung der schrä-
gen Erdachse. Am unteren Ende der
Blitzableiterstange ist eine kleine Kugel
als Abschluß angebracht, die den Mond
darstellt. Sie befindet sich im richtigen
Größen- und Entfernungsverhältnis zur
Erde, im Maßstab 1:30 Mio.

Projektleiter: Ulrike Feucht
Mitarbeiter: Sigurd Hauer, Katrin Hülk,
Mehra Mehrdadi, Sven Meller, Christian
Salewski

7. Myron Goldsmith,
Nationales Observato-
rium Kitt Peak, Arizona,
1962. (Photo: Ezra
Stoller.)
8. Innenraummodell
des Globussaals. (Pho-
to: Stefan Müller.)

7. Myron Goldsmith,
Kitt Peak National
Observatory, Arizona,
1962. (Photo: Ezra
Stoller.)
8. Model of the exhibi-
tion room with the
globe. (Photo: Stefan
Müller.)

9. Muster eines Profils
aus Gußaluminium.
(Photo: Stefan Müller.)

9. Sample for a panel
of cast aluminium.
(Photo: Stefan Müller.)

On the one hand our design has traditional and regional elements – such as
a rustic base, variations in the planes of
the outer wall, and rather than transpar-
ent steel balustrades profiled window
ledges and masonry parapets, on the
other hand the large expanse of glazing,
the exact cubic forms and the reddish
colour shimmering through the painted
clinker bricks are modern elements.

High above the park a polished
sphere of high-grade steel, symbolizing
the earth, has been placed on a lightning rod. It is exactly in the linear extension of the sloping axis of the earth. An
end-point is at the bottom end of the
lightning rod where a small sphere represents the moon. In its proportions of
size and distance from the earth it is to
scale 1:30 million.

Project architect: Ulrike Feucht
Collaborators: Sigurd Hauer, Katrin Hülk,
Mehra Mehrdadi, Sven Meller, Christian
Salewski

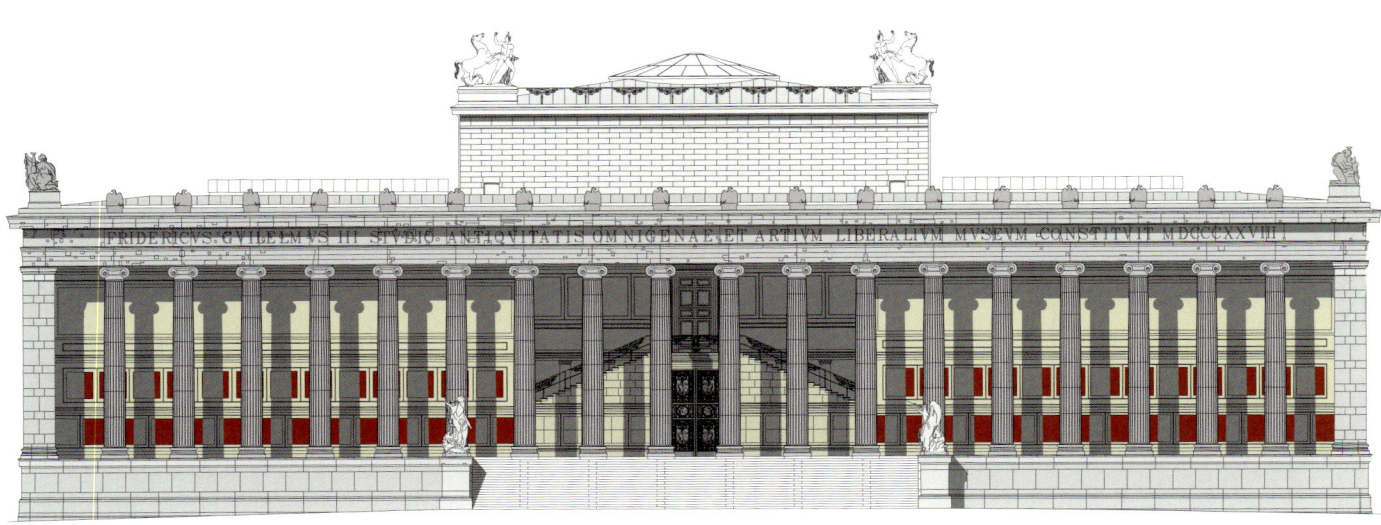

1. Aufriß des Gebäudes vom Lustgarten.

1. Elevation of the building from the Lust-garten.

Grundinstandsetzung des Alten Museums, Berlin-Mitte, 1999–2012

Das 1825 begonnene und 1830 vollendete wohl wichtigste Gebäude von Karl Friedrich Schinkel wurde ursprünglich als ein zweigeteiltes Museum entworfen: Im Hauptgeschoß mit der dem Pantheon in Rom nachempfundenen Rotunde wurden die antiken Vasen und Skulpturen gezeigt, während im Obergeschoß die Ölgemälde der europäischen Malerei mit Seitenlicht präsentiert wurden.

Eine prächtige, raffinierte Treppe im Freien hinter der zweigeschossigen Säulenreihe erschließt bis heute das Obergeschoß. Beide Ausstellungsebenen hatten ihren eigenen Zugang von außen. Dieses ungewöhnliche Konzept – zwei Museen in einem Haus – führte jedoch zu einer dauernden Folge von Umbauten zwischen 1860 und 1991. Die komplizierte und teilweise fragile Gründungssituation, eine authentische Pfahlgründung auf 3050 Kiefernstämmen, der beabsichtigte Anschluß an die archäologische Promenade, die alle Bauten auf der Museumsinsel miteinander verbindet, und der allzu verständliche Wunsch des jetzigen Nutzers, des Museums der Antikensammlung, nach einer umfassenden, nunmehr endgültigen Grundinstandsetzung des Hauses machen den Entwurfsprozeß zu einer höchst komplexen Aufgabe im dauernden spannenden Dialog mit der Denkmalpflege. Folgende Punkte sind unter vielen anderen Gegenstand der Planung:
– Die innere Verbindung aller drei Geschosse wird durch zwei zusätzliche

Renovation of the Altes Museum (Old Museum), Berlin-Mitte, 1999–2012

The Altes Museum, probably Karl Friedrich Schinkel's most important building, begun in 1825 and completed in 1830, was originally designed as a museum of two parts. Antique vases and sculptures were exhibited on the main floor with its rotunda inspired by the Pantheon in Rome, while on the upper storey side lighting was used for the presentation of European oil paintings.

A magnificent, ornate external staircase behind the row of two-storey columns still provides access to the upper storey. Both of the exhibition floors had their own external entrance. This unusual concept – two museums in one building – would, however, lead to an ongoing series of alterations between 1860 and 1991. The complicated and in parts fragile substructure, an authentic pile foundation on 3050 pine trunks, the planned link to the archaeological promenade connecting all the buildings on the Museumsinsel, as well as the understandable desire of the current user, the museum of the collection of antiques, for a comprehensive and conclusive renovation, all served to make the design process into a highly complex task, entailing a permanent and exciting dialogue with the office for the preservation of historical monuments. Amongst many others, the following points were objectives of the planning:
– Two additional stairwells, symmetrical to the rotunda, allow all three storeys to be connected on the inside. This means that the museum can now only be

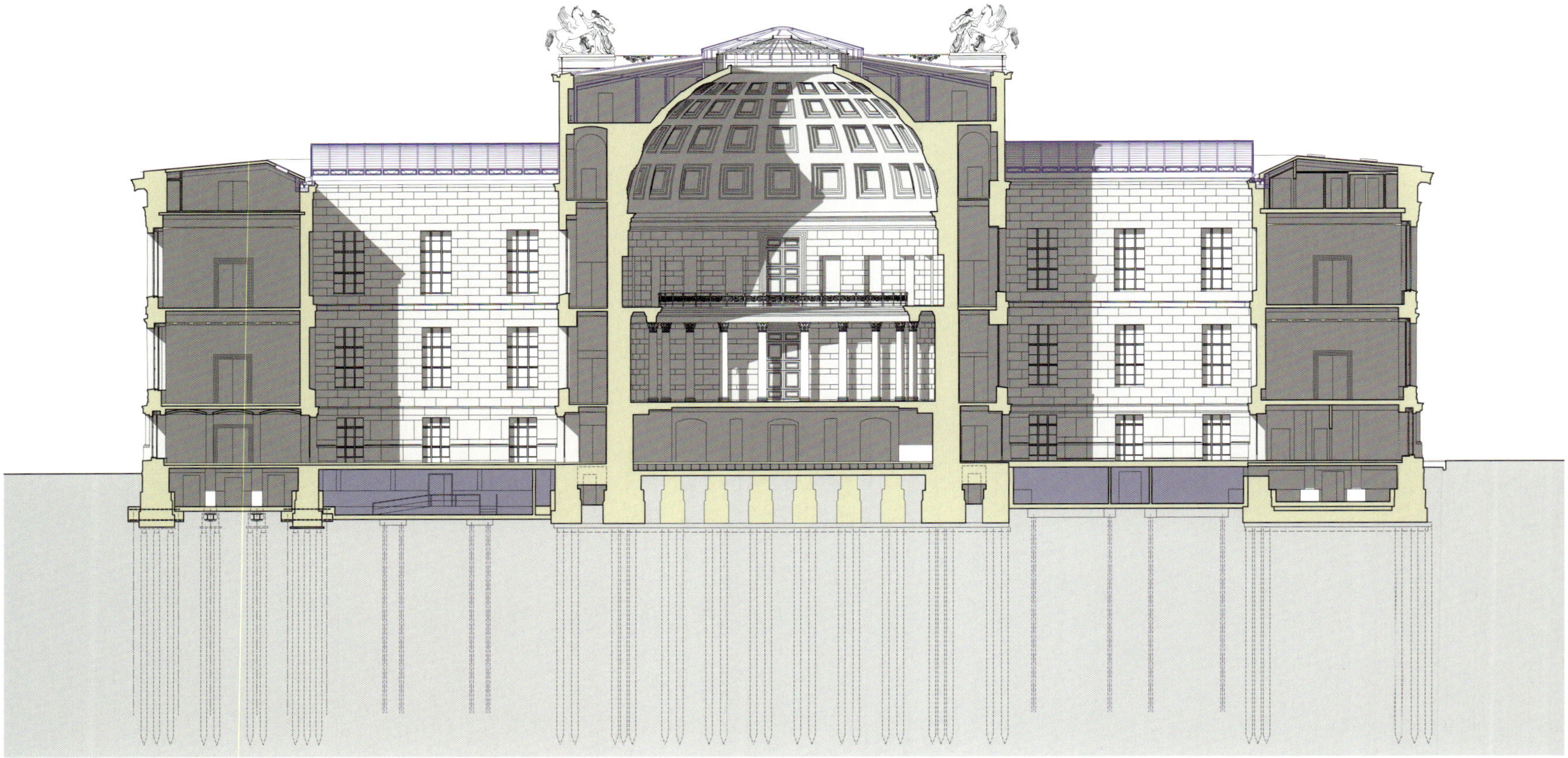

repräsentative Treppenhäuser geschaffen, die symmetrisch neben der Rotunde liegen. Dadurch wird erreicht, daß das Museum nur noch von einem einzigen Eingang im Hauptgeschoß erschlossen und die außenliegende Treppe nur noch bei besonderen Gelegenheiten benutzt wird.

– Die provisorische Glaswand vor dieser Treppe von 1991 wird entfernt.

– Alle Ausstellungsräume werden vollständig neu gestaltet.

– Die beiden bisher nicht genützten Lichthöfe werden mit einem filigranen Glasdach überspannt und dadurch in Innenräume umgewandelt.

– Der unter der Rotunde befindliche, ehemalige Kohlenkeller verbindet die jetzt neu geschaffenen Räume der Lichthöfe auf einer Ebene und wird ein zusätzlicher Ausstellungsraum.

– Das gesamte Sockelgeschoß, vormals Verwaltung, wird in ein drittes Ausstellungsgeschoß umfunktioniert.

accessed from a single entrance on the main floor and that the outside staircase is only used for special occasions.

– The temporary glass wall in front of this staircase, dating from 1991, is to be removed.

– All of the exhibition rooms are to be completely refurbished.

– The two air-wells that have not been used will be covered with a filigree glass roof and thereby made into inner rooms.

– The former coal cellar under the rotunda connects the newly created air-well rooms on one level and becomes an additional exhibition room.

– The entire ground-floor storey, formerly housing the administration, is to be turned into a third storey for exhibitions.

– A cafeteria, a museum shop and a variety of adjoining rooms are placed in the ground-floor storey in such a way that this building's status as a historical monument is not affected.

2. Längsschnitt.
3. Modell eines überdachten Innenhofes.

2. Longitudinal section.
3. Model of a covered court.

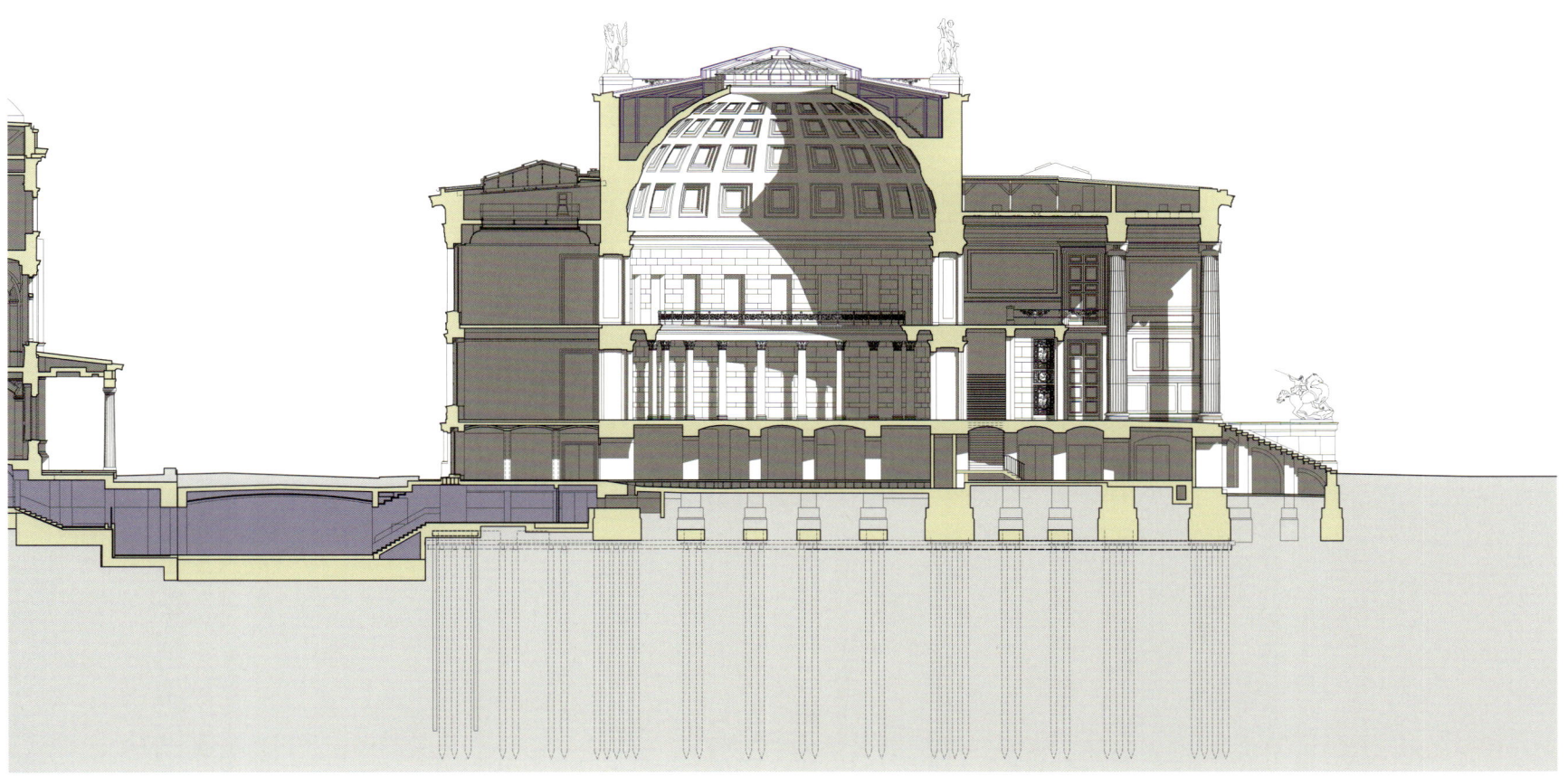

4. Querschnitt.

4. Cross section.

– Denkmalverträglich werden eine Cafeteria, ein Museumsladen und diverse Nebenräume im Sockelgeschoß untergebracht.

– Unter Beibehaltung der äußeren Erscheinung von 1830 werden neue Fenster sowie Klima- und Sicherheitstechnik eingebaut. Dächer und Wände werden saniert.

– Der hölzerne Pfahlrost wird durch zusätzliche Gründungsmaßnahmen verstärkt.

Gemeinsam mit allen Beteiligten ist es gelungen, die Vielzahl der Forderungen einvernehmlich in eine detaillierte Planung umzusetzen, die jetzt nur noch auf die Ausführung wartet.

Projektleiter: Frigga Uhlisch
Mitarbeiter: Peter Dörrie, Evelyn Galsdorf, Dietmar Husmann, Thomas Katzke, Christian von Oppen, Nina Otto, Ian Pautzke, Sebastian Treese, Peter Westermann

– The external appearance of 1830 will be retained, but new windows as well as air-conditioning and security systems will be added. Ceilings and walls will be renovated.

– The wooden pile grid will be strengthened with additional foundation work.

It was possible to reach a consensus with everybody involved and to set out the many requirements in detailed plans that now only have to be carried out.

Project architect: Frigga Uhlisch
Collaborators: Peter Dörrie, Evelyn Galsdorf, Dietmar Husmann, Thomas Katzke, Christian von Oppen, Nina Otto, Ian Pautzke, Sebastian Treese, Peter Westermann

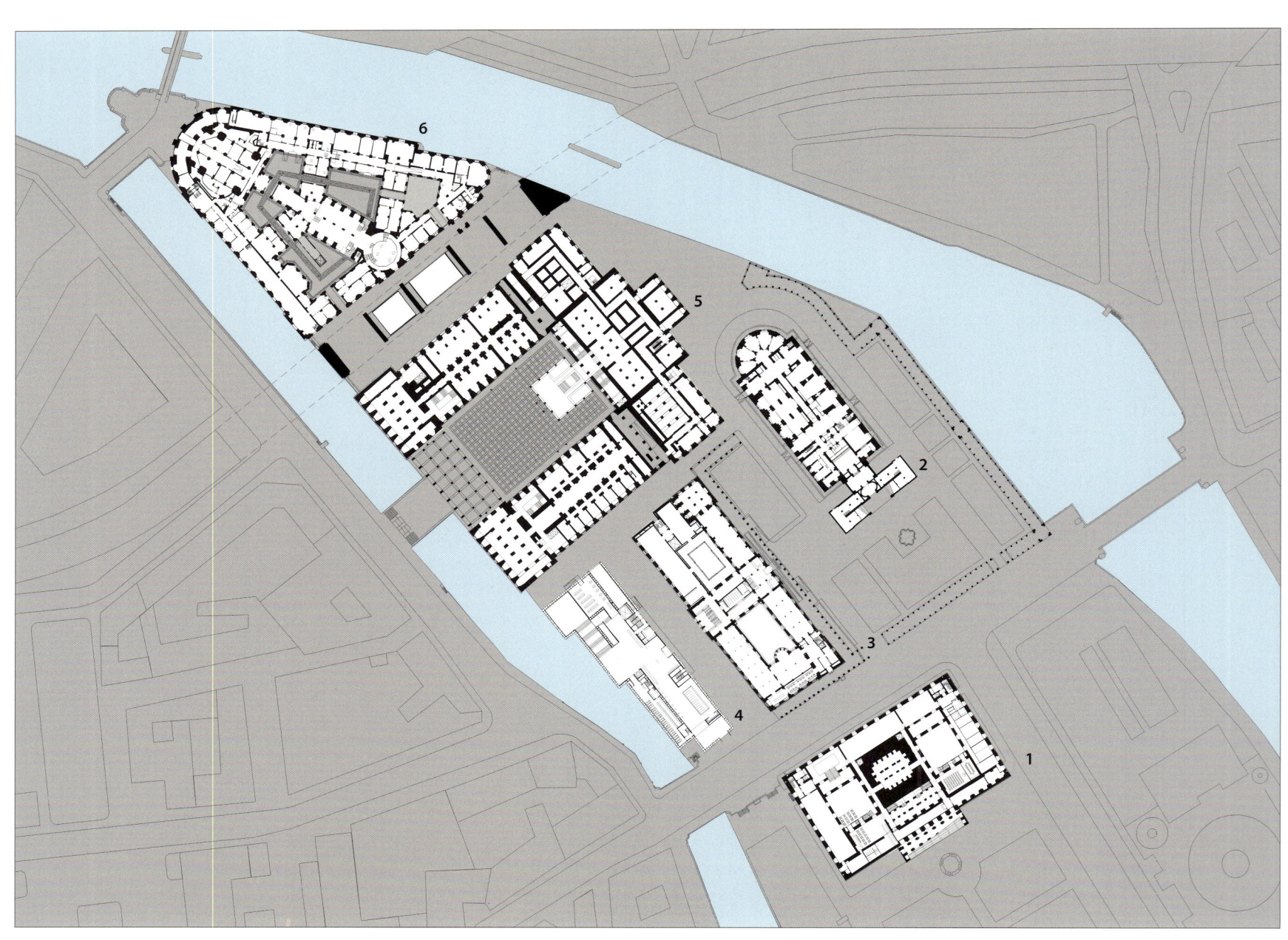

Masterplan für die Museumsinsel, Berlin-Mitte, 1998–2010

Mit der Beauftragung der Grundsanierung des Alten Museums begannen wir nicht nur mit dortigen Nutzern einen spannenden Dialog über die Frage, wie ein saniertes Museum idealiter auszusehen habe, sondern auch mit den anderen Architekten, die schon an der Museumsinsel arbeiteten.

Seit dem Jahr 1997 plante der Wiener Architekt Heinz Tesar die Sanierung des Bodemuseums, im selben Jahr gewann der Engländer David Chipperfield den Wettbewerb für die entsprechenden Maßnahmen am Neuen Museum. Da bei allen drei Museumsbauten ähnliche Fragestellungen auftraten, entwickelte sich ein regelmäßiger Dialog zwischen den drei beauftragten Architekten und den Nutzern. Dieser Gesprächskreis wurde vom damaligen Generaldirektor Wolf-Dieter Dube nicht nur angeregt und gefördert, sondern führte schließlich Ende des Jahres 1998 dazu, in einer separaten Beauftragung die sogenannte »Planungsgruppe Museumsinsel« ins Leben zu rufen, um bis zur vollständigen Fertigstellung aller Sanierungsarbeiten auf der Museumsinsel – also weit nach 2015 – übergeordnete Problemstellungen und gemeinsame Ziele zu definieren und so letztendlich ein zusammenhängendes und sinnvolles Gesamtensemble dieser nationalen Bauaufgabe zu erreichen. Die Planungsgruppe wurde als eine zusätzliche und unabhängige Planungsinstanz eingesetzt, parallel zum Nutzer, der Stiftung Preußischer Kulturbesitz, und zum eigentlichen Bauherrn, dem

Master plan for the Museumsinsel (Museum Island), Berlin-Mitte, 1998–2010

When we were commissioned with the renovation of the Altes Museum we not only entered into an interesting dialogue with its users on the question of the ideal appearance of a renovated museum, but also with the other architects who were already working on the Museumsinsel.

The Viennese architect Heinz Tesar had been involved in the renovation of the Bodemuseum since 1997. In the same year the English architect, David Chipperfield, won the competition for the renovation of the Neues Museum. Since similar questions arose for each museum building there was a regular dialogue between the commissioned architects and the users. This dialogue was not only initiated and supported by the general director at the time, Wolf-Dieter Dube, but also led to the formation at the end of 1998 of a planning group for the Museumsinsel, whose task until the completion of the renovation work on the Musemsinsel – well after 2015 – lay in defining larger problems and common goals and thereby achieving a coherent and meaningful, total ensemble of this national building task. This planning group was an additional, independent planning unit, parallel to the user, the Stiftung Preußischer Kulturbesitz, and the actual client, the Bundesamt für Bauwesen und Raumordnung (Federal Building Department).

The first large concrete task facing the planning group for the Musuemsinsel was the development, by June 1999, of

In Arbeitsgemeinschaft mit Heinz Tesar, David Chipperfield und Oswald Mathias Ungers

In cooperation with Heinz Tesar, David Chipperfield and Oswald Mathias Ungers

2, 3. Erschließungsstudien zum Pergamonmuseum.

2, 3. Studies for the entrance situation to the Pergamonmuseum.

Bundesamt für Bauwesen und Raumordnung.

Die erste große konkrete Aufgabe der Planungsgruppe Museumsinsel war die Entwicklung des sogenannten Masterplans I bis zum Juni 1999, der zunächst in verschiedenen Alternativen untersuchte, wie sich der jetzt schon beachtliche Besucherstrom nach der Sanierung aller fünf Museen auf der Insel entwickeln würde. Darüber hinaus wurde die Notwendigkeit gesehen, für den sogenannten »Kurzbesucher« einen eigenen kleinen Rundgang zu entwickeln, da auf der ganzen Welt ein großer Anteil der Museumsbesucher sich auf einer Bustour durch die jeweilige Stadt befindet und er das Museum nicht so sehr im Sinne einer kunsthistorischen Rezeption wie etwa die Gebrüder Humboldt wahrnimmt, sondern eher als ein modernes Event.

Da die Planung der Alten Nationalgalerie durch den Architekten HG Merz bei der Konstituierung der Planungsgruppe 1998 schon praktisch fertig war, wurde dieses Haus in seiner projektierten Form bei unseren Überlegungen als gegeben angesehen.

Im Mai 2000 ging aus einem Wettbewerb zur Instandsetzung und Ergänzung

the so-called Master Plan I. This plan, using different alternatives, examined how the already considerable number of visitors would develop after the renovation of all five museums on the island. In addition, it was recognized that a small tour should be especially designed for the so-called »short-term visitor« for all over the world a large portion of visitors to museums come from bus tours and the visitor does not so much experience the museum in the sense of an art-historical activity, for example as the Humboldt brothers would have, but rather as a modern event.

When the planning group 1998 was constituted, the architect HG Merz had practically finished his planning work for the Alte Nationalgalerie. In our point of view we accepted the project form of this building as given.

In May of 2000 the Cologne architect Oswald Mathias Ungers won the competition for the renovation of and extension to the Pergamonmuseum and joined the planning group.

The basic statements of the master plan were:

Firstly, the individuality of each of the five buildings should be safeguarded as far as possible. Each building will retain

des Pergamonmuseums der Kölner Architekt Oswald Mathias Ungers als Sieger hervor und trat der Planungsgruppe hinzu.

Die Grundaussagen des Masterplans waren:

Erstens, den individuellen Ausdruck der fünf einzelnen Häuser so weit als irgend möglich zu wahren. Jedes Haus behält seine charakteristische Eingangssituation und bekommt eine unverzichtbare, minimale Grundausstattung mit Cafeteria, Shop etc.

Zweitens sahen wir, daß neue, große Zusatzfunktionen nur in neu zu schaffenden Flächen unterhalb des Pergamonmuseums oder in einem separaten Eingangsgebäude unterzubringen sind.

its characteristic entrance situation and will be provided with an indisputable, minimal basic fit out with cafeteria, shop etc.

Secondly, we saw that new, large additional functions would have to be accommodated in newly created spaces under the Pergamonmuseum or in a separate entry building.

Thirdly, a sensible sequence for the gradual renovation of the different buildings was established, so that at least two museums would be open to the public at all times.

Fourthly, the area housing the former Friedrich Engels barracks, to the west of the Bodemuseum on the other side of the Kupfergraben would be designated

Drittens wurde eine sinnvolle Reihenfolge für die schrittweise Renovierung der verschiedenen Häuser festgelegt, die immer mindestens zwei Museen für das Publikum offen hält.

Viertens wurde die westlich des Bodemuseums, jenseits des Kupfergrabens gelegene Fläche der ehemaligen Friedrich-Engels-Kaserne als Funktions- und Erweiterungsfläche für die Museumsinsel vorgesehen, die den Namen »Museumshöfe« – in Anlehnung an die unweit davon gelegenen Hackeschen Höfe – erhält. Dort werden die Flächen der Nebenfunktionen aller fünf Museen zusammengefaßt, wie Verwaltung, Bibliotheken, Depots und Restaurierungswerkstätten.

Fünftens wurde vorgeschlagen, die Erdgeschoßflächen vom Alten Museum, Neuen Museum, Pergamonmuseum und Bodemuseum miteinander zu verbinden, um – wie vor 1940 – den fachübergreifenden Zusammenhang der Häuser und ihrer Sammlungen zu verstärken und ihre inhaltliche Verbindung erlebbar zu machen. Durch eine Folge von 23 Räumen kann der künftige Besucher so die vier hintereinander liegenden Museen durchschreiten, teils durch geschlossene Räume, teils in den jetzt glasüberdeckten historischen Innenhöfen.

Im weiteren Verlauf wurde der Masterplan konkretisiert und weiterentwickelt, so daß im Sommer 2000 ein sogenannter Masterplan II entstand. Außer den obengenannten – jetzt vertieften – Überlegungen sieht er einen großen zusätzlichen Museumsbau vor, der sich allerdings nicht mehr auf der Insel, sondern an der Südostecke des Kasernengeländes befindet – als weit in das 21. Jahrhundert blickende Vision.

Mitarbeiter: Francois von Chappuis, Peter Dörrie, Nina Otto

a functional area and an area for the future expansion of the Museumsinsel, which would be known as the »Museumshöfe« on the same lines as the nearby Hackesche Höfe. Here, the secondary functions – such as administration, libraries, depots, and restoration workshops – of all five museums will be concentrated.

Fifthly, it was proposed to link the ground floors of the Altes Museum, the Neues Museum, the Pergamonmuseum and the Bodemuseum: in order to reinforce the interdisciplinary link between the buildings and their collections, as had been the case before 1940, and allow for the actual experiencing of this connection. The future visitor can pass through a sequence of 23 rooms belonging to the four museums that lie beside each other. Partly he has to go through closed rooms and partly through historic courtyards that have been covered with glass roofs.

As things develop further, work was carried out on the master plan and it was put in more concrete terms so that in the summer of 2000 a so-called Master Plan II was ready. Further to the considerations mentioned above, which are now more consolidated, an additional museum was envisaged. This building would however not be located on the island but rather on the southeastern corner of the site of the former barracks, as a vision looking far into the 21st century.

Collaborators: François von Chappuis, Peter Dörrie, Nina Otto

4. Schnittmodell mit der Raumsequenz der archäologischen Promenade. (Photo: Planungsgruppe Museumsinsel.)

4. Sectional model with the room sequence of the archaeological promenade. (Photo: Planungsgruppe Museumsinsel.)

Skulpturenpräsentation in der Pfeiler-halle der Gemäldegalerie, Berlin-Tier-garten, 2003

Die 1998 eingeweihte Gemäldegalerie hat in ihrer Mitte einen 1500 m² gro-ßen, leeren Raum, in dem lediglich eine moderne Skulptur von Walter de Maria zu finden ist. Der Bauherr und frühere Generaldirektor Wolf-Dieter Dube achte-te streng darauf, die erfrischende Leere und Weite dieses Raumes als Spannungs-gegensatz zu den 60 Ausstellungsräumen mit ihren 1500 kostbaren Ölgemälden zu erhalten. Durch 32 Oculi fällt Son-nenlicht direkt in den Raum und bildet somit Licht und Schatten. Im Gegensatz dazu werden die Ausstellungsräume durch eine komplexe Glasdachkonstruk-tion mit diffusem Tageslicht versorgt.

Fünf Jahre nach der Einweihung sah der neue Generaldirektor Peter Klaus Schuster die Notwendigkeit, diesen wert-vollen Raum zumindest interimistisch für drei Jahre umzunutzen. Die seit 1997 magazinierte Skulpturensammlung der Stiftung Preußischer Kulturbesitz sollte bis zu ihrer endgültigen Präsentation im renovierten Bodemuseum der Öffent-lichkeit zugänglich gemacht werden.

Natürlich war es für uns emotional nicht ganz einfach, an diesem hart er-kämpften, fast sakralen Innenraum nach schon so kurzer Zeit Veränderungen vor-zunehmen.

Auf der anderen Seite wollten wir uns aber nicht wie manche Kollegen als die Hausmeister unserer eigenen Bauten fühlen, zumal uns das Anliegen der Skulpturenpräsentation allzu verständ-lich war.

Presentation of sculptures in the pillared hall of the Gemäldegalerie (Picture Gallery), Berlin-Tiergarten, 2003

In the middle of the Gemäldegalerie (picture gallery) officially opened in 1998 there is a large, empty room mea-suring 1500 m² containing only a mod-ern sculpture by Walter de Maria. The gallery's former general director, Wolf-Dieter Dube, who promoted the new building, was careful to maintain the invigorating emptiness and expanse of this room. It should act as a clear con-trast to the 60 exhibition rooms with their 1500 precious oil paintings. Sun-light enters the room directly through 32 oculi, creating light and shadow. In contrast, the exhibition rooms are lit by diffuse daylight through a complex glass construction.

Five years after the official opening the new general director, Peter Klaus Schuster, saw the necessity of putting this estimable room to a new use, at least for an interim of three years. The sculp-ture collection of the Stiftung Preußi-scher Kulturbesitz, in storage since 1997 and eventually be shown in the newly renovated Bodemuseum, should until this time be made available to the pub-lic.

Naturally it was emotionally not en-tirely easy for us to make changes after such a short time to an almost sacred, inner room that had been fought for so hard.

On the other hand, we did not want to feel the way some of our colleagues do – that we were the caretakers of our own buildings and in any case we cer-

217

Gleichzeitig bot sich bei dieser Gelegenheit die Chance, die bisherigen Beleuchtungskörper abzuändern, mit denen wir – offen gestanden – nicht wirklich zufrieden waren.

Für die ausgewählten Skulpturen mußten verschieden große Sockel geschaffen werden, die sich in den strengen Formenkanon der Galerie einfügen sollten. Als Material wählten wir, wie bei den Türgewänden und Sockeln in den Ausstellungsräumen, fein gegliederte, kubische Betonfertigteile, die – nicht verspachtelt – ihre industrielle Herkunft zeigen.

Über die Beleuchtung mußte völlig neu nachgedacht werden: Unter Verwendung der bisher vorhandenen Installationen wurden an jedem Pfeiler vier schwenkbare Spots ergänzt, die Grundhelligkeit der Halle wurde durch eine ausgeglichene Anstrahlung der Decke erreicht. Um diese Vielzahl an technischen Elementen zu kaschieren, entwarfen wir eine Verkleidung der Leuchten aus Gußaluminium.

Diese kapitellartigen Umfassungen konzipierten wir zwar in der äußeren Form streng rechteckig, die Flächen sind jedoch von organisch geformten Öffnungen durchbrochen, die den fließenden Vorgang des Gießens nachempfinden.

Projektleiter: Alexander Waimer

tainly sympathized with the wish to display the sculptures.

We were thereby also given the chance to change the existing lighting fixtures with which we were quite frankly not entirely satisfied.

The selected sculptures required pedestals of different sizes, that, however, had to conform with the gallery's strict canon of forms. The material we chose was a finely structured, cubic pre-fabricated concrete. This was also used on the doors and the pedestals in the exhibition rooms. The rough finish on these parts showed their industrial origins.

The lighting had to be thought through anew. Using the existing installations, we added four swivel spot-lights to each pillar. Balanced beams of light aimed at the ceiling make the hall bright. In order to conceal these many technical elements we designed a cladding for the lights out of cast aluminium.

Although we conceived these capital-like settings as absolutely rectangular in their outer form, their surfaces are perforated by organically formed openings that call to mind the flowing action of pouring.

Project architect: Alexander Waimer

2. Ansicht zweier Figuren. (Photo: Stefan Müller.)
3. Die Pfeilerhalle in ihrem ursprünglichen Zustand. (Photo: Stefan Müller.)

2. View of two figures. (Photo: Stefan Müller.)
3. The original condition of the pillared hall. (Photo: Stefan Müller.)

4. Leuchtenverkleidungen aus Gußaluminium. (Photo: Stefan Müller.)

4. Light fittings in cast aluminium. (Photo: Stefan Müller.)

1. Perspektive der rekonstruierten Nord- und Westfassade von Unter den Linden.

1. Perspective view of the restored north and west façade from Unter den Linden.

Das Berliner Stadtschloß, Berlin-Mitte, 1997 und 2002

Städtebau: Betrachtet man die historischen Ensembles in Berlin, so kann sich einzig der östliche Teil der Straße Unter den Linden mit der Öffnung der Blockrandbebauung zum Forum Fridericianum und mit dem Übergang zum Schloßplatz, zum Lustgarten und zur Museumsinsel mit der Qualität der großen Straßen und Platzkonfigurationen von Rom, Paris oder London messen. Wunderbare Bauten des strengen preußischen Barock stehen in spannungsvoller Beziehung zu den vier großen Beispielen des Schinkelschen Klassizismus: die Neue Wache, das Alte Museum, die Bauakademie und die Friedrichwerdersche Kirche.

Zwei weitere Elemente dieser städtebaulichen Situation wurden in jüngster Zeit wiederhergestellt, quasi als Ouvertüre: 1988 wurde auf der Brücke, welche die Straße Unter den Linden mit der Insel verbindet, der von Schinkel entworfene Figurenschmuck ergänzt. im Jahr 2003 entstand daneben die völlig zerstörte Kommandantur in ihrer äußeren Form.

Es fehlt jedoch das Bauwerk, auf das sich die Stadträume und Bauten dieses Ensembles beziehen und von dem sie abgeleitet sind: das Berliner Schloß. Das vorliegende Konzept geht daher von der Wiedererrichtung des Bauvolumens des Schlosses aus.

Architektur: Die Mitte Berlins wird in entscheidendem Maße von der vielfältigen Architektursprache des ausgehenden 20. und des beginnenden 21. Jahr-

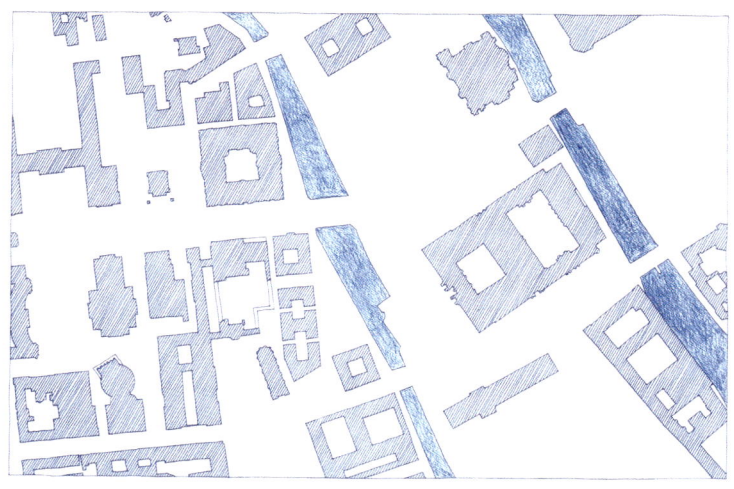

The Royal Palace, Berlin-Mitte, 1997 and 2002

2. Lageplan.

2. Site plan.

Urban Design: Of the historic ensembles in Berlin, it is only the eastern part of the boulevard, Unter den Linden – opening to the Forum Fridericianum and merging into the square surrounding the royal palace, as well as into the Lustgarten and the Museumsinsel – that has the quality of the great boulevards and the configuration of squares that can be found in Paris, Rome or London. Wonderful buildings in the pure Prussian Baroque style stand in contrast to the four great examples of Schinkel's Classicism: the Neue Wache (New Guard House), the Altes Museum (Old Museum), the Bauakademie (Academy of Architecture) and the Friedrichswerdersche Kirche.

Two further elements of this urban design were recently restored, quasi as an overture. In 1988 the statues designed by Schinkel on the bridge that connects Unter den Linden with the island were supplemented and in the year 2003 the

Das Berliner Stadtschloß, Berlin-Mitte, 1997
und 2002

hunderts bestimmt. Regierungsbauten im Spreebogen, Potsdamer Platz, Alexanderplatz und die Kriegslücken füllenden Neubauten der Friedrich- und Dorotheenstadt sind Architekturdokumente unserer Zeit. Die Mitte wird sich modern präsentieren.

Es zeugt somit nicht von mangelndem architektonischen Mut, sondern von einer Haltung gestalterischer Gelassenheit, wenn sich die Ergänzung des einzigen exzeptionellen Ensembles historischer Stadtstruktur Berlins heute auf die Rekonstruktion wichtiger Teile des Schlosses einläßt:

Die Nord- und Westfassaden und der Schlüterhof sind in diesem Projekt wiederhergestellt. Süd- und Ostseite und westlicher Innenhof des Schlosses erhalten ein durch Licht- und Schatten belebtes Relief im Putz. Die Gliederung von Fenstern, Portalen, Gesimsen und Pilastern wird hier artikuliert, trägt jedoch keine barocken Ornamentelemente in sich. Die Kuppel wird nicht rekonstruiert, um den historischen Bruch dezent zu zeigen.

In den ursprünglich je 7 m hohen Geschossen der ersten und zweiten Etage sind Zwischengeschosse vorgesehen. Dadurch entsteht eine Zweiteilung der historischen Kastenfenster, die von außen nicht spürbar sein wird.

Das kleine, torbildende Gebäude zwischen Schloß und Dom an der Brücke erhält eine moderne Fassade in kleinteilig gegliedertem Gußeisen.

Nutzung: Es handelt sich nicht um die Wiederherstellung des Hohenzollernschlosses oder des Schlosses der Deutschen Kaiser. Die Herausforderung besteht in der harmonischen Integration einer kleinen – neuen – Stadt in der Hülle des alten – traditionsreichen – Schlosses. Vergleichbar könnte das Resultat mit der im Krieg fast vollkommen zerstörten Münchner Residenz in ihrer

destroyed military headquarters were restored in their external form.

What is missing, however, is the building to which the urban spaces and the buildings in this ensemble relate. This building is the palace. Our concept, therefore, proceeds from the restoration of the palace's building volume.

Architecture: Berlin's centre has been largely defined by the diversity of architectural languages in the closing 20th and early 21st centuries. Government buildings in the Spreebogen, Potsdamer Platz, Alexanderplatz and the new buildings put up in Friedrichstadt and Dorotheenstadt in the empty spaces left by the war, document the architecture of our age. Berlin's centre will be modern.

It is, therefore, not a sign of architectural cowardliness but of equanimity to get involved in the reconstruction of important parts of the palace for one is thereby dealing with the only exceptional ensemble of Berlin's historic structure. This project restores the northern and western façades as well as the Schlüter courtyard. A plaster relief, enlivened through light and shadow, is placed on the southern and eastern sides as well as in the western, inner courtyard. While the structuring of windows, portals, ledges and pilasters is articulated, there is no attempt made at Baroque ornamentation elements. The historic breach will be indicated discreetly through the non-restoration of the dome.

Mezzanines are planned in the historic storeys of the first and second floors, each 7 m in height. This means that the historic box windows will be divided into two, an effect that will not be noticeable from outside.

The small building, that functions as a gate on the bridge between the palace and the cathedral, will be given a modern façade in cast iron, structured into small parts.

223

heutigen Nutzung oder dem Palais Royal in Paris sein.

Der Schlüterhof soll ein urbaner, belebter, öffentlicher Platz werden, im Ansatz ähnlich den Berliner Hackeschen Höfen auf einem dem Ort entsprechenden Niveau.

Alle Läden, Restaurants, Handelsbetriebe, Kommunikationseinrichtungen und Büros sowie öffentliche Ausstellungshallen und die ins Auge gefaßte große Bibliothek sind von diesem Hof aus erschlossen.

Der westliche Schloßhof ist in Größe und Architektur neu gefaßt und besitzt einen nahezu intimen Charakter. Vorgezogene Terrassen verkleinern ihn im Vergleich zum Eosanderhof. Ein Hotel mit Konferenzzentrum orientiert sich zu diesem Hof und den Terrassen. Aus dem großen Konferenz- und Festsaal blickt man auf den urbanen Schlüterhof und den exzellenten Risalit des großen Treppenhauses im Spreeflügel des Hofes.

Im Herbst 2002 ergänzten wir unsere Studie durch den Versuch, das Raumprogramm der Gemäldegalerie am Kemperplatz in den westlichen Teil des zweiten Obergeschosses unterzubringen, da im Sommer 2002 bei den Überlegungen zur Definition eines Raumprogramms für das neu zu bauende Schloß die Stiftung Preußischer Kulturbesitz Raumansprüche für die Dahlemer Sammlung angemeldet hatte.

Mitarbeiter: Frigga Uhlisch

Use: The goal here is not the restoration of the Hohenzollern palace or the palace of the German emperors. The challenge lies in the harmonious integration of a small – new – city in the shell of the old palace, so rich in tradition. This can be compared with today's use of the former royal residence in Munich, that was almost completely destroyed in the War or the Palais Royal in Paris.

The Schlüterhof should be an urban, lively space, similar to a place like Berlin's Hackesche Höfe.

All stores, restaurants, businesses, communication centres and offices as well as all public exhibition halls and the foreseen large library can be reached from this courtyard.

In both in its architecture and size the western courtyard has been newly conceived and now has an almost intimate character. In contrast to the Eosanderhof, this courtyard is made smaller by projecting terraces. A hotel with conference facilities is orientated towards this courtyard and terraces. The large conference-banquet hall affords a view of the urban Schlüter courtyard and the excellent salient of the great stairwell in the Spree wing of the courtyard.

In the autumn of 2002 we added to our study by examining the possibility of accommodating the spatial requirements of the Gemäldegalerie (picture gallery) on Kemperplatz in the western part of the second storey. This was in response to the claims made by the Stiftung Preußicher Kulturbesitz in the summer of 2002 for transferring the Dahlem collection to the planned palace.

Collaborator: Frigga Uhlisch

5–7. Studie zur Unterbringung der Gemäldegalerie im Stadtschloß, Schnitt und Grundrisse (Erdgeschoß, Ausstellungsgeschoß).

5–7. Study for the accommodation of the Gemäldegalerie collection in the Royal Palace, section and floor plans (ground floor, exhibition floor).

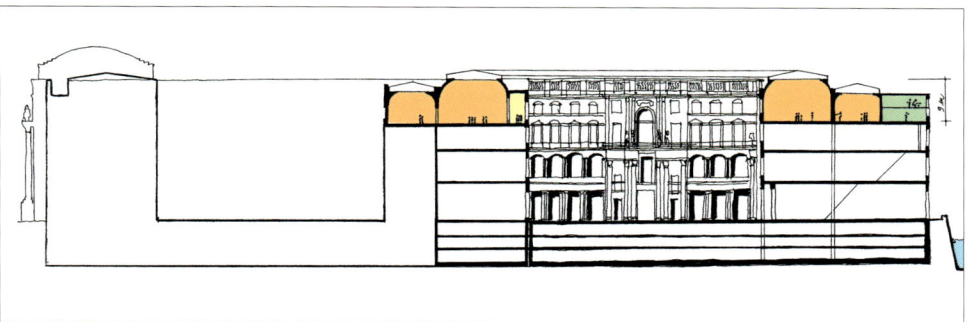

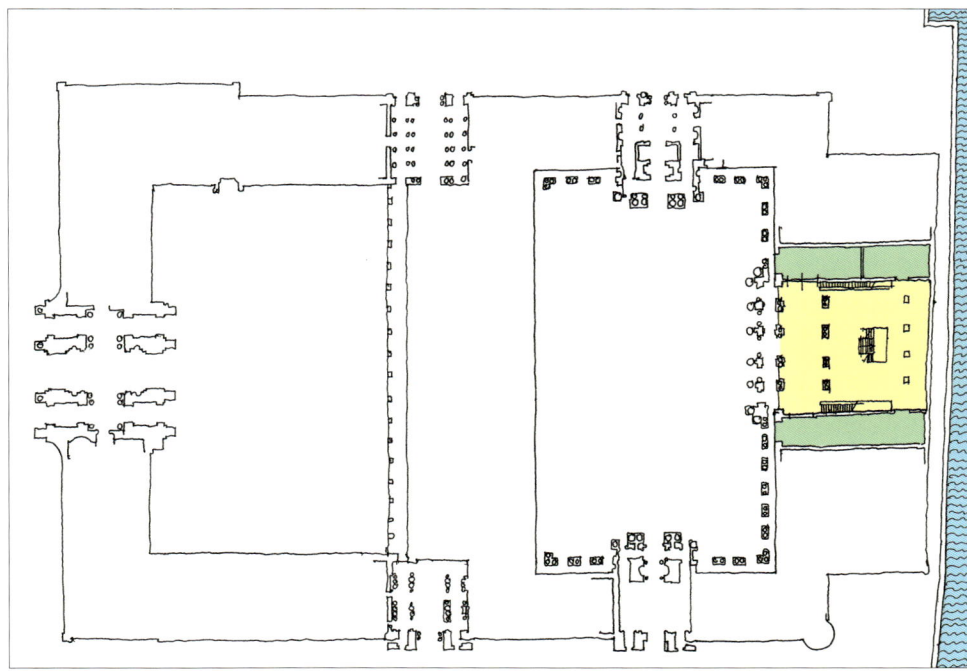

Blockergänzung am Warschauer Platz, Berlin-Friedrichshain, 1997

Block-addition at Warschauer Platz, Berlin-Friedrichhain, 1997

Das Quartier an der Oberbaumbrücke liegt östlich des Berliner Stadtkerns in einer ungewöhnlichen Situation: Im Süden wird es von der vielbefahrenen Stralauer Allee begrenzt, im Norden von einer großen Bahntrasse, im Westen von einem hochgelegenen Kopfbahnhof der U-Bahn, der direkt an die prächtige Oberbaumbrücke anschließt, welche die hier sehr breite Spree überquert.

Die im 19. und frühen 20. Jahrhundert erbaute Osram Leuchten- und Elektrofabrik hat die städtebauliche Grundstruktur eines quadratischen Blocksystems mit einer Traufhöhe von 18 m. Bis 1991 wurden die Gebäude als Narva Leuchtenfabrik in ihrer ursprünglichen Funktion als industrielle Produktionsstätte genutzt. Die gute Erschließung bietet dem Quartier interessante Entwicklungsmöglichkeiten als Bürostandort, die in Zukunft durch die günstige Lage zum neuen Berliner Großflughafen Schönefeld noch verbessert werden.

Seit 1996 wird das Quartier gemäß seiner Bedeutung als zusammenhängendes

The quarter around the Oberbaum Bridge, east of Berlin's centre, is in an unusual location. It is bordered to the south by the Stralauer Allee with its heavy traffic, to the north by a train route, to the west by an elevated underground terminus station directly connected to the grand Oberbaumbrücke spanning the Spree River, which is very wide at this spot.

In its urban design, the Osram lamp and electric factory that was built here in the late 19th and early 20th centuries had the basic structure of a square block system with an eaves' height of 18 m. Until 1991 the Narva lamp factory made use of the buildings' original function as industrial production centres. The quarter's good accessibility provides it with interesting possibilities for development as an office-centre, indeed its appeal will only be heightened in the future, when it is a convenient distance from Berlin's new Schönefeld airport.

In accordance with its significance as a multi-faceted industrial monument, the quarter has been undergoing care-

Industriedenkmal behutsam saniert und als Bürostandort genutzt.

1997 wurde ein Wettbewerb ausgeschrieben, der die städtebauliche Fassung und architektonische Gestaltung der unbebauten südwestlichen Quartiersecke zur Aufgabe hatte. Unser Vorschlag, der in den folgenden Jahren in den Bebauungsplan einfloß, sieht einen quadratischen, städtischen Platz vor, 40 m x 40 m groß.

Dieser wird im Norden und Osten von einer als Büro- oder Kaufhaus genutzten Blockergänzung begrenzt, die in Höhe und Form die vorhandenen baulichen Strukturen fortführt, sich aber zum Platz hin mit einer zweigeschossigen Arkade öffnet und dadurch in der Maßstäblichkeit vermittelt.

An der südöstlichen Platzecke schlagen wir einen Turm vor, welcher der Situation ein einprägsames architektonisches Motiv verleiht. Seine Fassade tritt leicht vor die Gebäudeflucht und staffelt sich nach oben hin mehrfach zurück. Seine relative Schlankheit kann er nur halten, indem er im oberen Drittel nicht den baurechtlichen und ökonomischen Zwängen eines Hochhauses gehorchen muß, da hier lediglich Haustechnik untergebracht ist.

Als Fassadenmaterial für Block und Turm wird eine Mischung aus Klinker und Terrakotta vorgeschlagen.

Die sechsspurige Stralauer Allee ist als Hauptausfallstraße Berlins Richtung Osten nicht zu »domestizieren«, deshalb ist hier – entgegen unserer sonstigen städtebaulichen Vorstellung – ausnahmsweise eine Fußgängerbrücke zur Anbindung der gegenüberliegenden Bebauung erwogen. Die Brücke nimmt ihren Ausgang im Turm und gibt ihm dadurch noch eine weitere Bedeutung.

Projektleiter: Alexander Waimer

ful renovation since 1996 and since this date has also been used as an office-centre.

In 1997 a competition called for the urban design and architectonic shaping of the undeveloped southwestern corner of the quarter. Our proposal which was used in the development plan in the following years envisioned a quadratic, urban square, 40 m x 40 m in size.

It is bordered to the north and east by a block-addition that can be used by an office building or a department store. Both the height and form of this addition are a continuation of the existing structures, it opens to the square with a two-storey arcade and thus conveys a sense of scale.

At the southeastern corner of the square we envision a tower. This lends the situation a strong and visible architectonic motif. Its façade projects slightly in front of the row of buildings and as it moves upwards it recedes backwards a number of times. Its relatively slender form can only be maintained, because its technical services have been placed in the upper third of the tower, and therefore it does not have to follow the constraints imposed on high-rise development by planning, building laws and economic considerations.

We propose a mixture of clinkers and terra cotta for the façades for the block and the tower

As Berlin's main arterial road in an eastward direction, the six-lane Stralauer Allee cannot be »tamed«. That is why we have made an exception here to our other urban designs. We have conceived of a pedestrian bridge leading to the buildings on the other side. The bridge begins at the tower, thereby lending it further significance.

Project architect: Alexander Waimer

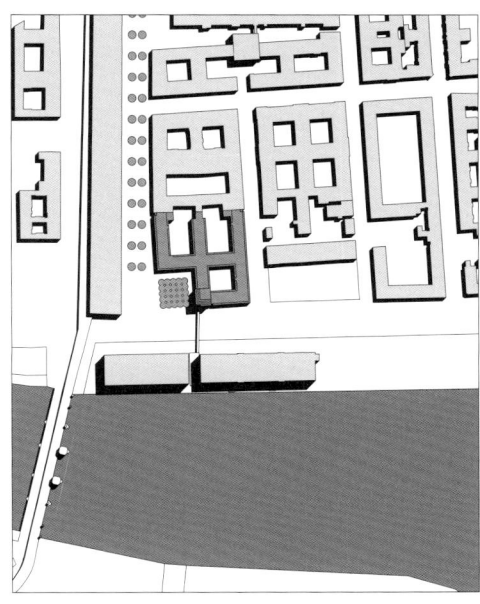

1. Perspektive des Gebäudes.

2. Lageplan.

2. Site plan.

1. Perspective view of the building.

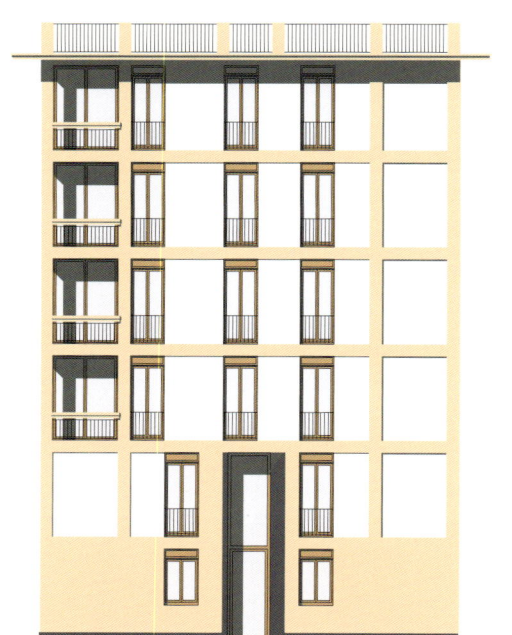
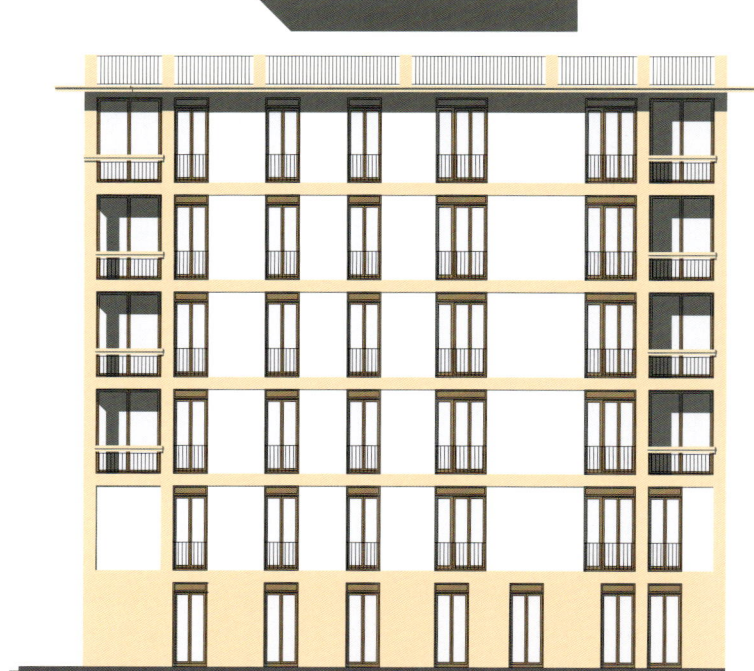

Wohnhaus im Olympischen Dorf, Turin, Italien, 2003–05

Otto Steidle, mit dem uns eine langjährige Freundschaft verbindet, gewann in Zusammenarbeit mit der Turiner Architektengruppe Camerana den Wettbewerb für das Olympische Dorf in Turin (Winterspiele 2006), das auf dem Gelände der ehemaligen Mercati Generali gegenüber Fiat Lingotto entstehen soll.

Um das internationale Dorf am Übergang von gewachsener Stadtstruktur und Peripherie als heterogenes, städtisches Gefüge entstehen zu lassen, wurden verschieden Architekturbüros an der weiteren Planung beteiligt: Das Gebiet wurde in drei einzelne Felder aufgeteilt, die von Steidle + Partner, Camerana und de Rossi beplant wurden. Innerhalb dieser Felder konnten dann auch Diener & Diener, Adolf Krischanitz, Ortner & Ortner und wir einzelne Häuser realisieren.

Residential building in the Olympic Village, Turin, Italy, 2003–05

Together with a Turin-based group of architects, Camerana, Otto Steidle – our friend of many years – won a competition for the Olympic Village in Turin (Winter Games 2006) that is to be built on a site, across from Fiat Lingotto, where the former Mercati Generali was located.

A variety of architectural firms were involved in the further planning of the transition of this international village with an evolved urban fabric at the city's outskirts into a heterogeneous urban structure. The lot was divided into three areas that were to be planned by Steidle + Partner, Camerana and de Rossi. Within these three areas, buildings were constructed by Diener & Diener, Adolf Krischanitz, Ortner & Ortner and by ourselves.

1, 2. Aufrisse der Fassaden von Nordosten und von Südosten.

3. Lageplan.

1.2. Elevations of the façades from the northeast and the southeast.

3. Site plan.

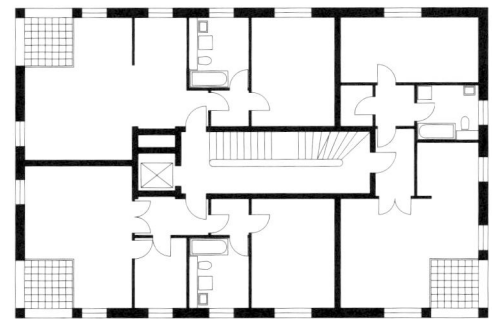

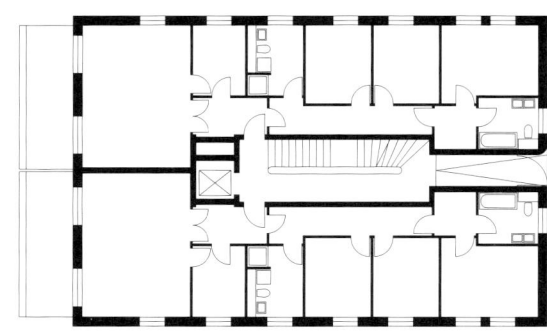

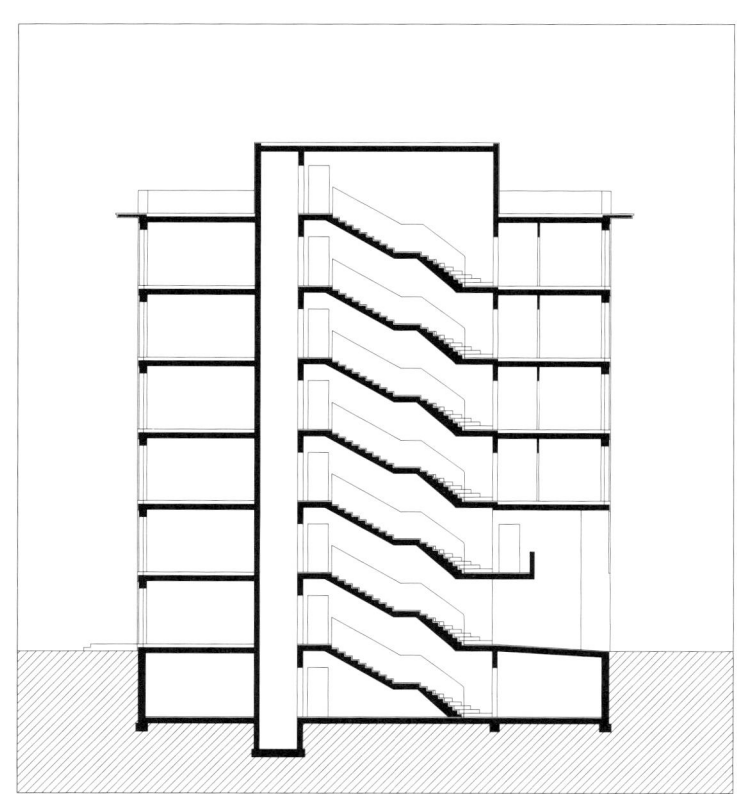

4–6. Grundrisse (Erd-
geschoß, Normalge-
schoß) und Schnitt.

4–6. Floor plans
(ground floor, typical
floor) and section.

Dem städtebaulichen Konzept liegen Gebäudetypen zugrunde, welche zwei Jahre zuvor während der gemeinsamen Planung von Otto Steidle, Ortner & Ortner, Adolf Krischanitz und uns für die Theresienhöhe in München entstanden waren (siehe S. 122–129). Der Typus des freistehenden Punkthauses mit innenliegendem Treppenhaus ermöglicht geschoßweise Variationen bei den Wohnungsgrößen. Nach den Olympischen Spielen werden nur noch geringfügige Änderungen vorgenommen, und es entsteht ein Angebot an Ein-, Zwei- und Vierzimmerwohnungen.

Für alle Häuser wurde aus Gründen eines rationellen Bauablaufs die Konstruktion vereinheitlicht: Vorgegeben war ein Stahlbetonskelettbau mit Achsmaßen von 4 m bis 5 m, ausgefacht mit kerngedämmten, zweischaligen Mauerwerkswänden.

Auf diese Weise erhielten wir den Auftrag für ein Wohnhaus in Italien, womit ein von uns langgehegter Wunsch in Erfüllung ging.

Projektleiter: Ulrik Hinze

The town planning concept is based on building types that we had developed two years earlier with Otto Steidle, Ortner & Ortner and Adolf Krischanitz, while we were drawing up the plans for the Theresienhöhe in Munich (see p. 122–129). The typology of the free-standing tower with inner stairwell allows for variations on each storey in the apartment size. After the Olympic Games, only small changes will be made and one-room, two-room and four-room apartments will be available.

In the interests of efficiency, the construction for all of the buildings was standardized. A frame of reinforced concrete on a grid layout of 4 m to 5 m was used, infilled with cavity insulated cavity wall construction.

In this way we could construct a residence in Italy and thereby make true a wish that we had had for a long time.

Project architect: Ulrik Hinze

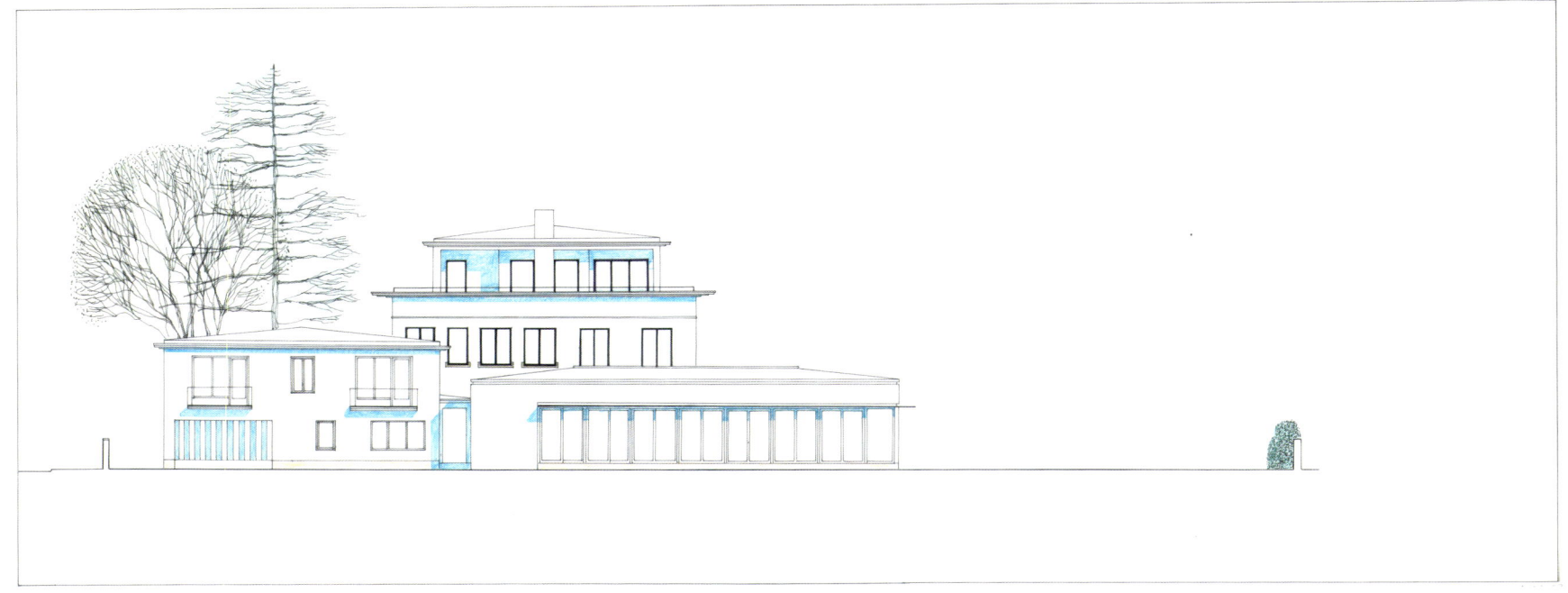

Haus an einem Park, 2003–05

Der Entwurf des großen Villengebäudes am Park ist geprägt von der Vorstellung, durch die Gruppierung der drei Bauteile Villa, Bedienstetengebäude und Badpavillon nicht eine Straßenrandbebauung, sondern statt dessen ein Raumensemble zu erstellen. Sowohl Raum- und Traufhöhen, als auch Fenstergrößen und Gliederungen des kleinen Wohn- und Garagenhauses im Vordergrund unterscheiden sich deutlich von denen der Villa, die mit ihren groß proportionierten Öffnungen, Natursteingewänden und ausladender Traufausbildung von der Straße zurückgesetzt ist. Da sich die beiden unterschiedlichen Häuser, die im rechten Winkel zueinander stehen, fast berühren, entsteht eine räumliche und maßstäbliche Spannung.

House by a park, 2003–05

The idea underlying the design for the large villa building on the park was to group the three building parts – a villa, a building for employees and a bathing pavilion – in such a way that instead of merely closing the street's periphery, a spatial ensemble would be created. The height of the rooms and the eaves' height, as well as the size of the windows and the configuration of the small residential and garage building at the front, clearly differ from the villa that is set back from the street with its large proportioned openings, natural stone claddings and overhanging eaves. A tension of space and scale results from the fact that these two different buildings, standing at a right angle to each other, are almost touching.

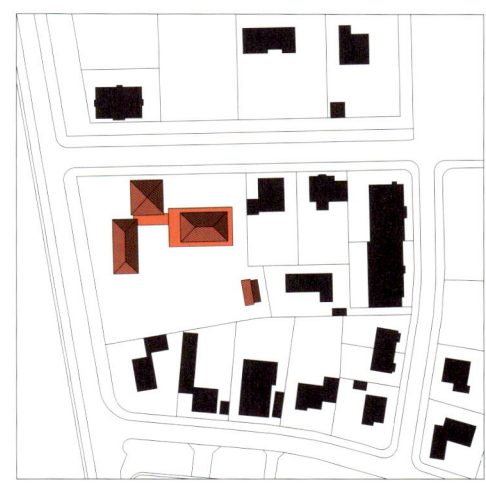

1, 2. Aufrisse der Fassaden von Süden und von Westen.

3. Die Eingangshalle.
4. Lageplan.

1, 2. Elevations of the façades from the south and from the north.

3. The entrance hall.
4. Site plan.

Im Inneren entwickeln sich sehr unterschiedliche Raumtypen in einer kontinuierlichen Abfolge: Die zweigeschossige Eingangshalle mit Galerie ist auch von außen erkennbar. Dahinter folgen der fast symmetrische Wohnraum mit angrenzender Bibliothek, auf der anderen Seite der Eßraum mit variierenden Wandbekleidungen und der Wintergarten als Verbindung zur Schwimmhalle.

Projektleiter: Fritz Treugut
Mitarbeiter: Daniel Türcke

Inside, there is an on-going sequence of different room types. The two-storey entrance hall with a gallery is also recognizable from the outside. Behind this, is the virtually symmetrical living space with an adjoining library. On the other side is the dining room with varying wall claddings and the winter garden leading to the swimming pool.

Project architect: Fritz Treugut
Collaborator: Daniel Türcke

5. Perspektive des Hauseingangs.
6. Das Bibliotheks-zimmer.

5. Perspective view of the entrance.
6. The library.

7–9. Grundrisse (Erd-geschoß, Oberge-schoß, Dachgeschoß).

7–9. Floor plans (ground floor, 1st floor, top floor).

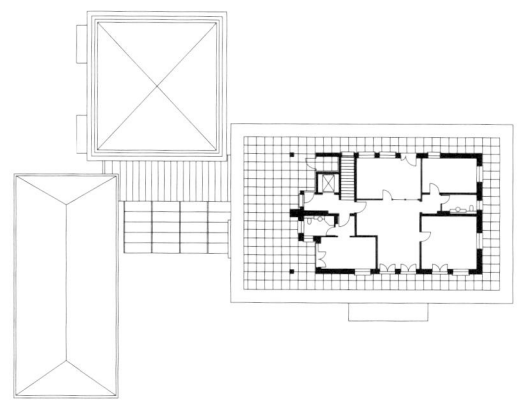

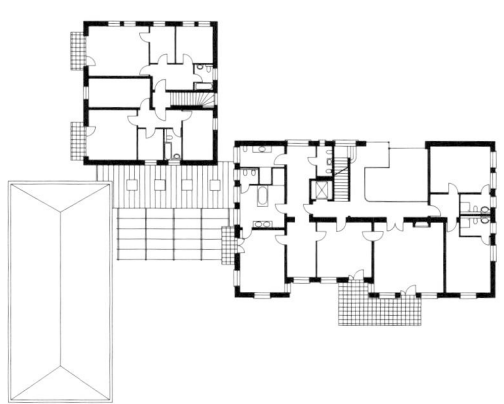

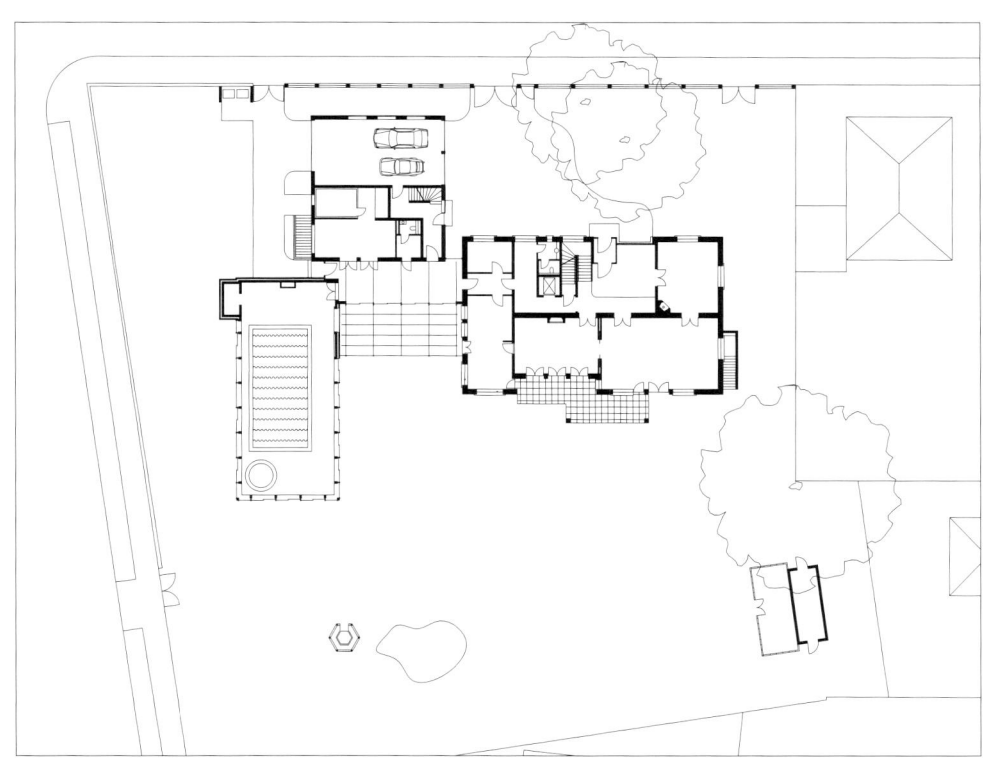

1991

2003

Vergleichende Betrachtung: Potsdamer Platz und Leipziger Platz, 1991 und 2003

»Nicht das weltweit verwendete amerikanische Stadtmodell der Hochhausagglomeration, sondern die Vorstellung von der kompakten, räumlich komplexen europäischen Stadt liegt dem Entwurf zugrunde.« (Erster Satz aus dem Erläuterungstext unseres Wettbewerbsbeitrags vom Juli 1991.)

Es handelte sich 1991 um ein höchst eigenwilliges Areal im Zentrum Berlins, freigesprengt von all jener Bebauung,

A comparison: Potsdamer Platz and Leipziger Platz, 1991 and 2003

»Our design is not based on the internationally used, American urban model of a conglomerate of skyscrapers but rather on the concept of the compact, spatially complex European city.« (First sentence in the commentary to our design for the competition, July 1991.)

The competition in 1991 dealt with an extremely unconventional area in the centre of Berlin, whose buildings, which were completely demolished, took on

1. Lageplan Potsdamer Platz und Leipziger Platz, Berlin, 1991, nach dem Wettbewerbsprojekt von Hilmer & Sattler und Albrecht (1. Preis).

2. Lageplan Potsdamer Platz und Leipziger Platz, Berlin, 2003.

2. Site plan Potsdamer Platz and Leipziger Platz, Berlin, 2003.

1. Site plan Potsdamer Platz and Leipziger Platz, Berlin, 1991, in accordance with competition project of Hilmer & Sattler und Albrecht (1st prize).

die das besonders an dieser Stelle pulsierende Berliner Leben von vor dem Krieg aufnahm: freies Brachland, vor kurzem noch vom Mauerstreifen durchkreuzt, das sich ausbreitete zwischen der Friedrichstadt mit dem barocken Straßengrundriß und der meist gründerzeitlichen Bebauung und dem neuen Kulturforum im Westen, diesem losen, landschaftlich gedachten Zusammenwirken mächtiger architektonischer Einzelformen von Scharoun, Mies van der Rohe und Gutbrod.

Das zukünftige urbane Leben sollte sich nicht im Inneren großstrukturierter Gebäudekomplexe, wie es später die beiden Investoren debis und Sony realisierten, sondern auf Straßen und Plätzen entfalten.

Die großen gliedernden Elemente des Entwurfs sind:
– die Leipziger Straße in ihrem alten Querschnitt und 22 m Traufhöhe;
– der Leipziger Platz auf dem ursprünglichen, oktogonalen Grundriß mit der Gebäudehöhe des neuen Stadtteils von 35 m;
– der Potsdamer Platz mit einer Gruppe spitzwinkliger Hochhäuser als schlanke, vertikale Zeichen in der Silhouette Berlins;
– die breite, boulevardartige neue Potsdamer Straße zum Kulturforum hin, an der sich die Bauten für die öffentlichen und publikumsintensiven Nutzungen aufreihen;
– die Freiräume mit der Wasserfläche im Süden und dem Grünkeil vom Potsdamer Platz zum Tiergarten im Norden.

Als Bebauung zwischen diesen gliedernden Elementen ist nicht an einen ge-schlossene Block mit Parzellierung und Randbebauung gedacht, sondern es sind große Häuser von 50 m mal 50 m Seitenlänge vorgesehen, deren Zwischenräume nur 17,5 m breite Straßen bilden. Die Häusertraufe liegt bei 35 m. Hier-

the pulsating pre-War lifestyle of Berlin particularly associated with this locality. Until quite recently it had been cut cross by the Wall. It was spread out between Friedrichstadt, with its Baroque street grid and its predominantly late-19th century buildings, and the new Kulturforum – a loose, scenic collaboration of powerful and detached architectonic forms by Scharoun, Mies van der

durch beträgt die Proportion von Traufhöhe zu Straßenbreite 2:1. Die Kürze der
Seitenabmessungen dieser Häuser läßt
häufige Unterbrechungen der Straßen-
fronten entstehen, wodurch sich vielfäl-
tige Lichtwirkungen ergeben. Durch diese gute Belichtungssituation sehen wir
die neue Höhe des Stadtteils legitimiert,
der an Proportionen von Stadterweiterungen des späten 19. Jahrhunderts in
Wien, Mailand oder Madrid erinnert.
Die Durchdringung des Blocks mit engen, kurzen öffentlichen Straßen, die
nach nicht mehr als 60 m in die großen
Stadträume münden, verhindert die Ver-
einheitlichung in der Wirkung, die bei
Großinvestitionen naturgemäß entsteht.

Die beträchtliche Größe der Häuser
von 15 000 m² bis 20 000 m² Geschoß-
fläche entspricht den künftigen Nutzungen wie Wohn- und Geschäftshaus, Kaufhaus, Konzernzentrale, Musiktheater,
Hotel etc. und garantiert Überschaubar-
keit. Benötigt ein Nutzer größere Flächen, erhält er zwei Häuser.

Auch die Individualverkehrs- und An-
lieferungserschließung ist nicht vereinheitlicht, sondern dezentral konzipiert,
mit Rampen in jedem der Häuser. Der
Anteil an Wohnnutzung soll 30 Prozent
nicht unterschreiten.

Realisierungsprozess: Unser Plan war als
städtebauliches Schema gedacht, nicht

Rohe and Gutbrod – to be found in the
West.

The urban life of the future should
not take place inside large building complexes, as it was later realized by the investors debis and Sony, but should un-
fold onto streets and squares.

The main organizing elements of the
design are:
– Leipziger Straße with its old cross
section and an eaves' height of 22 m;
– Leipziger Platz on the original, octag-
onal ground plan with the building
height for the new district of 35 m;
– Potsdamer Platz with a group of
sharp-cornered skyscrapers as slender,
vertical elements in Berlin's silhouette;
– The broad, boulevard-like Potsdamer
Straße, leading to the Kulturforum,
where the buildings for public use have
been lined up;
– The free spaces with an expanse of
water in the south and the green trian-
gular area between Potsdamer Platz and
the Tiergarten in the north;

The type of development envisaged
between these organising elements is
not that of the closed block, divided into lots and built up at its borders, but
rather large buildings whose periphery
measures 50 m by 50 m. The spaces between these buildings are made up of

als architektonische Ausformung, anders
etwa als die Wettbewerbsbeiträge von
Hans Kollhoff mit den sieben freistehenden Hochhäusern oder Daniel Libes-
kinds intellektuelles Baukörperverwirr-
spiel. In den Jahren 1992 und 1993
folgten nun die Hochbauwettbewerbe
für die Einzelbereiche auf der Grundlage unseres Masterplans.

Bis zum Jahr 1994 wurde dann von
uns der letztendlich verbindliche Bebauungsplan ausgearbeitet, unter Berück-
sichtigung der Wettbewerbe und der weiteren Planungen für die einzelnen Teilgebiete.

Wenn man die beiden Stadtpläne von
1991 und 2003 miteinander vergleicht,
so erkennt man den Wucherungscharak-
ter, mit dem sich die Entwicklung dieses
Stadtteils vollzieht. Wir, die Verfasser des
ersten Plans, beobachten dies mit einer
Mischung aus Neugierde und wohlwol-
lender Verzweiflung. Der Vergleich zeigt
aber auch, daß Renzo Pianos debis-Are-
al, Helmut Jahns Sony-Bebauung und

streets that are only 17,5 m wide. The
height of the buildings is 35 m. This
means that the proportion of the eaves'
height to street width is 2:1. The short
length of the sides of these buildings
allow for many breaks in the street-front,
which produce a variety of light effects.
For us, this good lighting situation legit-
imizes the district's new height, a height
that recalls the proportions of late 19th
century expansions of cities such as Vienna, Milan and Madrid. The permeation
of the block with narrow short public
streets, with no more than 60 m between
their junctions with large urban spaces,
hinders the monolithic effect that is
always a risk where large investors are
involved. The considerable size of the
buildings, measuring between 15,000 m^2
and 20,000 m^2 in floor area, corresponds
to their future use as residential and
commercial building, department store,
business headquarter, musical theatre,
hotel etc., and also guarantees a compre-
hensibility. If a user requires a larger
floor area, then he is allotted two buildings. The individual traffic and delivery
systems are not standardized, but rather
have been decentralized, with ramps in
each of the buildings. The proportion of
residential use should not fall below 30
percent.

Giorgio Grassis ABB-Projekt nicht die Grunddisposition zerstören, sondern daß nun individuelle Handschriften den Entwurf vom städtebaulichen Schema hin zum konkreten Plan verändern.

Positiv zeichnet sich nach zwölf Jahren, im Jahr 2003, ab:
– Das Zusammenwachsen der beiden Stadtteile Ost und West beginnt.
– Im Westen erkennt man, daß sich das Kulturforum in ehemals desolater Randlage vor dem Hintergrund der unerhört verdichteten neuen Bebauung um den Potsdamer Platz zu einem offenen, jedoch zentralen städtischen Raum verändert.
– Es gibt gelungene Stellen, wie etwa die fünf Hochhäuser vorne am Potsdamer Platz: das dichte Nebeneinander von Pianos gewebehafter Fassadentextur aus Terrakotta, Helmut Jahns gekrümmten Ganzglas-Flächen und Hans Kollhoffs kraftvollem, festen Bau in der Mitte, der die beiden Nachbarn aufrecht hält.
– Noch kaum, aber in Ansätzen, erfaßt man die Idee für das Quartier: die Abfolge gänzlich unterschiedlicher Stadtraumtypen, nämlich: aus dem gründerzeitlichen Stadtraum der Leipziger Straße kommend, das weite, hohe Oktogon des Leipziger Platzes, die leicht hysterische Hochhausbündelung am Potsdamer Platz, der breite, hohe Boulevard der neuen Potsdamer Straße und die offene Landschaft des Kulturforums. Es sind bereits südlich und nördlich dieser Raumfolge einzelne Straßenräume entstanden, die in ihrer stark verdichteten Proportion für Berlin neu sind.

Als Fehlentwicklung erscheint uns:
– das Verlegen der für das städtische Leben attraktiven Nutzungen ins Blockinnere, bei Sony in den glasüberdachten, ovalen, introvertierten Platz, bei debis an die Rückseite der Staatsbibliothek, anstatt diese Nutzungen an der neuen

The process of realization: Our design was conceived within the context of town planning and not that of architectonic form. In this we differed from the competition entries of, for example, Hans Kollhoff, with his seven freestanding high-rise buildings or Daniel Libeskind and his intellectual game with the perplexity of building form. In 1992 and 1993 the first competitions were held for the high-rise buildings in the individual areas based on our master plan.

By 1994 we had worked out the final and binding development plan, thereby also taking into consideration the competitions and the further planning of the individual areas.

When one compares the plan of 1991 with that of 2003, one immediately sees the great growth in the development of this district. As the creators of the first plan we look upon this with a mixture of curiosity and bemused despair. The comparison also shows, however, that Renzo Piano's debis area, Helmut Jahn's construction for Sony and Giorgio Grassi's ABB project have not destroyed the plan's basic disposition but rather that individual scripts are changing the design of the town planning scheme into a concrete town plan.

After twelve years, the year 2003 shows some positive signs:
– The eastern and western parts of the city are beginning to grow together.
– In the West one recognizes that the Kulturforum, which was once in a desolate peripheral location, now with the incredible density of the new development around Potsdamer Platz as its background, is changing into an open but still central urban space.
– There are successful areas, such as the five high-rise buildings at the front of Potsdamer Platz. Close to each other are the woven-like texture of the façade of Piano's terracotta high-rise, Helmut

10. Blick vom Beisheim-Center zum Potsdamer Platz. (Photo: Stefan Müller.)

10. View from the Beisheim-Center towards Potsdamer Platz. (Photo: Stefan Müller.)

Potsdamer Straße anzusiedeln, der Verbindung zwischen Ost und West, zwischen Innenstadt und Kulturforum.

– die zentralisierte, labyrinthische unterirdische Erschließung, die von den durchgehenden Parkdecks ausgeht, die im Gegensatz steht zu den Gruppierungen von einzelnen großen Häusern im Stadtraum.

– das Verlassen dieser Gliederung in »große Häuser« im südlichen debis-Abschnitt und statt dessen die Zusammenfassung von vier Häusern zu zwei Großeinheiten.

– der willkürliche Standort des südlichen debis Hochhauses am Landwehrkanal, welcher der Konzentration von Hochhäusern um den Potsdamer Platz zuwiderläuft.

– der zu geringe Anteil von Wohnungen am Gesamtbauvolumen (20 Prozent).

– das Verlegen der Wasserfläche aus dem großen Freiraum im Anschluß an den Potsdamer Platz in die Restfläche zwischen der Rückseite der Staatsbiblio-

Jahn's bent glass surface and Hans Kollhoff's strong, solid building in the middle strengthens the two neighbouring buildings.

– First impressions allow one to just barely grasp the idea behind this quarter – a succession of completely different types of urban space. These are the wide high octagon of Leipziger Platz that belongs to the late 19th century urban space of Leipziger Straße; the somewhat hysterical cluster of high-rises at Potsdamer Platz and the open landscape of the Kulturforum.

Individual streets have been created to the north and south of this spatial sequence and are, in their considerable density and proportion, new to Berlin.

Deviations in our opinion are:

– The activities, attractive in terms of urban living, are positioned in the block's interior, as by Sony in the glass-covered, oval, introverted square and by debis at the back of the Staatsbibliothek. These uses should have been located on the new Potsdamer Straße, the connection between East and West, between inner city and Kulturforum.

– The centralized, subterranean parking decks, which are labyrinthine in their succession, contradict the grouping of individual large buildings in the urban space.

– One of the principles behind the structuring – that of »large buildings« – has been given up in the southern debis segment and four buildings have been incorporated into two large units.

– The arbitrary location of the southern debis high-rise building at the Landwehrkanal contravenes the concentration of high-rise buildings at Potsdamer Platz.

– The proportion of residences to the total volume (20 percent) is too low.

– The placement of the expanse of water in the leftover space between the

thek, debis-Verwaltung und Landwehrkanal.

Ein abschließendes Gesamturteil wird
sicherlich erst möglich sein, wenn das
gesamte Oktogon des Leipziger Platzes
vollendet ist und sich die zwei großen,
räumlich sehr verschiedenen Charaktere
des Potsdamer- und Leipziger Platzes in
ihrer Gänze zeigen.

rear of the Staatsbibliothek, the debis
administration and the Landwehrkanal
instead of at the large open area connected to Potsdamer Platz.

A final judgement is of course only
possible when the entire octagon of
Leipziger Platz is completed and the two
large, spatially very different characters
of Potsdamer Platz and Leipziger Platz
are fully apparent.

Umbau der Neuen Wache zur Zentralen Gedenkstätte der Bundesrepublik Deutschland, Berlin-Mitte, 1993

Umbau und Erweiterung des Schlosses Elmau, Mittenwald, 1993–2004

Haus der Bayerischen Wirtschaft, München, 1993–98

Regionalbahnhof Potsdamer Platz, Berlin-Tiergarten, 1995–2006

Bürogebäude Glinkastraße, Berlin-Mitte, 1996, Wettbewerbsprojekt

U-Bahnhof Mendelssohn-Bartholdy-Park, Berlin-Tiergarten, 1996–98

Seniorenwohnhaus, Passauer Straße, Berlin-Schöneberg, 1996–99

Seniorenwohnhaus Jahnstraße/Klenzestraße, München, 1996–2000

Zwei Wohnhäuser im Tiergartendreieck, Berlin-Tiergarten, 1997–2000

Umbau des Verlags- und Redaktionsgebäudes der *Frankfurter Allgemeinen Zeitung*, Berlin-Mitte, 1997–99

Städtebaulicher Entwurf Theresienhöhe, München, 1997, Wettbewerbsprojekt (2. Preis)

Blockergänzung am Warschauer Platz, Berlin-Friedrichshain, 1997, Wettbewerbsprojekt (1. Preis)

Das Berliner Stadtschloß, Berlin-Mitte, 1997 und 2002, Studien

Buchhandlung Hacker & Presting, Berlin-Charlottenburg, 1997

Neugestaltung Kulturforum / Kemperplatz, Berlin-Tiergarten, 1998, Wettbewerbsprojekt

Zwei Wohnhäuser an der Außenalster, Hamburg, 1998/99

Graphikmuseum Pablo Picasso, Münster, 1998–2000

Generalsanierung des Martin-Gropius-Baus, Berlin-Kreuzberg, 1998/99

Masterplan für die Museumsinsel, Berlin-Mitte, in Arbeitsgemeinschaft mit Heinz Tesar, David Chipperfield und Oswald Mathias Ungers, 1998–2010

Grundinstandsetzung des Alten Museums, Berlin-Mitte, 1999–2012

Bürohäuser am Karl-Scharnagl-Ring, München, 1999–2003

Wohnbebauung am Olympiaberg, München, 1999–2002

Wohn- und Geschäftshaus Salvatorstraße, Fünf Höfe, München, 1999 bis 2003

Wohnhäuser auf der Theresienhöhe, München, 1999–2002

Bürogebäude der Münchner Rückversicherung, München, 1999, Wettbewerbsprojekt (2. Preis)

Stadtbibliothek und Jugendmusikschule, Pforzheim, 1999–2002

925 Lounge Bar, Berlin-Mitte, 2000

Wohnhaus in den Bergen, 2000–03

Beisheim-Center – städtebauliche Konkretisierung, Berlin-Tiergarten, 2000–03

Ritz-Carlton Hotel und Apartment-Tower, Beisheim-Center, Berlin-Tiergarten, 2000–03

Bürogebäude, Beisheim-Center, Berlin-Tiergarten, 2000–03

Wohn- und Geschäftshaus Leipziger Platz 8, Berlin-Mitte, 2000–03

Wohnhaus in der Nördlichen Auffahrtsallee, München, 2000–03

Wohnungsbau Orsoyer Straße, Düsseldorf, 2001, Wettbewerbsprojekt

Campus am Jungfernsee, Potsdam, 2001, Wettbewerbsprojekt

Einstein-Kongress, St. Gallen, Schweiz, 2001–06

Wohn- und Geschäftshaus am Oberanger, München 2001–04

Neues Globushaus bei Schloß Gottorf, Schleswig, 2001–03

Städtebaulicher Entwurf Siemens-Hofmannstraße, München, 2002, Wettbewerbsprojekt

Kommandantur, Unter den Linden 1, Berlin-Mitte, 2002, Wettbewerbsprojekt

Wohnungsbau, München-Riem, 2002–04

Leipziger Platz Carrée, ehemaliges Kaufhaus Wertheim, Berlin-Mitte, 2002–05

Skulpturenpräsentation in der Gemäldegalerie, Berlin-Tiergarten, 2003

Bürohäuser Gabriele-Tergit-Promenade, Berlin-Tiergarten, 2003–06

Fassadenentwurf für Karstadt-Oberpollinger, München, 2003, Wettbewerbsprojekt

Wohngebäude im Köbis-Dreieck, Berlin-Tiergarten, 2003–06

Wohnhaus im Olympischen Dorf, Turin, 2003–05

Conversion of the Neue Wache to the Central Memorial of the Federal Republik of Germany, Berlin-Mitte, 1993

Renovation and extension to Schloß Elmau, Mittenwald, 1993–2004

Haus der Bayerischen Wirtschaft (House of Bavarian Economy), Munich, 1993–98

Potsdamer Platz station, Berlin-Tiergarten, 1995–2006

Office building Glinkastraße, Berlin-Mitte, 1996, competition project

Mendelssohn-Bartholdy-Park underground station, Berlin-Tiergarten, 1996–98

Retirement home, Passauer Straße, Berlin-Schöneberg, 1996–99

Retirement home, Jahnstraße/Klenzestraße, Munich, 1996–2000

Two apartment houses in the Tiergartendreieck, Berlin-Tiergarten, 1997–2000

Renovation of the *Frankfurter Allgemeine Zeitung* publishing and editorial offices, Berlin-Mitte, 1997–99

Urban design for Theresienhöhe, Munich, 1997, competition project (2nd prize)

Block addition at Warschauer Platz, Berlin-Friedrichshain, 1997, competition project (1st prize)

The Royal Palace, Berlin-Mitte, 1997 and 2002, studies

Bookshop Hacker & Presting, Berlin-Charlottenburg, 1997

Remodelling of the Kulturforum/Kemperplatz, Berlin-Tiergarten, 1998, competition project

Two residential buildings on the Außenalster, Hamburg, 1998/99

Pablo Picasso Graphics Museum, Münster, 1998–2000

Renovation of the Martin-Gropius-Bau, Berlin-Kreuzberg, 1998/99

Master Plan for the Museumsinsel, Berlin-Mitte, in cooperation with Heinz Tesar, David Chipperfield, Oswald Mathias Ungers, 1998–2010

Renovation of the Altes Museum, Berlin-Mitte, 1999–2012

Office buildings Karl-Scharnagl-Ring, Munich, 1999–2003

Residential development Olympia-berg, Munich, 1999–2002

Residential and commercial building Salvatorstraße, Fünf Höfe (Five Courtyards), Munich, 1999–2003

Three residential buildings on the Theresienhöhe, Munich, 1999 to 2002

Office building for the Münchner Rückversicherung, Munich, 1999, competition project (2nd prize)

City library and youth music school, Pforzheim, 1999–2002

925 Lounge Bar, Berlin-Mitte, 2000

Residence in the mountains, 2000 to 2003

Beisheim-Center – development of the urban form, Berlin-Tiergarten, 2000–03

Ritz-Carlton Hotel and apartment tower, Beisheim-Center, Berlin-Tiergarten, 2000–03

Office building, Beisheim-Center, Berlin-Tiergarten, 2000–03

Residential and commercial building Leipziger Platz 8, Berlin-Mitte, 2000–03

House in Nördliche Auffahrtsallee, Munich, 2000–03

Residential complex Orsoyer Straße, Düsseldorf, 2001, competition project

Campus on the Jungfernsee, Potsdam, 2001, competition project

Einstein-Kongress, St. Gallen, Switzerland, 2001–06

Residental and commercial building, Am Oberanger, Munich, 2001–04

The new Globushaus (house for a globe), Schloß Gottorf, Schleswig, 2001–03

Urban design Siemens-Hofmann-Straße, Munich, 2002, competition project

Kommandantur, 1 Unter den Linden, Berlin-Mitte, 2002, competiton project

Residential complex, Riem, Munich 2002–04

Leipziger Platz Carrée, Berlin-Mitte, 2002–05

Presentation of sculptures in the pillared hall of the Gemäldegalerie, Berlin-Tiergarten, 2003

Office buildings Gabriele-Tergit-Promenade, Berlin-Tiergarten, 2003–06

Design of a façade for Karstadt-Oberpollinger, Munich, 2003, competition project

Two residential buildings, Köbis-Dreieck, Berlin-Tiergarten, 2003–06

Residential building in the Olympic Village, Turin, Italy, 2003–05

Fritz Treugut	1986–	Mehra Mehrdadi	2001–2003
Peter Dörrie	1988–2003	Christian von Oppen	2001–2003
Johannes Rößler	1991–1997	Stefano Magistretti	2001–2002
Rita Ahlers	1994–	Natalie Friedrich	2001–2002
Christian Winter	1994–2003	Christiane Gabler	2002–2003
Ulrike Flacke	1994–1998	Sabina Krause	2002–2003
Ursula Gonsior	1994–2002		
Ulrich Greiler	1994–	**Praktikanten/Trainees**	
Alexander Waimer	1997–		
Ulrike Feucht	1997–	Anne Katrin Treugut	1996
Philipp Althammer	1997–2002	Julian Sattler	1997
Britta Greese	1997–1998	Ariane Wolf	1997–2000
Sigurd Hauer	1997–	Florian Schätz	1998
Peter Solhdju	1997–	Harald Kettner	1998–2000
Daniel Türcke	1997–	Volker Schmid	1998–2000
Michael Andreotti	1997–1999	Myriam Decker	1999–2000
Michael Maurer	1997–1999	Helena Albrecher	1999–2000
Bettina Otto	1997–2000	Christian Salewski	2000–2001
Peter Westermann	1997–	Ulrich Heine	2001–2002
Alexandra Stepanienko	1997–	Jens Rott	2001–2002
Peter O'Callaghan	1998–	Meredith Weems	2001–2002
Ulrik Hinze	1998–	Katrin Hülk	2002
Andreas Schindhelm	1998–2000	Robert Tholl	2002
Frigga Uhlisch	1998–	Sebastian Treese	2002–2003
Herman Duquesnoy	1998–	Evelyn Galsdorf	2002–2003
Jan Pautzke	1998–	Silke Kapust	2002–2003
Ayhan Ayrilmaz	1998		
Kirsten Händel	1998	**Sekretariat/Secretary's office**	
Veronika Barth	1998–2001		
Martin Waldorf	1998–2001	Barbara Reitzlein	1993–
Isabelle Heide	1999	Angela Schülke	1994–2002
Janka–Karita Guhl	1999–2000	Nora Engelberg	2002–
Gerhard Bolkart	1999–2003		
Barbara Schindhelm	1999–2000		
Nadine Zietlow	1999–2001		
Ruth Schroers	2000		
François von Chappuis	2000–2001		
Carsten Baur	2000–		
Frauke Blasy	2000–		
Jens Förster	2000–2001		
Till Roggel	2000–		
Myriam Wiedemann	2000–2003		
Veronika Praxmarer-Breuer	2000–2001		
Jan Faller	2000–		
Daniel Kahala	2000		
Wolfgang Metschan	2000–2001		
Peter Adrian	2000–2002		
Henrik Eichler	2001–2002		
Dietmar Husmann	2001–2002		
Thomas Katzke	2001–2002		
Sven Meller	2001–2003		